THE NORTHEAST CORRIDOR

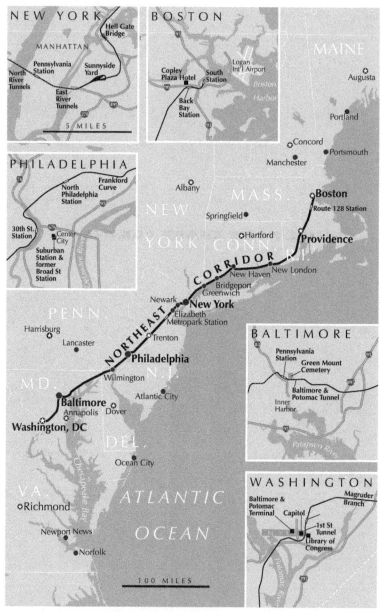

The northeast corridor rail line and region. Map courtesy of Chicago CartoGraphics.

THE
NORTHEAST
CORRIDOR

THE TRAINS,
THE PEOPLE,
THE HISTORY,
THE REGION

DAVID ALFF

THE UNIVERSITY OF CHICAGO PRESS

Chicago and London

The University of Chicago Press, Chicago 60637
The University of Chicago Press, Ltd., London
© 2024 by David Alff
Published 2024
Printed in the United States of America

33 32 31 30 29 28 27 26 25 24   1 2 3 4 5

ISBN-13: 978-0-226-82283-9 (cloth)
ISBN-13: 978-0-226-82284-6 (e-book)
DOI: https://doi.org/10.7208/chicago/9780226822846.001.0001

Library of Congress Cataloging-in-Publication Data

Names: Alff, David, author.
Title: The northeast corridor : the trains, the people, the history, the
    region / David Alff.
Other titles: Trains, the people, the history, the region
Description: Chicago : The University of Chicago Press, 2024. |
    Includes bibliographical references and index.
Identifiers: LCCN 2023037502 | ISBN 9780226822839 (cloth) |
    ISBN 9780226822846 (ebook)
Subjects: LCSH: Railroads—Northeastern States. | Northeastern
    States—History.
Classification: LCC F106 .A44 2024 | DDC 974—dc23/eng/20230905
LC record available at https://lccn.loc.gov/2023037502

♾ This paper meets the requirements of ANSI/NISO Z39.48-1992
(Permanence of Paper).

FOR MY PARENTS AND THEIRS

CONTENTS

GREATEST ASSET

The corridor is one great compression of industrial shapes,
industrial sounds, industrial air.
JOHN MCPHEE[1]

Three days before he entered the White House, Barack Obama stood on a platform at Philadelphia's 30th Street Station. The president-elect studied his train. It had two diesel engines, nine stainless steel Amtrak carriages, and one royal blue Pullman observation car. Lanyarded passengers filed aboard. Reporters scribbled in pads. Secret Service agents orbited.[2] 30th Street Station is famous for its waiting room, a pale-honey travertine gallery brightened by portico windows and pendant chandeliers. But none of this radiance reaches the platforms, where riders come and go through creosote-scented gloom.

Obama boarded his Pullman. The train blasted its airchime horn, shuddered into sunlight, and rumbled off toward Washington. Crowds gathered on the Chestnut Street overpass. Onlookers clung to chain-link fences, clambered onto car hoods, and scampered up embankments. They came to see a journey that had no practical purpose. The Obamas already lived in Washington. They had resided in suites at the Hotel Hay-Adams and Blair House for weeks.[3] In late January the incoming first family left the capital so they could arrive again, by rail.

Their so-called Inaugural Express promised bystanders and television viewers an American panorama, from bustling cities to sleepy whistle-stops. Obama found patriotic poetry in a route that linked Philadelphia, where "farmers and lawyers, merchants and soldiers, gathered to declare their independence," with Delaware, the first state to ratify the Constitution, and Baltimore, birthplace of the "Star-Spangled Banner." Obama invited aboard people he met campaigning in Ohio, Georgia, Montana, and elsewhere. The delegation embodied his hope that Americans "from the north and the south and the east and the west" would join to "seek a better world in our time."[4]

Despite its geographical outreach, Obama's steel parade could not help but highlight one particular region: the northeast. There were no fruited plains or majestic peaks here, just a washed-out collage of polyvinyl cable, cracked rebar, rigidized metal, and leafless trees beside the gray chop of the Delaware River. Cathedrals spired over rowhomes. Stone-crushing plants shouldered up against scrapyards and algal ponds. Freeways clogged with rigs and sedans. So many petroleum refineries hugged the tracks in Marcus Hook that Greenpeace urged the train's cancellation lest it provoke "the terrorist release of ultrahazardous chemicals."[5]

The scenery looked nothing like the romantic railscapes that Americans often conjure: a lone locomotive chuffing over prairie or threading alpine passes, its forlorn whistle haunting pioneer wilderness. Obama's journey was no Kodak canyon excursion or rocket ride into space but a banal act of transit through lands so familiar they hid themselves. What spectators saw behind the Inaugural Express was a place used to get other places, an architecture of anticipation, an inglorious backdrop on which to project a perfected union— a convergence called the Northeast Corridor.

In its most literal sense, the corridor is a fistful of train tracks that solder Boston to Washington via Providence, New Haven, New York, Philadelphia, and Baltimore. The rails are hot-rolled steel beams. Spikes bind the beams to ties made of treated oak or prestressed concrete. The ties rest in a bed of crushed limestone called ballast. Above this gravel path hangs the copper catenary that feeds current to electric trains. Bridges carry this cat's cradle of rail and wire over rivers and ravines. Tunnels inject it into downtown cores. Cuts and embankments keep things level in between.

In 2019 corridor trains carried 820,000 riders each day—a head count greater than the populations of San Francisco or Denver.[6] Trains delivered those people to hundreds of thousands of jobs (including one-third of Fortune 100 firms), 263 colleges within five miles of a station, and over a third of civilization's most visited museums.[7] The line links the world's leading financial hub with its most consequential political capital. Economists estimate that closing the corridor for a single day would sacrifice one hundred million dollars' worth of lost labor to gridlock. In congressional testimony, Drexel University president John Fry called the corridor the "epicenter of American rail travel" and "America's greatest transportation asset."[8]

So great is this asset that the word *corridor* has grown synonymous with its region. People do not simply ride the corridor but live there too. Amtrak's tracks anchor a socioeconomic enclave that extends 457 miles from Washington to Massachusetts. Once home to tens of thousands of Algonquians, this coastal band became a beachhead for colonial conquest, a testbed of the Industrial Revolution, a fiscal laboratory, and a fount of global policy. The corridor today holds fifty million people, including Indigenous Americans, descendants of European colonists and the Africans they enslaved, and immigrants from everywhere.[9] Despite their numbers and clout, northeasterners have also weathered recessions, abandonment, and decay. Part hearth, part ruin, the corridor has always been a place to live and to leave.

Rhode Island senator Claiborne Pell saw the region as an "unbroken sea of twinkling lights that signifies a continuous chain of human habitation and human activity."[10] Pell was obsessed with *Megalopolis*, a 1961 book by French-Ukrainian geographer Jean Gottmann, who deemed the northeast a "new order in the organization of inhabited space."[11] Unlike European nations, which developed around dominant capitals (London, Paris, Rome), the northeast's "polynuclear" structure scattered people across a single urban conglomeration (New York–Philadelphia–Baltimore).[12] The proximity of northeastern cities unleashed a "tidal current of commuting" between them, which Gottmann saw firsthand while riding trains between his appointments at Johns Hopkins University, Princeton's Institute for Advanced Study, and Manhattan's Rockefeller Institute.[13]

Gottmann's megapolitan thesis endures today in the work of Richard Florida, whose jarring phrase "Bos-Wash Mega Region" refers to a biosphere of knowledge workers who convene in seaboard cities for high salaries, bourgeoise amenities, and proximity to one another.[14] Demographics support this impression. Residents of the corridor's thirty trackside counties are 5.5 times more likely to take public transportation than the average American.[15] They earn almost $13,000 a year over the median national income and attain graduate degrees 31 percent more often than those who live outside the region.[16] In 2020 corridor residents cast over 70 percent of their presidential ballots for Joe Biden (who received 51 percent of all American votes).[17]

This profile explains why *corridor* has become a conservative swear word. In 1961 Barry Goldwater claimed the country "would be better off if someone sawed off the eastern seaboard and let it float out to sea."[18] In 2017 White House deputy assistant Sebastian Gorka sneered at the "Acela Corridor of wonkery," imagining the Trump administration's deep state enemies as train riders.[19] Conservative law professor F. H. Buckley railed against the "lawyers, academics, trust-fund babies and high-tech workers, clustered in the Acela Corridor."[20] "I'm the kind of patriot whom people on the Acela corridor laugh at," claimed J. D. Vance in *Hillbilly Elegy*.[21]

Corridor bashing, observes Paul Krugman, is a new way of proclaiming the northeast too godless, refined, and self-absorbed to qualify as "real America."[22] Like the Rust Belt, the Bible Belt, the Deep South, Silicon Valley, and Appalachia, the word *corridor* assigns culture to soil. The train line has become a signpost. A product of manufacturing might and can-do public works, the railroad now represents the region's postindustrial ambivalence: its groundbreaking ingenuity and brooding workaholism, its ethnic diversity and flimsy introspection, its difference-seeking globalism and homogenized bubbles.

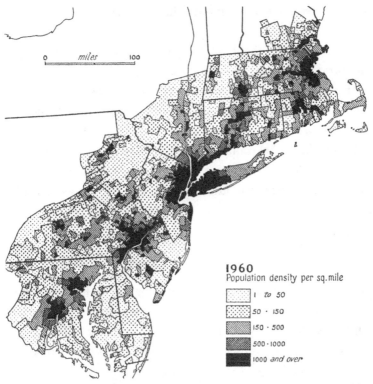

FIGURE 0.1 Northeastern megalopolis depicted through population density. Map of population density of the Northeast, 1960, in Gottmann, *Megalopolis*. Twentieth Century Fund, Inc., by permission of the MIT Press.

Such contradictions have led some to give up on the idea of a cohesive northeast. In 1981 journalist Joel Garreau divided the seaboard into "New England" and a mid-Atlantic "Foundry" to gratify his nagging sense that a better map "had been there, like a piece of corn stuck in your teeth."[23] More recently, author Colin Woodard called the northeast "meaningless," a cartographic fairy tale that ignores "the continent's actual settlement history and sectional rivalries."[24] His map dices the coast into ethnic-religious "nations": Puritan Yankeedom, Dutch New Netherland, Quaker-Germanic Midlands, and an English Tidewater.

Such Eurocentric partition stories miss something that Gottmann gleaned from his research and that Pell pictured as a luminescent sea:

the northeast is defined by motion. Its chief characteristic has never been a common creed or shared blood but an interest in elsewhere—a ceaseless to-and-fro that binds the region to itself and to the world. The corridor descends from a restless heritage that includes Lenape pathbreakers, Dutch traders, Boston mariners, Maryland couriers, and the drivers, pilots, and engineers who steer people through the region today. Examining America's "greatest transportation asset" reveals a northeast that cannot be seen standing still. A northeast that never rinses down to a straight story because it is also a ride—one taken by millions of commuters who, on January 17, 2009, included the next president.

"Happy birthday, kid, welcome to Wilmington! Hi buddy, how are ya? It is cold. It is cold. Yeah. Great." Delaware's seven-term senator bear-hugged Michelle Obama (who turned forty-five that morning). Barack stared at his running mate. "You look sharp, Joe." "So do you, man. So do you."[25]

No one could inhabit an element more than Joe Biden at Wilmington Station. The incoming vice president had spent a lifetime waiting on trains in its brick and terra-cotta confines. Wilmington, a seventeenth-century Swedish fur-trading post turned modern corporate tax haven, was where Biden launched his legendary passenger career, one that spanned two million miles aboard sixteen thousand trains. "Amtrak Joe" was riding the rails to Washington when Amtrak was barely a year old, its hand-me-down coaches still bearing the faded logo of their previous owner, the Penn Central.

Biden's prodigious travels began in tragedy. The former Scrantonian had just defeated Delaware's incumbent senior senator when his wife, Neilia, and infant daughter, Naomi, were killed in a car crash. Biden entered Congress but chose to commute to Washington, ninety minutes each way, so that he could raise his surviving sons in Delaware. The junior senator became a club car regular, holding court in vinyl booths, bottled water or virgin cranberry cocktail in hand.[26]

Thousands gathered to watch Obama's arrival and Biden's send-off in a Wilmington park named for the local abolitionist, Thomas Garrett, and the Underground Railroad's most famous conductor, Harriet Tubman. The first speaker at Tubman-Garrett Riverfront Park was an Amtrak conductor. Gregg Weaver had worked Biden's morning train for decades. "Laptops to lunch cans, blue jeans to custom-fit suits, he knows we're all in this together," said Weaver through the belt-sanded consonants of a Philadelphia accent. "It is my honor to introduce Amtrak's number one commuter."[27]

"Now what [Gregg] didn't tell you," Biden began, "occasionally he'd be standing outside the door as the Acela came up. I'm coming down Martin Luther King Boulevard. I'd call in here to Ron and say, 'Ron, I can see the light. I'm only two away. What do you think?' And he said, 'I'll check with Gregg.'" Biden grinned. "There was always some mechanical difficulty that lasted for a minute or two"—a phantom delay that gave the tardy senator enough time to catch his train.

Biden's aw-shucks schtick was familiar to his constituents, as were his sharp turns to tenderness. "There's a great thing about my love affair with Amtrak. It's truly close and personal. It used to be before it got too big, we used to have a Christmas party." Biden shuffled between yarns, character sketches, one-liners, and policy points with self-effacing ease. The crowd hung less on his every word than on the tidal drift of his candor. Biden clinched his lightly scripted amble by pointing back to the station: "This is more than an ordinary train ride. This is a new beginning."

After Biden, Obama sounded metrical, like train wheels on bolted rail. "I chose Joe because I knew where he came from, even if I haven't spent much time here, because you can learn a lot about a person's hometown through the deeds they have done." Obama reintroduced the Indiana machinists, Michigan truckers, and Colorado teachers who became his stump speech staples. "Irish Catholics in Wilmington and African Americans in the South Side of Chicago" again discovered their common values. This inclusive portrait of national striving played well in Wilmington as it would have in Wichita or West Palm Beach, and that was the point. Obama spoke to the north and the south and the east and the west.

But then, turning trackside, the president-elect delivered a fresh refrain: "To the conductors who make our trains run, and the workers who laid down the rails. To the parents who worry about how they're going to pay the bills next month while on the commute to work. And to the children who hear the whistle of the train and dream of a better life. That's who we're fighting for. That's who needs change."

Obama drew listeners off into allegory, then back to a cold Delaware morning. His tribute addressed all Americans but echoed in the presence of railroaders: Biden's conductor, Gregg Weaver, and the Inaugural Express's conductor, Noel Powell. Had he stepped outside his locomotive cab, engineer Carlyle Smith, who sported a suit and fedora, could have heard as well.[28] Obama summoned the flesh and blood that lives behind the railroad a hundred yards behind him. Who conducted those trains, after all? Who rode them to work and heard their whistle? Who laid the rails? Who laid *those* rails?

Who knows? The line that carried Obama to Washington was first built in the early 1800s, when sledge-wielding crews drove horse trams into wilderness, leaving timber ties and strap iron in their dusty wake. The conversion of these makeshift stubs into a high-speed railroad required over a century of toil: hand-dug culverts, welded truss bridges, palatial stations, state-of-the-art signal systems, high-voltage transmission networks, vast managerial hierarchies, herculean feats of paper processing—and a dauntless commitment to keeping everything operable.

That a train line this old and intricate still functions is miraculous. And yet today's riders dwell less on the corridor's longevity than on its defects. The rails curl and contort, a legacy of antebellum engineering and long-lost eminent domain battles. Writer Joseph Vranich calculates that the "pretzel-like track" between New York and Boston could form ten full circles.[29] Some of the corridor's oldest catenary wires droop in summer heat, occasionally snagging the trains they power.[30] The line's movable bridges, which lift and swing to let fishing charters enter Long Island Sound and waste barges putter down the Hackensack River, have a habit of jamming. The corridor's tunnels seep and sometimes flood. At a 2013 congressional field hearing, planner Robert Yaro described a railroad held together by "Band-Aids and bailing wire."[31]

Yaro's language, unusually colorful for the buttoned-up realm of federal subcommittee reports, cuts to the corridor's central paradox: the line appears ultramodern one moment then prehistoric the next, especially when compared with systems elsewhere in the world. The twenty-first-century global boom in high-speed rail projects has shown how aggressive transportation spending gives nations a state-of-the-art sheen. The corridor has less sheen than patina. Unlike systems from scratch in China, Japan, France, Spain, Italy, Saudi Arabia, and South Korea, America's corridor came together intermittently over two centuries. None of the line's original builders knew what it would become.

The corridor right of way retains this history. Its rails read like the rings of an oak tree. In Wilmington, the line that Obama mentioned received its original charter from Delaware's legislature, its sandstone embankment from the share-held Pennsylvania Railroad, its catenary from a package of Public Works Administration loans, and its trains from the federally owned corporation Amtrak and the municipal transit authority SEPTA.

The corridor's absorption of private capital and public subsidy and its operation under for-profit carriers and government bureaucracy epitomizes the kind of compromise that has come to define American infrastructure. And yet when Americans dream of riding their own trains of tomorrow, they usually see them zipping between DC and Boston. The country's most crowded region remains the most obvious place to imagine passenger railroading's future even when the railroad itself can seem like a duct-taped relic.

Obama's Inaugural Express embraced these contradictions by finding in trains the holiness of heritage and the promise of innovation. As his charter pulled away from Wilmington, it seemed that America's historical crossroads had become a rail junction, the line's endless interlocking of past and present personified in the postcard snapshot of the first Black president waving goodbye to Delaware from the back of a vintage business car.

Maryland is dormant fields and bare woods. A lacrosse net stands in one yard. An outboard motor rusts in another. The Inaugural Express rolled on through rural counties that McCain and Palin won by double digits. An hour's ride from Philadelphia reveals a different northeast, more spread out and conservative, anchored not by downtowns but defense contractors, big-box stores, and office parks. The landscape brims with brackish creeks and bird habitat, Rite Aids and Dunkin' Donuts.

Obama's express crossed an estuary where the Susquehanna River drains into Chesapeake Bay. The granite piers of an abandoned bridge rise next to the tracks.[32] In summer, herons roost on these bleached pedestals, which once bore trains. Before this older bridge opened in 1866, passengers transferred from rail coaches to ferries. These riders included Frederick Douglass, who escaped slavery by forging free papers, disguising himself as a sailor, and catching a northbound train from Baltimore. "The train was moving at a very high rate of speed for that time of railroad travel," Douglass recalled, "but to my anxious mind, it was moving far too slowly."[33]

After miles of dreamy piedmont, Baltimore formstone punches through the horizon. Cable commentators took this occasion to remark that Obama's express was retracing the last leg of Abraham Lincoln's own inaugural journey. When Lincoln steamed out of Springfield in 1861, six states had already left the Union, and pro-slavery Maryland appeared poised to secede. Despite his resounding victory in 1860, Lincoln won just 2.5 percent of Maryland ballots.[34] Months later, he had no way of reaching Washington but through the hostile Chesapeake region and its temperamental chief port, nicknamed Mobtown.

The Philadelphia, Wilmington, & Baltimore Railroad hired Allen Pinkerton to investigate plots against the president-elect. Pinkerton caroused around Baltimore until he allegedly uncovered a conspiracy to assassinate Lincoln. The purported plot, masterminded by a Corsican barber, exploited the railroad's lack of continuous track through Baltimore. When Lincoln arrived at Calvert Street Station, his carriage would be hitched to a horse team, towed over rails grooved in Pratt Street, then coupled to a connecting train at the Baltimore & Ohio Railroad's Camden Station. This interlude gave assassins crowd cover and a clear shot.

Though he hated the idea of stealing into Washington "like a thief in the night," Lincoln revised his itinerary.[35] Instead of riding his ceremonial charter through Maryland by day, he boarded an ordinary 11 p.m. departure from Philadelphia. The future emancipator hid behind drapes in a sleeping berth. When the other riders exited in Baltimore, Lincoln's car was decoupled from its train, towed by horse through the harbor basin, and parked at Camden Street Station. Lincoln waited for his connection behind carriage blinds while predawn drunks belted out "Dixie."[36] The hours dragged on until a whistle shriek told Lincoln that his locomotive had arrived. By 6 a.m., the next president was in Washington.

Lincoln faced threats throughout his presidency until the night John Wilkes Booth shot him. The slain president was loaded aboard a funeral train beside the exhumed casket of his son Willie for the 1,654-mile journey home to Illinois. In Baltimore, mourners crammed crepe-lined streets in such numbers that the cortege took three hours to move nine blocks. Ten thousand grieving Baltimoreans filed through the Merchant's Exchange Building to see the man so many Marylanders once defied.

Eight years later, Baltimore's horse tram transfers were a thing of the past. Trains now rolled continuously under Mobtown through tunnels and cuts. The tunnels' tight turns and low clearances limited trains to thirty miles per hour. In later years seepage chewed through the bore linings. Ice caked the walls in winter and weeds bloomed by the portals each spring. And yet like so much other corridor masonry, the tunnels outlived their builders. It was these frozen shafts that Obama's train negotiated in the moments leading up to his next rally.

Forty thousand people filled War Memorial Plaza under a dim orange sun.[37] Obama paid homage to the "sailors, militia men, and even a runaway slave" who defended Fort McHenry during the War of 1812. And that fight, he suggested, continued through present strife: "an economy that's faltering. Two wars: one that needs to be ended responsibly [Iraq], and one that needs to be waged wisely [Afghanistan]. A planet that's warming (although you cannot tell today) from our unsustainable dependence on oil."

Compared to his Delaware benediction, this speech sobered listeners with its allusion to foreign war and domestic recession, its dire warnings and open address to those "starting to lose faith in the country," CNN analyst David Gergen explained.[38] Obama's severity owed something to the seriousness of the presidency, now just three days and thirty-eight miles away. "And yet, while our problems may be new, what is required to overcome them is not new . . . what's required is a new Declaration of Independence." Obama closed by inviting his audience to "seek a better world in our time." His entourage left War Memorial Plaza. What came next was Washington, the White House, the dawn of "our time," but first, a waiting train.

Night fell as the Inaugural Express approached Washington. The crowds dwindled. Obama and Biden remained inside their Pullman, a varnished blue treasure chest on wheels emblazoned "Georgia 300." Obama first encountered Georgia 300's brass fixtures and diamond-patterned carpet on a primary junket through Pennsylvania. The car had previously hosted Jimmy Carter, George H. W. Bush, and Bill Clinton. John Kerry and John Edwards rode Georgia 300 from Missouri to Arizona during their 2004 campaign.

Before its refurbishment for private excursions, Georgia 300 carried ordinary passengers between New York and New Orleans on the Southern Railroad's Crescent Limited. The car was painted bright apple green and christened "General Polk" in honor of Leonidas Polk, an Episcopal minister and Confederate lieutenant general. "Sewanee's Fighting Bishop" fought at Shiloh, Perryville, and the rail junction of Atlanta, where he was blown apart by a Union shell. In its previous life, Obama's gleaming flagship honored a rebel commander who enslaved at least 215 people on his Tennessee plantation.[39]

Reporters covering the Inaugural Express stressed the pivotal role that train attendants known as Pullman porters played in building an African American middle class. The passenger coach, they implied, told a story of racial uplift. But railroads retain many pasts — in their paths, their paint, and the worlds they convene. No commentator mentioned the legacy of Leonidas Polk, still honored by a memorial society whose website proclaims, "our work is unfinished."[40]

The Obamas emerged at Union Station looking tired — like they had ridden a very delayed train. The typical two-hour journey from Philadelphia had, one reporter observed, "stretched into more than seven."[41] Barack waved to the cameras, shook his conductors' hands, and rode off in a limousine to the presidential guest house where his family already lived. The inauguration was now seventy hours away. This cathartic celebration would draw over a million people to the National Mall, creating one of the busiest days in corridor history.

Railroads gave the Obama administration something to rally around during its first hundred days: an epic infrastructure program to match the president's heroic rhetoric and a new New Deal to put machinists, electricians, drivers, inspectors, and surveyors back to work after the 2008 financial crash. The American Recovery and Reinvestment Act allocated eight billion dollars to passenger rail projects. "There's no reason," Obama declared in his first State of the Union, "Europe or China should have the fastest train."[42]

The stimulus act called for new high-speed lines serving Raleigh, Richmond, Topeka, Tulsa, El Paso, and Flagstaff — passengers in "the north and the south and the east and the west," and not just a blue state seaboard.[43] But the president's high-minded dispersal of recovery grants blew up in his face when Republican governors in Wisconsin, Ohio, and Florida shipped their money back to Washington rather than lay rails. After canceling a proposed line between Milwaukee and Madison, Governor Scott Walker advised Obama to put "those funds into the use for roads and bridges."[44]

The Department of Transportation diverted Wisconsin's money not to roads, as Walker wanted, but to rail projects, including California's attempt to link Los Angeles and San Francisco with high-speed rail, and the northeast corridor, where it paid for new overpasses, transmission upgrades, and interlocking tower demolitions.[45] Stimulus-funded maintenance refurbished parts of the old line as its traffic began to surge: Amtrak corridor ridership leapt by 33 percent during Obama's two terms.[46] While the president entered office intending to build something new, he settled for shoring up an inheritance.

Today the corridor's capacity to keep pace with its region will go a long way toward determining whether the northeast remains a traversable place—a place that in 2010 hosted 17 percent of the country's inhabitants and 20 percent of its trade on just 1.4 percent of its land.[47] The I-95 Corridor Coalition calculates that 60 percent of the thruway's urban sections are already congested and predicts that car traffic will increase by 85 percent by 2035.[48] Nearly half of the nation's domestic flight delays originate in New York, New Jersey, and Philadelphia.[49] Seventy percent of the country's chronically delayed flights navigate the corridor's contrail-streaked airspace.[50]

Claiborne Pell warned his Senate colleagues that a megalopolis "can flourish mightily—or it can stagnate."[51] The outcome depended on the country's willingness to provide transit for the masses. Once surpassed by the speed of jets and the convenience of cars, northeastern trains are mounting a comeback. Their rally is visible in packed park and ride lots and trackside condo developments from Maryland to Massachusetts. The railroad resurgence is most conspicuous in the corridor's busiest hub: New York. In 2019, six hundred fifty thousand passengers scuttled through Penn Station each day, more people than flew out of Kennedy, LaGuardia, and Newark airports combined, more people than took the Lincoln and Holland Tunnels.[52]

The electric trains that carry those riders expend less energy per passenger mile than planes and automobiles while emitting a fraction of the carbon exhaust.[53] If, as architects suggest, the greenest building is one that already exists, then perhaps the most ecological infrastructure is already up and running. In a time of combustion-driven climate change in a region afflicted by chronically high child asthma rates, the compact, fuel-efficient corridor is a gift from history and a tool for survival.[54] Yet it wobbles on the brink of ruin.

How did the corridor come to be what it is? Can it get better? Can it be enough? Answering these questions requires a story— a tale of politics, demographics, regionalism, ideology, technology, and the countless tactile impressions that make up transit. The Acela Lounge's corporate blue serenity, the chlorine stench of terminal toilets, the cherry almond scent of Amtrak soap, the passive aggression engulfing every Quiet Car, the faux-oak interiors of battered commuter coaches, the platform storm blast of an express train, the coach-seat daydreaming of what life is like through each passing window, the look of 30th Street Station in winter sunlight, and the smell of Trenton after summer rain.

How can we hold on to what we have while waiting for something better to arrive? How can we "stay with the trouble" of old infrastructure, learning to care for something imperfect, without retreating into futuristic fantasies?[55] How can we muddle through? The story that answers these questions begins before the United States was a country. It begins before the northeast was even a thing at all.

I. TRACES

· 1 ·

A SOMEWHERE-ELSE FEELING

So there it was, the light of day.
It walks the road each morning, that light of day.
MUNSEE LENAPE CREATION STORY[1]

The first easterners took their name from an Algonquian word meaning "dawn." Wampanoags saw the sun rise off the coast of present-day Massachusetts. As shore dwellers, they received solar priority and so called themselves "people of the first light," which also meant "eastern people."[2] The Wampanoags settled the dawning tip of a vast alcove that winds like slack rope from Nantucket Shoals to the Outer Banks. Oceanographers call this cove the Middle Atlantic Bight.[3] Between Cape Cod and Chesapeake Bay, the bight bends around a disc of open sea. This coastal arch is the American northeast.

The Wampanoag were indigenous to the bight, but their land came from elsewhere. Twenty-five million years ago, tectonic plates heaved the microcontinent of Avalonia against the coast of proto–North America. Avalonia crumpled against a layer cake of lava that bubbled through the ocean floor 415 million years ago. Geologists refer to most of New England as "exotic terranes" to distinguish its beds of alien magma from the continent's native alluvium flats and rift basins.[4]

Forged from fire, the land was then scoured by ice. The Pleistocene sent a snowy blue crust creaking over the continent. The glacier reached what became Central New Jersey, where it dumped its spoils along a ridge that snakes between Edison and Metuchen. The ice sheet gouged popsicle-shaped kettle ponds and carved a fjord to-day known as the Hudson River. It shaved Canada like a razor and dumped its trimmings in the ocean to build Nantucket, Cape Cod, and the outwash plain of Long Island. The ice's retreat littered New England with loaves of gneiss and quartz that Yankee farmers plucked from fields and stacked into walls.

By the time the Wampanoags settled their headlands, the ice had receded, and plants grew. Manhattan alone burst with oak, beech, hornbeam, juniper, cedar, walnut, ash, linden, birch, elm, and poplar. Roses decked the island's meadows and grape vines coiled around its trunks. To nature's arboretum Dutch colonists added apple and pear. They pressed tulip bulbs into topsoil and scattered an invasive bouquet of peonies, hollyhocks, and carnations.[5] "It was indeed a spot," Washington Irving later wrote, "on which the eye might have reveled forever."[6]

After the last dinosaur plodded across Hartford or Newark Basin, it left the land to beavers, minks, cougars, and bears. From the dark underbrush glowed the white eyeshine of wolves ("not as big and ferocious as those in the Netherlands," assured seventeenth-century colonist Adriaen van der Donck).[7] Canopies filled with fathomless wingbeats. The waters teemed with wriggling profusions of fish. Ale-wives glimmered in creeks like spilt coins. Humpback whales spouted in the East River. Oyster reefs carpeted river mouths.

The Wampanoag shared the bight with others who spoke Algonquian languages, raised winter longhouses, and practiced a slash-and-burn husbandry that seeded the three sisters of maize, beans, and squash. To their north were the Massachusett and the Abenaki, who called their beachfront "dawnland."[8] To the west Narragansetts controlled the bay that bears their name. To *their* west were the Pequot and Quinnipiac, who fished and crabbed the gentle surf of Long Island Sound. Lenaphoking, homeland of the Lenape people, stretched from the marble-laced Taconics to the pine dunes of Cape Henlopen. The Piscataway occupied the Chesapeake tidewaters.

Their Nacotchtank confederates raised wigwams on the knoll later christened Capitol Hill.

European visitors grafted themselves into Indigenous America before seizing it for themselves. The English Calvinists who found their New Jerusalem on the sea-blasted terranes helped Chief Massasoit fight the Narragansett. Mohawk-harvested beaver pelts stocked a Dutch emporium on Lenape Manhattan. Across the North River, Low Country farmers diked the spartina marshes in an attempt to recreate Holland in the Hackensack meadows. To their southwest, William Penn's "holy experiment" called on its Quaker settlers to "live soberly and kindly" with the Lenape on whom they imposed Pennsylvania.[9] A downriver colony of Swedes, Finns, Danes, and Dutch trapped beaver and harpooned whales with Lenape permission and squared logs so precisely that their cabins stood "without a nail or a spike."[10] Beyond New Sweden, Lord Baltimore orchestrated Maryland within a sinuous plot that snaked from the Blue Ridge peaks to Pocomoke Sound.

Mid-Atlantic people answered different gods and leaders. They built homes from disparate timbers and cajoled crops from diverse mixtures of clay, sand, and glacial scrap. They forged distinct ideas of kinship and local "conceptions of life."[11] But they shared the sea. The northeast saw its silhouette in the ocean — in the tumbling main that gave English colonists a "bridge to Great Britain" and in the tidal estuaries that pulsed inland to Hartford, Albany, Trenton, and Alexandria.[12] The ocean received Pequot messengers in sycamore canoes, seasick New Yorkers in yawing packet boats, and the pirate Blackbeard, who hunted the inlets of Delaware Bay. Jean Gottmann credits the "deep harbors of a drowned shoreline" with making the land of first light a vestibule between the "rich heart of the continent and the rest of the world."[13] A leaky coast gave northeasterners access to elsewhere.

Footpaths complemented the water. Native couriers conducted trade and diplomacy over a vast network of woodland trails. Observing that Lenape shell beads have been excavated "deep in the continental interior," historian Daniel Richter concludes that eastern trade reached the Great Plains.[14] Trails linked seaboard societies "hinged on mobility," writes William Cronon, connecting people already accustomed to "breaking up and reassembling" their communities in pursuit of spawning fish, migrating fowl, and fertile soil.[15] The paths must have been busy since only habitual footfalls would have kept them from vanishing into scrub.[16]

Some trails became the interstates of their day. The Pequot Path ran from Shawmut (Boston) down Narragansett Flats and along Long Island Sound before entering Manhattan via a roiling creek ford that the Dutch called "Spuyten Duyvil." Europeans hired native trail guides but still found overland travel terrifying. "Each lifeless Trunk, with its shatter'd Limbs, appear'd an Armed Enyymie, and every little stump like a Ravenous devourer," trembled Sarah Kemble Knight, a Boston teacher who survived a round trip to New York in 1704.[17] Knight feared violent death at every turn on an itinerary through Stamford, Norwalk, and Fairfield that now carries the mundane familiarity of a Metro-North timetable.

The Lenape linked the Shatemuc (Hudson) and Lenapewihittuck (Delaware) Rivers with two paths. The Lower Assunpink Trail wound through the Mill River Valley between Aquehonga (Staten Island) and the Council Fires of the Unami (Crosswicks, New Jersey). The Upper Assunpink Trail originated in the Palisades, merged with the Lower Trail in what is now Metropark, then split off toward Assunpink Village through the future sites of New Brunswick, Princeton, and Trenton. At the height of Holland's imperial power, so many traders schlepped furs along the Upper Assunpink that people took to calling it the Old Dutch Trail.[18]

In 1667 the Treaty of Breda ended the Second Anglo-Dutch War, giving England control of New Netherland. The war had gone disastrously for England, but Charles II's fleets managed to capture New Amsterdam, which they renamed in honor of the king's brother, James, Duke of York. Charles tried to draw his colonial subjects into a "strict Allyance and Correspondency" by converting their foot trails into carriage highways.[19] The king believed that good roads and a regular post could unite Virginian planters, Pennsylvania Quakers,

FIGURE 1.1 Corridor tracks run beside a canalized remnant of Assunpink Creek in Trenton. Lenape travelers beat a path alongside this stream to form part of a trail network that connected the Lenapewihittuck (Delaware) and Shatemuc (Hudson) Rivers. Photograph by Henry Rowan.

New York merchants, and Rhode Island zealots into a cohesively English New World.

Charles, who committed much of his waking life to parties, plays, and vigorous adultery, proved a halfhearted infrastructuralist. The "Merry Monarch" sired a dozen children out of wedlock without issuing a single legitimate heir. Absorbed by his raucous court at Whitehall Palace and the trials of the Great Plague and London Fire, Charles did little more than rebrand existing colonial paths as a "King's Highway." Despite its regal designation, the "highway" still heaped with winter snow that thawed into spring mud. Tree roots tripped feet and hooves. Salmon swam over some sections during high tide. To withstand the trials of the road, mail carriers had to be "active, stout, and indefatigable."[20]

For all its shortcomings, the royal fiction of the King's Highway suggested a common project for trade and defense. When Pennsylvania's Provincial Council authorized a new road between Philadelphia and Bristol, members believed the track would double as a segment of the King's Highway. William Penn put his Quakers to work on the road and its stone bridges over the Poquessing and Pennypack Creeks. New York ratified a law for the "better laying out, ascertaining, and preserving the Publick Common and general highways."[21] New Jersey started a lottery to fund roads.[22] The highway nurtured intercolonial society along its piecemeal spine. "A meeting-house would appear, then a tavern, then a marketplace," notes Eric Jaffee, "and soon the route conferred upon its New World residents a sense of permanency, safety, and hope."[23]

One such hopeful traveler left Boston in 1723. Benjamin Franklin, age seventeen, broke an apprenticeship to his brother, the printer and gazetteer, James. Benjamin so feared punishment that he made up a story about impregnating a "naughty girl" to wheedle his way aboard an outbound sloop.[24] The *Speedwell* blew around the tip of Cape Cod and entered New York Harbor three days later. Franklin could not find printshop work in Manhattan, and so he followed a lead to Philadelphia.

This journey began on the Battery docks. Franklin's autobiography recounts that as soon as the ferry shoved off a "squall tore our rotten sails to pieces."[25] Wind drove the boat toward Brooklyn's jagged beaches, where the last glacier dumped its load before melting back to Canada. "Some people came down to the water edge and hallow'd to us, as we did to them, but the wind was so high, and the surf so loud, that we could not hear so as to understand each other."[26] The captain dropped anchor. Passengers grew seasick, then thirsty, having embarked without "any drink but a bottle of filthy rum, and the water we sail'd on being salt."[27] They pitched over the churn for thirty hours before reaching Perth Amboy, where a "very feverish" Franklin stepped onto solid ground.[28]

Amboy now belongs to a sulfurous portscape known as the Chemical Coast. The brown spool of Arthur Kill slinks behind gantries, ethanol tanks, and grids of incandescent asterisks. Franklin disembarked to a quaint village where oyster rakers combed the shallows and shell mounds piled outside vestigial Dutch taverns. He gulped down cold water to ease his fever, then hiked off across the cinched waist of New Jersey. Franklin later complained that the road's sandy surface exhausted horses, and its route "was not well inhabited, nor the Inns well supply'd with provisions."[29] Rain pattered the lonely track. Franklin "cut so miserable a figure, too, that I found, by the questions ask'd me, I was suspected to be some runaway servant, and in danger of being taken up on that suspicion."

In Burlington Franklin bought gingerbread (a salve against sea sickness) and split oxcheek and ale with an old woman. One evening, while killing time by the docks, waiting on the next ferry to Philadelphia, Franklin spied a small vessel—not a scheduled ferry but a rowboat. He hailed the crew who "took me in, and as there was no wind, we row'd all the way."[30] As night fell the crew wondered whether they passed Philadelphia in the darkness. They docked in a creek in what turned out to be Camden and spent the night shivering around a bonfire of stolen fenceposts. At sunrise, Franklin crossed the Delaware to the wooden planks of Market Street wharf. With only a "Dutch dollar, and about a shilling copper," he bought three "great puffy rolls" and set about becoming Philadelphian.[31]

Franklin traveled between English North America's three largest cities by sloop, ferry, foot, and oar. Other routes were available. Franklin could have walked west out of Boston over a post road to Hartford or followed Sarah Kemble Knight's footsteps along the Pequot Trail (now grandiosely reimagined as a King's Highway). He could have ferried across the Hudson River and avoided the stygian crossing to Amboy. He could have bypassed New Jersey altogether in the ocean packet that carried his luggage. He could have taken the Old Dutch Road from Amboy and lodged under the sign of the White Hart at New Brunswick or the Indian Queen at Princeton or the Royal Oak at Trenton. He could have entered Philadelphia over a 1697 masonry arch erected by order of William Penn—a span so strong that it still carries traffic over Frankford Creek today.

"Early America was a busy tangle of travelers, couriers, sailors, and riders," writes historian Katherine Grandjean, "a mess of motion."[32] Northeastern logistics have grown only messier since 1723. Were

Franklin to attempt the same getaway today, he would encounter highways, skyways, boulevards, and turnpikes. He would pass under high-tension power lines sizzling with alternating current and over pipelines coursing with pressurized petroleum. He would cross tracks clattering with stainless steel trains, freight yards brimming with gondolas and boxcars, and rusted spurs framing weeds like box gardens. He would have heard the shoreline drone with tankers, trawlers, and garbage barges. He would have seen jets, medivacs, and news choppers flock the same sky where dawn shone over the Wampanoags.

The northeast has given so much of itself to transit, to the corridors that make the region more than a sum of cities and wilds. Few colonists took to these corridors more avidly than Franklin, who washed up on the wharves of Philadelphia as a bedraggled teenager, who surveyed almost every inch of the King's Highway as postmaster general to the Crown then to Congress, who crossed the Atlantic Ocean eight times, and who wagered at the age of seventy-nine that he could handle a coach ride over the "sandy road between Burlington and Amboy."[33] In his private affairs and public career, Franklin exhibited a restlessness that antiquarian Seymour Dunbar called a "somewhere-else feeling."[34] Franklin was hardly the first northeasterner to feel this affliction — or the last.

PROMISING
PASSAGE

Intercourse throughout the Union will be facilitated by new improvements. Roads will everywhere be shortened, and kept in better order; accommodations for travelers will be multiplied and meliorated; an interior navigation on our eastern side will be opened throughout, or nearly throughout, the whole extent of the thirteen States.

JAMES MADISON[1]

"We are the Athens of North America," proclaimed poet, *salonnière*, and Philadelphian Elizabeth Graeme.[2] Seventy years after Benjamin Franklin staggered down Market Street to stuff his face with popovers, William Penn's "green countrie towne" flourished. Philadelphia's pebble-paved, lamplit streets hosted the country's first philosophical society, subscription library, and medical school.[3] Clockmaker David Rittenhouse watched the transit of Venus through a homemade telescope and later became vice provost of the University of Pennsylvania.[4] Poet Philip Freneau arrived from New York to launch the *National Gazette*.[5] His neighbors included future novelist Charles Brockden Brown and eventual steamboat pioneer Robert Fulton, still training as a portrait miniaturist.

Philadelphia cut its reputation as a federalist laboratory by hosting the symposia that hammered out the Declaration of Independence and the Constitution. In 1790 William Penn's urban arbor became the nation's temporary capital while a new federal canton congealed in the Potomac backwaters. The District of Columbia at first felt so desolate, its residents so dusty and dispirited, that some Philadelphians hoped government would remain forever at 6th and Chestnut. Anyone who heard George Washington deliver his 135-word second inaugural address before Congress Hall or spent a Friday night at one of Martha Washington's punch-fueled drawing room parties had good reason to imagine Philadelphia as the lasting locus of national life.[6]

The summer of 1793 roasted Pennsylvania. Rivers dropped in their beds. Creeks curdled into slime.[7] People noticed black billows of mosquitos swarming the docks. By July they complained of symptoms: weariness, chills, and a "frequent propensity to puke," noted William Currie, fellow of the College of Physicians.[8] Severe cases left patients with a "cadaverous appearance . . . succeeded by a deep yellow or leaden colour of the skin and nails; the eyes become suffused with blood, and the countenance appears like that of one strangled."[9] By winter, one in ten Philadelphians had died of yellow fever.

Pathogens had always been a cost of transacting business in the Atlantic sphere. Harbors, like lungs, absorb the outside world. Philadelphia's docks received sacks of coffee, bolts of taffeta, crates of port, cords of sandalwood, enslaved people—and the viruses that caused measles, smallpox, and influenza. Residents steeled themselves for the late summer "sickly season," when wealthy citizens retreated to the high ground and cool breezes outside town. But the sickness of 1793 moved faster and struck harder than anything people remembered. Philadelphians tried the usual plague prophylactics: firing muskets to purify the atmosphere, chewing garlic to induce sweat, and wearing tar-coated ropes to ward off distemper.[10] But nothing worked, and no one knew why.

Chestertown, Maryland, was the first community to ban travelers from Philadelphia. Its councilors feared that a disease they heard spread "to Trenton, Princeton, Woodbridge, and Elizabeth-town, on the post road to New York" could also swim through the blood of southbound passengers.[11] In Havre de Grace, constables required everyone crossing the Susquehanna River to show certificates proving they had come from somewhere other than Philadelphia.[12] Baltimore officials pledged to prosecute anyone foolish enough to host a Philadelphian. New York threatened lurking fever refugees with quarantine on Governor's Island.[13] Fears of a regionwide pandemic exposed the northeast as a league of rival city-states that would sever common ties to save themselves. The King's Highway that Charles II decreed for "strict Allyance and Correspondency" now extended the flimsiest promise of passage.[14]

Travel was hard even in more trusting times. The King's Highway lay strewn with mud clots pitched from verging fields. Cattle hooves dimpled its surface. Rain carved gullies through the right of way.[15] In 1773 the surveyor Hugh Finlay described the highway east of New London as a "bed of rocks."[16] Each rut and cobble rattled the ribs of passengers on plank-bench wagons slung over tar-greased wheels.[17] The rivers that linked northeastern ports cut northeastern roads to shreds. Bridges required a combination of statecraft and carpentry that few eighteenth-century officials could muster. It was not until 1804 that Theodore Burr supervised construction of the first permanent span across the Delaware River. He learned during the project that his cousin, the vice president, had shot Alexander Hamilton.

America's impasse stemmed from a lack of money, a dearth of knowledge, and what Philadelphia economist Tench Coxe decried as "detached local interests."[18] Though constitutionally bound to "provide for the common defence, promote the general Welfare, and secure the Blessings of Liberty," states clung to colonial-era grudges, and usually built their own roads, canals, breakwaters, and lighthouses. Philadelphia, Boston, Providence, New York, and Baltimore paid less attention to each other than to the task of turning their hinterlands into cargo bound for Europe, Africa, the Caribbean, and Canada. The nineteenth-century Bostonian Henry Adams lamented that "each group of states lived a life apart."[19]

The country's third president, Enlightenment disciple and Virginian enslaver Thomas Jefferson, sought order. When Jefferson moved to Washington in 1801, the White House looked across a ragged "mall" to the Potomac River, which jittered down from the Alleghany highlands. Where older cities vied for maritime supremacy, Washington, nestled just below the fall line merge of coastal plain and foothill, faced west. Jefferson dreamed of linking the Great Lakes, the Gulf of Mexico, and the Potomac, Ohio, and Mississippi Rivers into a great fluvial freight system.[20] Fifty-seven days into office, he purchased the right to bargain for Indigenous lands west to the Rocky Mountains. The Louisiana Purchase doubled US territory and deepened the need for federal transportation planning.

Jefferson chose a western settler to author his plan. Albert Gallatin immigrated from Geneva in 1780 bearing a letter of recommendation from Benjamin Franklin. He left Boston to command a fort in Machias, Maine, then purchased a Pennsylvania farm overlooking the Monongahela River. Gruff, balding, and brilliant, Gallatin embraced the doctrine of internal improvements as Jefferson's treasury secretary. In 1808 he submitted to Congress a report discussing potential improvements to the nation's roads, canals, harbors, and rivers. Gallatin's public works proposals included an early version of the Intercoastal Waterway and a "great turnpike extending from Maine to Georgia."[21] "Good roads and canals," Gallatin proclaimed, "will shorten distances, facilitate commercial and personal intercourse, and unite by a still more intimate community of interests the most remote quarters of the United States."[22]

Gallatin believed that only the federal government could harness America's improving impulse. He wanted central planning to subsume the haphazard ventures that states and joint-stock companies had been cooking up for decades. His vision of integrated federal works enticed senators, but no one knew whether Congress had the authority to repair roads without state consent, much less construct new interstate arteries. Article 1, Section 8 of the Constitution authorized legislators to "establish post Offices and post Roads," but it was unclear whether the verb "establish" authorized government to pave actual strips of land or merely to carry mail over existing routes.

And what of those Americans who did not want improvers beating paths to their doors for tax collectors and military recruiters? What about the Scots-Irish mountaineers who savored the chance to remain ungoverned in their Appalachian hollows, or the surviving Lenape of the Midwest, already evicted from their ancestral lands, now warily watching Europeans encroach again?[23] Transportation projects polarized America because they compelled its people to decide on the country they would have—to name those works that would formulate the national public.

While Americans dithered over the question of improvement, calamity forced them into motion. In 1812, the United States again went to war with Britain. Unlike the Revolution, which engaged the seaboard, its sequel raged across the interior from Detroit to New Orleans. The US Army struggled to transport troops and supplies across wilderness. The British Navy blockaded Atlantic ports, diverting marine cargo onto congested highways.[24] A British coal embargo spurred Pennsylvanians to mine anthracite from the Wyoming Valley, an early stab at national energy independence that required new canals and fortified roads. John C. Calhoun, US war secretary, equated public works with a "more complete defence of the United States."[25]

Less than two months after the Treaty of Ghent ended hostilities, the Indonesian volcano Mount Tambora erupted, spewing ash, dust, rock, and cubic miles of sulfur into Earth's atmosphere. Ten thousand people died on the Dutch East Indies island of Sumbawa. Volcanic haze blotted skies around the globe. The air over the North Atlantic chilled. In May 1816, frost crept as far south as Trenton. A June snowstorm blanketed Albany. Cisterns crusted with ice in Virginia. The "year without a summer" hit hardest in New England, where farmers sick of coaxing "food from stone" packed up for Ohio, Indiana, and Illinois—heartland territories dealt pleasant weather by the roulette wheel of climate change.[26]

As easterners marched west, Congress enacted just one of Gallatin's projects, a mountain portage linking the Potomac and Ohio Rivers. The Cumberland—or National—Road was completed in 1820. Its broad grade, macadamized surface, and drainage culverts impressed passengers, but the cost of maintaining a ridgeline route to Ohio strained the federal budget. Congress surrendered the road to Maryland, Virginia, and Pennsylvania, which installed tollgates, thereby diminishing the great work's publicness. The federal government's reluctance to sponsor improvements intensified competition among states, who now raced each other toward the moving target of the American West.

Pennsylvanians met their match in the Alleghenies, a sandstone range that cartographers denoted with black bars and cone pickets. The leading lights of the American Philosophical Society pondered how to pierce the rock chain separating Philadelphia from Pittsburgh. In 1826 legislators authorized a Rube Goldberg machine of turnpikes, portages, rope inclines, and railways. The Main Line of Public Works proved as cumbersome as its title.[27] While early sponsors delighted in the prospect of "mountain sailing" through high-altitude canals, most Main Line passengers found their journeys tedious.[28] Harriet Cheeney reported being "dragged along in the canal at a slow rate of forty miles a day, the distance of 300 miles. No water to drink but the water of the canal, and other things as dirty accordingly."[29] Cheeney found the portage rails "very icy," shrugging, "it is curious to see what is invented by man."[30]

New York, by contrast, enjoyed a landscape tailor made for freight. The Hudson River drilled through the Appalachians, leaving a nautical route to the interior that no other port possessed. Were this gift of the glaciers not enough, the Mohawk River scooped a gentle valley west through the plains. New Yorkers could reach the Great Lakes without scaling mountain peaks (like the projectors of Pennsylvania's Main Line) or involving other states (like the architects of the Cumberland Road and Potomac River navigation). Though canal diggers dealt with malarial swamps, tree trunks, and the Niagara Escarpment, their trough rose scarcely six hundred feet over its 363-mile course.[31]

The ditch to Buffalo was a coup for Manhattan merchants who made New York America's transshipment king. The rest of the country would play catch-up for decades.

By May 1825 barges floated across upstate New York from a temporary canal head near Rochester to the city of Troy, where they were roped to paddle steamers and tugged down the Hudson River. The Hudson wound south from its Adirondack source, Lake Tear of the Clouds, through the Saratoga Sand Plains and granite highlands. It slipped past the Catskills and lapped against the slender island whose mercantile bazaar had finally eclipsed Philadelphia.

Life was quieter across the river from Manhattan on a bucolic New Jersey headland known to Hackensacks as Gamoenapa ("village of the shore"); to Dutch colonists as Pavonia, Communipaw, and Bergen; and to English settlers as Hoboken. Washington Irving doted on these gentle coves sprinkled with oyster shells. He relished the cabbage gardens shaded by sycamores and the taverns full of pipe smoke, all dramatically cast against the Palisades' serpentinite wall. He called Hoboken a "wonderful little place unchanged, though in sight of the most changeful city in the universe."[32]

The timeless strand belonged to John Stevens, a Continental Army colonel who purchased part of "Hobuck Island" in 1784. Stevens cleared a terrace, built a villa for himself, and erected a hotel for travelers crossing to Manhattan aboard his steam ferry, the *Juliana*. The colonel plotted a residential grid and hawked lots to speculators at Wall Street's Tontine Coffee House. With its flower-studded meadows, gladed river walk, and grotto gurgling with magnesium-infused spring water, Castle Point tantalized city dwellers across the harbor. Manhattan tourists arrived by the boatful.[33]

In May 1825 Stevens gave his pleasure grounds their newest wonder: a mechanical road. Workers laid an oval of logs six hundred feet in circumference. To this oblong corduroy they nailed two iron-plated wooden bars, and between them a toothed rack. On these bars rested a platform mounted to five wheels (two spoked numbers on each side and a pinion gripping the rack). The platform held benches, a slim cast-iron boiler, and a whiskey barrel filled with water that the boiler turned to steam. At Stevens's command, the boiler released a wraith of pitchy smoke. The pinion clawed the rack, pushing the platform forward. The machine built speed slowly, percussively, until it orbited the lawn at six miles per hour.[34]

Stevens believed water vapor would propel the new age of commerce, a ludicrous thought at a moment when mule barges filled New York wharves with western spoils. While Americans used steam to twirl boat propellers, drain copper mines, saw timber, and grind plaster of paris, no one had successfully rigged boilers and cylinders to a land vehicle. When Stevens invited the faculty of Columbia College to test-drive his wagon, only two professors came.[35] The colonel's sense of defeat peaked that October, when a relay of cannon blasts saluted the Erie Canal's completion. Stevens knew that New York's ditch was already obsolete. But he could not sell people on its replacement.

Railroads themselves were nothing new. Greek soldiers grooved a limestone cartway through the Isthmus of Corinth six hundred years before Christ. The Corinthian *diolkos* (portage machine) carried cargo on trolleys between the Aegean and Ionian Seas, shaving miles off white-knuckle navigations through the Greek Isles. In Central Europe, medieval engravings depict extravagantly bearded Germans pushing coal hopper "hunds" out of mine shafts over plank rails. In 1604 England's Chancery Court credited Huntington Beaumont of Nottingham with inventing a "speedy and easy conveyance" by "breaking the soyle for laying of rayless."[36] Beaumont's wooden wagonway became standard mining equipment in Britain's coal belts. Horses hauled empty wagons from river docks to hillside drifts. Bituminous-laden carts returned to water by gravity like Renaissance roller coasters. Daniel Defoe called them "artificial roads."[37]

America had a few artificial roads of its own. In 1762 British military engineer John Montresor fashioned a rope and pulley incline to lift furs out of Niagara Gorge. In 1805 Silas Whitney built an incline railway to wheel gravel away from Beacon Hill. Mining railways hauled Lehigh Valley anthracite from pitheads to canal barges and granite along Crum Creek. Tracks laid in Quincy, Massachusetts, carried the granite blocks that became Bunker Hill Monument. Albert Gallatin's 1808 *Report* included an appendix on "Rail Roads" written by architect Benjamin Latrobe. Latrobe credited tracks with a "diminution of friction in the greatest degree" but concluded that such systems were suited only as "temporary means of overcoming the most difficult parts of artificial navigation."[38]

Stevens saw railroads as more than stepchildren to canals. The colonel considered Britain, where Scottish inventor James Watt patented a coal-fired steam engine in 1784 and, twenty years later, Richard Trevithick built a locomotive strong enough to pull wagon trains. Stevens tried to convince New York governor Dewitt Clinton to lay tracks across his state. He touted the advantages of a Buffalo–Albany railway that required no freshwater source, could operate in winter when canals were "locked by frost," and would permit each "suit of carriages" to run without pausing at every lock.[39] Where canal barges moved at the speed of mule — tolerable for flour sacks but torture for mosquito-bitten passengers — Stevens saw "nothing to hinder a steam carriage from moving on these ways with a velocity of one hundred miles an hour."[40]

No amount of arguing could stop the Erie Canal. But five days before the War of 1812 ended, New Jersey legislators granted Stevens permission to build a railroad between Burr's Delaware River bridge at Trenton and New Brunswick's Raritan River landing.[41] Politicians placed their hopes in trains following a war that shut down ports and jammed roads with landlocked "wagon fleets."[42] Boxed in by Pennsylvania, New Jersey had no delusions of conquering the West. Lawmakers instead saw an opportunity to squeeze revenue from the exploding commerce crossing its borders. Positioned between New York and Philadelphia, New Jersey became a thoroughfare for through traffic.

On January 3, 1814, Stevens paced the route for himself. With rods and chain, the sixty-four-year-old entered the woods outside New

Brunswick. He scurried around sand mounds. He forded creeks. He crossed the properties of Stats Van Dusen, George McKay, Vander Veer, Enos Ayres, and Andrew McDowell.[43] He marked off road crossings and graves. When Stevens reached Trenton twenty-six miles later, he had completed the first railroad survey in United States history. Stevens celebrated over whiskey and cider at the Steamboat Hotel, certain he had beaten a path for trains "between the different parts of our country, safe from the risks of the sea or the power of the enemy."[44] In 1815 Stevens received a charter to lay the first piece of what would become the northeast corridor.

But the charter failed. Stevens could not convince speculators to invest in his scheme. Were grading a flat right-of-way through New Jersey's forests not daunting enough, prospective sponsors could not yet wrap their heads around the technology. Was it a tool for miners? A portage patch between rivers? A winter workaround for frozen canal beds? Would tracks act like a mechanized King's Highway to which passengers brought their personal vehicles? Or would they behave like the Erie Canal, a state-owned conduit serviced by private barge lines? The age of iron and steam could not begin until these administrative questions had answers. Trains would have to wait for someone to invent the American railroad.

After several futile attempts to revive his Trenton–New Brunswick line, including a direct appeal to President James Monroe, Stevens retreated to Hoboken. His next persuasive essay took the form of a carnival ride. Spectators came and went during the summer of 1825. They sipped drinks on the Piazza Hotel veranda, peeked over the fence on Hudson Street, and requested rides on the wagon as it puffed around an impossibly romantic terrace. But the investors and legislators who might free the wagon from its eternal loop and send it streaking down the coast never came. Hoping to transport the world, Stevens managed only to divert his guests.

In 1825 an autumn cold snap froze the water in the steam wagon's cast-iron boiler. The boiler ruptured. Stevens was soldering new copper piping when he learned that his daughter, Mary Sands, had died two weeks after giving birth to a son.[45] The heartbroken colonel quit his experiments. The engine was parked in a warehouse. The tracks were pried up. For a time, one could see their waffle imprint in the matted grass beside a harbor speckled with grain barges from Buffalo.

The rail dream that flickered out in Hoboken reignited in Baltimore. On Independence Day, 1828, fifty thousand people paraded out to Gwynns Falls. On a podium flanked by mulberry trees sat a snow-haired, fire-eyed man of ninety.[46] Charles Carroll outlived every other signer of the Declaration of Independence. He had aged into a living fossil and civic mascot while retaining the clout of a planter who enslaved three hundred people on his ten-thousand-acre estate. After prayer, speeches, and song, Maryland's surviving signatory thrust a silver spade into the earth.[47] The crowd—sweaty, sunburned, half drunk—cheered.

A marble chest was wheeled into place, then sprinkled with wine and corn kernels as part of a masonic blessing.[48] This ceremonial stone launched an epic venture. It proclaimed the coming construction of a new bridge, the Carrollton Viaduct, that one day would carry trains across Gwynns Falls, across the Shenandoah Valley, through the Appalachians, and perhaps someday over the Great Plains all the way to the Pacific Ocean. This visionary project announced itself through four words engraved on the marble trunk: BALT & OHIO RAIL ROAD.

Marylanders had good reason to build America's first common carrier railroad. Like New Jersey, Maryland was squashed between larger states and lacked New York's drainpipe to the interior. Unlike New Jersey, Maryland at least kissed the Ohio Valley with its panhandle of Allegheny Plateau. Baltimore & Ohio investors, who included Carroll himself, imagined this strip as an iron gateway to the west. They embarked on a heedless experiment remembered more for its missteps than triumphs. Track workers laid rails atop granite stringers rather than the wooden cross ties that became standard. Engineers tinkered with a "sail car" that notched twenty miles

an hour but stalled in headwind.[49] Equine power predominated until
Peter Cooper delivered the Tom Thumb locomotive, a more powerful rendition of Stevens's wagon.

The Baltimore & Ohio figured out railroading on the fly. Its visionary boasts, managerial fiascos, and insatiable hunger for capital
anticipated by 150 years the trials and turbulence of Silicon Valley
startups. Two summers after Carroll flung aside the first shovel of
ceremonial dirt, the line had advanced only thirteen miles toward
Ohio.[50] And yet even this minimal progress inspired Americans who
wanted to believe in an age of improvement and its renewed promise of passage. In January 1832 a new periodical, the *Railroad Journal*,
predicted that trains would carry easterners to the Ohio River in less
than twenty-four hours "at all seasons of the year—a distance little
short we believe of 350 miles!!"[51]

A month before this article appeared, French diplomat Alexis de
Tocqueville rambled through Baltimore during his American tour.
Tocqueville had trekked across the country on dark paths, rock-strewn
roads, and ice-choked rivers. His travelogue described the jumbled
nature of United States transportation: "No exclusive system, then,
is known here. Nowhere does America exhibit the systematic unifor-
mity so dear to the superficial and metaphysical minds of our day."[52]
Baltimore's railroad had sprung from a hodgepodge of speculative
schemes, civic visions, provincial resentments, urban rivalries, and
cunning frauds—a land, Tocqueville surmised, where "everything
is in constant motion and every change seems an improvement."[53]

THE GREAT
CHAIN

Dreamlike traveling on the railroad. The towns which I pass between Philadelphia and New York make no distinct impression. They are like pictures
on the wall. The more that you can read all the way in a car a French novel.

RALPH WALDO EMERSON[1]

Railroaders rarely sign their creations. The tracks they lay and the
paths they embank remain anonymous. A railroad is not a novel or a
fresco but an artifact of many hands lost to time. Canton, Massachusetts, is the exception. Here, an arcade wall carries corridor trains over
the Neponset River. If you park by the Honey Dew Donuts and walk
down Neponset Street, you will come face to face with a stone wall
full of strange graffiti: diamonds, triangles, plusses, hourglasses. Each
mark belongs to an ancient masonic alphabet. Each scratch identifies,
credits, and holds culpable whoever cut the stone. Each autograph
signifies someone who built the corridor.

Many masons carved granite in Canton in 1834. Over hilltops and
cedar bogs carried the ring of bladed hammer on rock, the clop of
oxen, the bray of horses, and the brogue of ballast crews. By day Canton ravine echoed with the toil of Scotch and Irish immigrants, the
new New Englanders replacing those Yankee farmers who fled west.
At dusk the workers retired to camps, where they drank so much
beer and brawled so fiercely that the commonwealth militia twice
deployed to quell riots.[2]

The workers came to Canton to raise a stone curtain. This solid-seeming but actually hollow wall cast its shade over the river, the meadow where cows browsed, and the foundry where Paul Revere's son, Joseph Warren, melted copper ore into sheets that sheathed naval hulls and the state house dome. The wall would fuse two track segments in the sky: one track from the India Point docks in Providence and the other from Park Square, Boston.

The viaduct sprang from the minds of three West Point graduates. The North Carolina brevet major William Gibbs McNeill oversaw the project. His classmate and brother-in-law, George Washington Whistler, assisted. Whistler had just fathered an infant, James, who would grow up moody and get drummed out of West Point by academy superintendent Robert E. Lee, before blossoming into one of the era's most exquisite painters. McNeill and Whistler were joined by Isaac Ridgeway Trimble, a passionate artillery engineer from Virginia.

McNeill and Whistler learned their trade in that great laboratory of American train craft, the Baltimore & Ohio, then traveled to Britain, where they took pointers from the reticent "father of railways," George Stephenson. The men returned the favor in Canton by hosting two Russian engineers, Pavel Petrovich Melnikov and Nikolai Osipovich Kraft, faculty at the St. Petersburg Institute of Transportation, sent by Czar Nicholas I to study construction techniques.[3] The Massachusetts foothills became a global technology expo as cubic tons of granite were chipped off New England's volcanic shelf to make way for trains.

The connection could not come soon enough for Boston. From atop Canton's Great Blue Hill one could see the state house dome glimmering in the distance where oak forest verged on the sea. This picturesque panorama belied the fact that New England's capital had fallen on hard times. Boston still held the world at its fingertips, launching sails toward Greenland's whaling grounds, around the Horn to the South Pacific, and into the ports of China. (Canton took its name from the popular miscalculation that it was antipodal to Guangzhou.)[4] No northeastern port was closer to Europe. None could boast as plentiful a protein source as its cod fishery. Boston's docks brimmed with local exports and worldly goods: flour barrels, molasses kegs, marble cubes, coffee sacks, tea chests.

But as the 1800s dragged on, Boston's oceanic orientation became a liability "for want of an easy and cheap channel of communication with the interior."[5] The city was too east for its own good during the throes of Erie Fever, when New York's canal made it cheaper for Rhode Island merchants to ship cargo through Long Island Sound and up the Hudson River than to boomerang through the choppy water off Point Judith to reach Boston.[6] Manhattan seemed poised to claim Providence as its satellite. "How," wondered one commonwealth legislator, could Massachusetts "keep pace with our sister states?"[7]

To some the answer seemed obvious: dredge a channel between the Charles River and Albany, thereby patching Boston into the Erie Canal system. The Berkshire Mountains discouraged this project as did local pride. Bostonians resented any scheme that would reduce them to New York's clients. They needed to preserve both the Providence trade and their dignity as a sovereign maritime metropolis.

Boston journalist Nathan Hale proposed another solution. Since Massachusetts was "extremely ill-suited to the construction of Canals," it made more sense to lay rails to Albany and Providence.[8] Hale's plan endures in the smudgy print and water-stained pages of an old pamphlet that describes horses towing carriages between Back Bay and India Point at three miles an hour. Hale proposed cutting the rails from Massachusetts's ubiquitous granite intrusions and packing the gaps between ties with "earth and gravel, so as to form a path for the horses."[9] Each train would have a platform car "on which the horse himself may ride" on downhill sections.[10] The road would pay for itself by levying fifty cent "tolls" on passengers.[11]

By the time state legislators granted their charter, steam locomotives had replaced horses and wooden ties succeeded granite stringers. In 1828 James Hayward surveyed the route.[12] The line originated in South Boston beside a turnpiked section of the Old King's Highway. It wound toward Providence between Dr. Richmond's Church and Boyce's Factory, ducking south of Fowl Meadows,

FIGURE 3.1 Canton Viaduct. As of 2023 the viaduct has carried corridor trains over the Canton River Valley for over three-quarters of United States history. Historic American Engineering Record, Library of Congress.

north of Massapoag Pond, then south of Thomas Clarke's House. Trains would skirt Purgatory Swamp and the home of Willard Comey before barreling straight through Attleboro's Old Kirk graveyard.[13]

Hayward sought the most direct route, though he also considered political costs. Joseph Warren Revere sat on the railroad's board and wanted trains to serve the Canton cooperage he inherited from his father.[14] The metalworks sat at the bottom of a ravine. Initial plans called for rigging an incline plane up the Neponset hillside, which would have obliged passengers to transfer to funicular cars. Wary of begetting another Frankensteinian contraption like Pennsylvania's Main Line of Public Works, the Boston & Providence Railroad (B&P) resolved to lay a single band of iron through the air. It took McNeill, Whistler, Trimble, and their workers two years to complete the viaduct, which the *Providence Journal* hailed as an "enduring monument" to New England resilience.[15] Boston answered New York with a landmark that would outlast the age of canals.

The viaduct has carried trains ever since. Today, Acela Expresses, Amtrak Regionals, Boston commuter trains, and CSX freights rumble over Canton's deck like low-flying jets. The B&P is long gone, but thousands of riders rely on its masonry. Thousands retrace the route that James Hayward jotted on parchment the same year the typewriter was invented. Thousands click-clack past pilgrim bones in Attleboro's Kirk Yard.[16] Nathan Hale may have boasted that his railroad would save Boston, but he could not have foreseen the line's longevity. The men who scratched their signs in Canton Viaduct never imagined what those stones would carry.

An 1832 article in *Railroad Journal* predicted that these tracks would eventually form a "great chain which, is in our day to stretch along the Atlantic coast, and bring its chief capitals into rapid, constant and mutually beneficial relation."[17] Rail segments in New England, New Jersey, Pennsylvania, and Maryland reached for each other like houseplants toward sunlight. They seemed destined to mesh into something greater than their parts. But nineteenth-century railroaders thought in more local terms. They could not yet recognize their individual epics as chapters of a single volume. No one knew they were building a corridor.

In 1817 the former King of Spain moved to Bordentown, New Jersey.[18] By all accounts, Joseph Bonaparte detested his brief reign on the Madrid throne, during which Bourbon partisans attacked him as a dynastic puppet and habitual drunk. When the Russian-Austrian Coalition crushed Napoleon's army in 1814, Joseph hoped his brother's defeat would let him return to private life. Bonaparte absconded back to France with the Spanish crown jewels and sailed for America. He pawned his coronal loot in Philadelphia and bought an estate on the Delaware River called Point Breeze.

Bonaparte converted this land into South Jersey's Versailles. He dredged a lagoon, stocked it with swans, then bisected the water with a brick causeway. He planted Tuileries-style gardens. He imported violet seeds, artichoke shoots, and apricot saplings from France.[19] He raised pheasants in an aviary and decked his three-story mansion with Van Dycks, Rubens, Titians, and one of the country's most intimidating libraries. Bonaparte entertained dignitaries including the Marquis de Lafayette, Secretary of State Henry Clay, and President John Quincy Adams, who requested discretion, lest his visit irk the French empire's old enemies.

Bonaparte relished his bizarre retirement until surveyors of the Camden & Amboy (C&A) Railroad appeared at Point Breeze. The crew planned to lay tracks between Bonaparte's mansion and Crosswicks Creek. The deposed sovereign raged. As a foreigner, Bonaparte owned land only by special permission of the state assembly. Despite his tenuous standing, the Frenchman petitioned for a federal injunction against the railroad. In 1830 Judge Henry Baldwin ruled that "trespass is destruction, in the eye of equity," even in the case of an "alien resident."[20] The surveyors diverted their tracks around Bonaparte's park. The man who gladly surrendered the Spanish crown yielded not one inch of New Jersey soil.

The C&A rarely gave ground to anyone. Eighteen years after John Stevens's charter lapsed, his son, Robert, presided over a new company that laid an "almost mathematically straight" line from Raritan Bay to the Delaware River.[21] The rails traced the same sandy road that Franklin trudged to Burlington and the Lower Assunpink Trail that once carried Lenape messengers. The C&A's tracks shot through orchards, wheatfields, and villages like Jamesburg and Spotswood that happened to be in the way. The railroad reached Bordentown in 1832, then in 1834 extended its tracks to Camden, across the Delaware River from Philadelphia.

The *Newark Advertiser* praised the C&A's "thoroughfare of communication" as a "most desirable accommodation."[22] *Railroad Journal* marveled that trains made day trips possible between Philadelphia and New York.[23] In his *Practical Treatise of Rail-Roads*, Nicholas Wood called the C&A "one of the most important works in the

Union."[24] After centuries of riding stagecoaches over mud ruts and rock rivers, northeasterners now flowed over iron beams spiked to sleeper stones cemented from gravel or hacked from marble by Sing Sing chain gangs.[25]

With its exploding ridership and exclusive charter, the C&A soon overpowered the lawmakers who created it. Stevens's railroad greased its monopoly with bribes, kickbacks, and patronage promises. Candidates who defied the C&A fell off nomination tickets, replaced by friendly shareholders. "There never was a more complete master anywhere of the destinies of a State than was this monster monopoly of the affairs of New Jersey," wrote journalist William Edgar Sackett. He continued, "there came a time when the State that had taken the corporation to its bosom as a child began to fear it as a master."[26]

The C&A monopoly incensed citizens in Elizabeth, Newark, and Jersey City, upstate industrial centers without tracks. Legislators chartered a second railroad to redress North Jersey's train desert but assured C&A executives that this carrier would not steal their riders. The New Jersey Railroad (NJRR) ran only from New Brunswick to a point "no more than fifty feet above the high-water mark" of the Hudson River.[27] Where the C&A ploughed through New Jersey, the NJRR had to scrape together its right-of-way by buying old turnpike charters. Between Newark and Elizabeth, the NJRR sprinkled ballast atop the Essex & Middlesex Turnpike, a former crown highway graded over the Upper Assunpink Trail. Like the C&A, the NJRR followed an Indigenous artery.

Beyond Newark, the NJRR's tracks extended over the dregs of a glacial lake. The squelching Meadowlands were no place to build a railroad. Winter littered the wash plain with clods of frozen mud. Spring floods refilled the Pleistocene lakebed. Summer bred mosquitos. Engineers watched embankments "sink out of sight" into the bottomless loam as track gangs sickened with malaria.[28] In the same flats where seventeenth-century New Netherlanders harvested salt hay, German immigrants now slogged through root-matted muck, dumping load upon load of fill into the morass as if it were runny cake batter.

After taming the Meadowlands, NJRR engineers ran headlong

into the basaltic wall of Bergen Hill. The mushy landscape grew im-
placably hard. Crews pickaxed and dynamited their way through a
mile of solid rock. When the line opened in 1838, passengers departing Jersey City marveled at the artificial ravine. British travel writer
Alexander Mackay claimed it "in every way more formidable than the
celebrated cutting on the Birmingham line."[29] The icicles that clung to
Bergen Hill's rock reminded Scottish geologist Charles Lyell of "huge
stalactites pendent from the roofs of limestone caverns in Europe."[30]

All this chipping, blasting, and wadding prepared New Jersey for
the age of steam, which dawned when a crate of machine parts arrived at the Hoboken shops of Isaac Dripps. Born in Belfast, Dripps
had tinkered with engines since he went to work for a steamboat
manufacturer at the age of sixteen. By twenty-three, Dripps was the
C&A's master mechanic, the kind of intuitive genius who could jigsaw
a package of parts into a functioning locomotive without assembly
instructions or an operating manual. Initially dubbed the Stevens
(after Robert), this engine achieved immortality under the Britannic
moniker, John Bull. The John Bull was the fastest, most sophisticated
locomotive that Americans had ever seen. It chugged up to forty
miles an hour and lasted thirty-five years in service.[31] In 1981, the
Smithsonian celebrated the John Bull's sesquicentennial by firing up
its boiler and joyriding through Washington, DC.[32]

Passenger accommodations kept pace with locomotive technology. Stagecoach style berths gave way to rectangular coaches. The
drab flicker of sperm whale candles was replaced by gas fixtures that
projected "cheerful, bright and uniform" light, "rendering all parts
of the car distinctly visible."[33] Onboard stoves warmed passengers
in winter as they rocketed through ice-crusted cuts and crystalized
meadows. The C&A advertised "gentlemanly and attentive agents,
comfortable fires, spacious cars, and a good cup of coffee."[34] The
railroad reserved coaches for women to liberate "ladies from the dis-
agreeables of tobacco juice and contact with the grosser sex, which,
it is well known, they do so much abhor."[35]

Steam trains destroyed the peace of trackside residents. "It appears
in the woods, suddenly shattering the harmony of the green hollow,

like a presentiment of history bearing down on the American asylum," wrote literary historian Leo Marx of the locomotive's arrival.[36]
No event typified the collision of rail and rustic ways more than livestock strikes, which occurred whenever free-ranging cattle plopped
down on rights of way. The John Bull hit a hog on its first test run.
Strikes occurred so often that Dripps outfitted C&A engines with
pilot grates called cowcatchers. Though meant to shunt animals off
tracks, it was common to find an impaled "sheep or a hog dead or
dying in" the catcher.[37]

Passengers reclining in gaslit, stove-warmed coaches ran their own
risks. The coal-burning railroad could be indifferent to its soft-tissued
cargo. Engine smoke billowed through carriages, choking passengers
and spoiling garments. Open windows allowed riders to peek out
and decapitate themselves on bridge piers. Iron strap rails sometimes
peeled loose under the weight of trains and jabbed through coach
floors, forking passengers to the roof—a lethal mishap called "snake
heads."

The era's most fatal accident stemmed from a single burned rod.
The touring Irish actor Tyrone Power recalled the events of November 8, 1833, in his memoirs. Power woke in his Manhattan hotel
room to a "warm sun just tempered by a breeze balmy and soft" and
boarded the ferry to Amboy.[38] From here, his train gusted off over a
"dreary, barren-looking country" brightened by "little mountains of
apples destined chiefly for the cider press."[39] In 1838, another traveler,
Andrew Bell, characterized this landscape as "uninteresting a country
as it was ever my fate to travel on."[40] In 1848 Archibald Prentice dis-
paraged the "barren sand" and "miserably thin" rye before acknowledging that the tract held "beauty of a certain sort."[41]

Passengers calculated the train's speed by counting the seconds between each milestone. One of Power's seatmates deduced a velocity
of twenty miles per hour. A few coaches back, former president John
Quincy Adams, returning to Washington to represent Massachusetts's
11th Congressional District, clocked another segment at thirty-eight
miles per hour.[42] Eyes darted between windows and pocket watches
when someone cried "stop the engine!"[43] The train shuddered. Power

looked out his window. The carriage behind him had exploded into a
tangle of wood, metal, and flesh. "One man was dead, another dying,
and five others had fractures, more or less serious; a couple of ladies
(sisters) dreadfully wounded, the children of one of them; two little
girls, with broken limbs."[44]

Among the injured was a twenty-nine-year-old Staten Islander
who broke his leg, punctured a lung, and swore he would never ride
a train again.[45] (Cornelius Vanderbilt came around, however, and
later became president of the New York Central Railroad.) Representative Adams took charge. The congressman, sixty-four years old, all
but bald, his remaining whiskers melded into mutton chops, ordered
a coroner's inquest. "The scene of sufferance was excruciating," he
recorded in his diary that night. "Men, women, and a child, scattered
along the road, bleeding, mangled, groaning, writhing in torture and
dying." He described the ordeal as a "trial of feeling" and the "most
dreadful catastrophe my eyes beheld."[46]

The culprit was an undergreased carriage axel, which ground
against its wheel until it glowed red then snapped. The axel's bearing
rested within a compartment stuffed with oily rags called a journal
box. For some reason, the journal failed to lubricate the axel, a mal-
function known as hot boxing. The grind of shaft on plate ignited the
undercarriage, snapping the rod and derailing the train. Two people
died. Twenty-one suffered injuries. The wreck occurred in the sandy
nowhere west of Spotswood but entered history as the "Hightstown
Rail Accident," after the next stop where the train awaited a coroner.

After discharging its dead and wounded passengers and detaching
the damaged carriage, Power's train proceeded toward Bordentown
"with a character mournfully altered since our first departure."[47] The
coaches rolled over Crosswicks Creek and wrapped around Bonaparte's Point Breeze, regal as ever, even in the absence of its proprietor,
who had moved to London the previous year.[48] Former President
Adams, still processing the trauma of train wreck, passed the grounds
where he once dined with the ex-king of Spain in New Jersey's greatest palace.

Little of the C&A line survives today. In Hightstown, a stub of asphalt named Railroad Avenue recalls the first iron throughfare between the country's two greatest cities and the first train accident to claim American life. Beside Railroad Avenue is a wooden sandbox lined with marble chips and twenty-two iron oxide cubes that once cradled the C&A's rails. These original sleeper stones are still shot through with spike holes. You can straddle the stones today, though it's hard to see the railroad of Railroad Avenue through the sprawl that has claimed its path or to picture the John Bull chugging through Anthony's Chicken and Grill or Wayne's Wash World laundromat.

When the C&A opened a new route to Philadelphia in 1839, Hightstown lost much of its traffic. When Conrail ripped up the tracks in the 1980s, the station grew dormant, like a volcano that drifted past its fault, or an oxbow lake severed from flow. The "great chain" had changed course. The corridor carried on elsewhere.

The Philadelphia & Trenton (P&T) Railroad touched neither Philadelphia nor Trenton. Incorporated by Pennsylvania's general assembly in 1832, the company laid track along Bristol Turnpike between Morrisville (a Delaware River trading post opposite Trenton) and Kensington (a suburb outside Philadelphia's city limits). Without a bridge to Trenton or permission to enter Philadelphia, the railroad languished as a scenic horse tram. While the C&A barreled through New Jersey with a puff of impunity and the NJRR parted rock and water east of Newark, the P&T lugged its smattering of passengers through drowsy hinterland.

When an 1834 Kensington district ordinance let the P&T lay a single track down Frankford Road to Philadelphia's Liberty Lands, it forbade the railroad from employing a "locomotive engine propelled by steam" or from running any car over "five miles per hour."[49] Pedestrians, carts, wagons, and market fairs got in the way of trains. Businesses affixed homemade spurs to the track like illegal cable hookups.[50] Philadelphians strutted between the rails, treating them as what historian Joel Schwartz calls "whimsical spectacle for common use."[51]

Despite their clogged and curtailed right-of-way, P&T executives dreamed of dominating mid-Atlantic rail travel. In December 1833, the company bought a controlling share in New Jersey's Brunswick Turnpike. The gravel road between Trenton and New Brunswick was the rare conduit to impress Albert Gallatin, whose 1808 report commended the highway's razor-straight path and gentle grade.[52] The P&T intended to turn the turnpike into a railbed, connecting itself to the NJRR in New Brunswick to form an unbroken line between Philadelphia and New York Harbor.

The impetuous railroad had overreached. With the backing of New Jersey power broker Robert Stockton, the C&A answered this usurpation by acquiring a majority share of its upstart rival. The P&T became a docile subsidiary. The C&A spiked rails to the towpath of the Delaware and Raritan Canal between Trenton and New Brunswick. Acting at the C&A's behest, the P&T laid tracks over a rebuilt Delaware Bridge in 1839 to complete a line from Jersey City to Philadelphia's outskirts. All that stood between the Hudson docks and the heart of William Penn's "green countrie town" was Kensington.

Kensingtoners came from Ireland mostly. Protestants arrived first, followed by droves of Roman Catholics. They made cloth on home looms, spinning yarn into carpets, drapes, and upholstery. Their weaving gave work to dyers, carders, carters, and machinists. Glass works and chemical plants opened to support woolens production. Kensington became a local, then regional, then national textile center, an industrial embryo that would make North Philadelphia the "workshop of the world."

But the Kensingtoners who sent their woven wares around the globe lived local lives. They cherished their tight-knit community, a theological haven salvaged from seas of nativism. They looked suspiciously on outsiders, intrusions, and the appearance of train tracks on Frankford Road. Kensingtoners worried that the P&T's pathetic tram had become a placeholder for something more dangerous. They had read the journalists prophesizing a "great chain" and could see its tracks coming for them—through them.

The same steam trains that slaughtered swine in the countryside wreaked havoc in cities. In 1842 Charles Dickens watched an engine run "slap-dash, headlong, pell-mell, down the middle of the street; with pigs burrowing, and boys flying kites and playing marbles, and men smoking, and women talking, and children crawling, close to the very rails; there comes tearing along a mad locomotive with its train of cars, scattering a red-hot shower of sparks (from its wood fire) in all directions."[53] In 1856 the English tourist Isabella Bird looked down from her Albany hotel window into the "funnel of a locomotive, and all night was serenaded with screams, ringing of bells, and cries of 'All aboard' and 'Go ahead.'"[54]

In Kensington, a broadside warned: "Mothers look out for your children! Artisans, mechanics, citizens! When you leave your family in health, must you be hurried home to mourn a Dreadful casualty!"[55] The poster showed a scowling steam engine (its tender stamped "Monopoly" in reference to the C&A) severing a child's leg and toppling a cart. The author stoked Philadelphia's inferiority complex—in full flower during Manhattan's meteoric rise—by asking, "do you consent to be a suburb of New York!!!" The insinuating whisper of small type confided that "rails are now being laid on Broad Street to connect the Trenton Rail Road with the Wilmington and Baltimore Road." Kensington, the text implied, would become a "mere right of way."[56]

Kensington's conversion into a train corridor began when the state assembly allowed the P&T to replace its inset tram rails with edge rails, which jutted out from the street. Edge rails tripped hooves and caught cartwheels. They turned local streets over to intercity passengers and far-bound freight. In July 1840, P&T crews clawed apart Front Street with pickaxes and sledges. A Kensington alderman arrested the workers for "riot." A judge released the men after consulting their written court authorization. But when the crew returned to Front Street, neighbors encircled their worksite. The crowd, mostly women and teenage boys, chased off the workers. The women picked up the dislodged pavers and set them back in place, restoring the street as theirs.[57]

When Judge John Gibson ruled that Kensington could not obstruct an interstate rail line, the P&T resumed prying up Front Street. On the night of July 27, "an immense gang of women immediately went out and ordered the workmen to 'quit.'"[58] The crew dropped their tools. Neighbors tore up the tracks and stacked them in a bonfire. When a sheriff's posse arrived, rioters pelted them with upturned paving stones, which they called ground apples.[59] Kensington Commissioner John Painter led the rebellion, which drove the sheriff into a Front Street tavern owned by P&T president John Naglee. Ground apples pelted the saloon. Someone set the building on fire. When firefighters arrived, they met a barrage of rock, and so stood down while the bar burned.

Track work ceased. Residents wondered whether the P&T would press its luck a third time. Pennsylvania's general assembly considered whether the "great chain" of seaboard commerce could raze one community to bind others. Their debates carried on for months. While Kensington awaited its fate, William Henry Harrison entered the White House and died thirty-two days later. Philadelphian Edgar Allan Poe sold "The Murders in the Rue Morgue" to *Graham's Magazine*. Hightstown train wreck survivor Tyrone Power drowned at sea when his ship sunk off Nantucket.

After two years, word came from Harrisburg: Pennsylvania had revoked the P&T's right-of-way. Kensingtoners rejoiced. They lit candles. They paraded. Residents and business owners on Front Street hung paper silhouettes in their windows displaying the message, "Free passage to all."[60] Their papercraft hangings "brilliantly illuminated" the sidewalks, conveying delight, relief, and a warning to anyone tempted to meddle with Front Street.[61] Their riot showed that the corridor could be stopped.

The P&T terminal remained on Philadelphia's fringes, "a good way from the centre of business."[62] Arriving passengers transferred to hackney carts and ferries to reach downtown. These rides were so inconvenient that most passengers from New York preferred to arrive in Camden via the old C&A line, then cross the Delaware River directly to Market Street wharf.

When Philadelphia obtained a throughline in 1867, its route avoided Kensington like yellow fever, skimming overtop the ward, then crossing the Schuylkill River twice before wrapping back to City Hall. Corridor trains today approach Philadelphia over the old P&T. They bear down on the glinting skyscrapers of Center City before jerking west from Frankford Junction. The route grows circumferential, as if seeking a backdoor to downtown. Trains sway through turns as their passengers pay for a nineteenth-century borough's fight to save itself. Kensington stayed off the corridor. Its absence manifests in the twenty-eight minutes it takes Amtrak trains to run between Philadelphia and Trenton.

In December 1859, seven miles from Kensington, a train clattered through the covered drawbridge linking Philadelphia to everything southwest of the Schuylkill River. The bridge replaced a log pontoon that George Washington plashed over enroute to his first inauguration.[63] The pontoon replaced a ferry operated by George Gray, a Quaker revolutionary who planted the riverbank with lemons and pineapples to refresh his passengers.[64] The train rolled off the bridge onto rails engraved in Gray's Ferry Avenue, then turned up the factory canyon of Prime Street past a naval asylum to the Southern and Western Station.

Behind the station's opera house facade waited what one reporter called "quite a crowd of colored persons and a few white sympathizers."[65] Mayor Alexander Henry examined his citizens. As leader of the "most northern of southern cities," a cold-weather Quaker port crawling with proslavery agitators, Henry did all he could to keep a civil war from erupting on the streets of Philadelphia.[66] He knew that the arriving train carried a man who left the city two months earlier with a mouth full of exhortation and a brain teeming with plots and who now returned as the antebellum's most incendiary cargo. Even reduced to freight, John Brown still set fires.

After raiding the federal arsenal at Harper's Ferry, Old Brown of Kansas was towed to his Virginia scaffold in a luggage wagon. Mary Ann Day Brown petitioned to save her husband's corpse from surgeons who wanted to parade it from town to town. She convinced Virginia's governor to release the body for burial on the family's Adirondack farm. The plan had been to dress Brown in Philadelphia. But Mayor Henry, who held "himself responsible to have the body carefully taken across the city to the New York Station," would stand no delay.[67] He surveyed the waiting room crowd, considered its enemies outside, and saw his city in flames. Old Brown needed to go.

But Philadelphia lacked through track. All railroads that approached the city stopped on its periphery, forming a depot atoll. To proceed north, Brown's body required a transfer. The mayor conferred with those escorting the coffin. A deerskin-wrapped box appeared and was laid onto a cart hitched to an old bay, who clopped north toward the city Anti-Slavery Office, or maybe the P&T terminal in Tacony. The crowd couldn't tell, and it didn't matter, because they were chasing a toolbox. When the waiting room emptied, a pinewood coffin bearing Brown's real remains was slid onto another cart, rushed to the Walnut Street docks, and ferried to Camden, where a steam train took it to Amboy.

Mayor Henry had exploited his city's Mason-Dixon Line of stunted track. At Kensington, passengers stared down the P&T rails to Bucks County, New Jersey, and New York—the industrial core of a coalescing North. The smoky shed on Prime Street, by contrast, looked west onto the domain of the Philadelphia, Wilmington, & Baltimore Railroad. The PW&B connected three mid-Atlantic ports that shared the same subtropical humidity, fixation on oceanic trade, and wary sense of scrapping in New York's shadow. And yet in 1859 these sibling entrepots existed worlds apart, a difference summarized by the fact that slavery became legal just 17.8 miles from Philadelphia at the Delaware State Line.

Upon crossing this border, British journalist James Silk Buckingham perceived a "marked difference, in the wretchedness of the huts or dwellings, the bad state of fences, and the slovenly and neglected appearance of the whole country."[68] English abolitionist Joseph Sturge contrasted the "industry and prosperity" of free states with the impoverished territories governed by enslavers.[69] Alexander Mackay noticed two things when his Washington-bound train departed Philadelphia. First, the coach floor became "incrusted with tobacco spit" to the point "one might almost smoke a pipe from its scrapings."[70] Second, the conductor removed a mixed-race man from his coach to the Blacks-only car, a "cold comfortless-looking box" lodged between the luggage and tender.[71]

For enslaved Africans, the PW&B offered a potential ride to freedom on an overground railroad. Frederick Douglass escaped servitude on the PW&B in 1838. Six years later, an enslaved Virginian named Henry Brown shipped himself over the line in a dry goods crate. Brown emerged in the home of a Philadelphia abolitionist and recited a psalm of deliverance. Witnesses to his "resurrection" included Underground Railroad conductor William Sill and James McKim, a minister who later accompanied John Brown's body and whose toddler, Charles, grew up to codesign New York's Pennsylvania Station. Henry Brown later reenacted his flight in the English Midlands, a stunt that infuriated Douglass, who lamented, "had not Henry Box Brown and his friends attracted slaveholding attention to the manner of his escape, we might have had Thousands of *Box Browns* per annum."[72]

One year after John Brown's body slipped through Philadelphia, southern states began leaving the Union. South Carolina seceded first, followed by Mississippi, Florida, Alabama, Georgia, Louisiana, and Texas. When Virginia joined the Confederacy in April 1861, attention turned to Delaware and Maryland, the northernmost states that practiced slavery. Delaware lawmakers ruled out secession. But Maryland reached no such consensus. Because the Old Line State's withdrawal would engulf Washington in Confederate territory, the PW&B grew indispensable, delivering troops, supplies, and intelligence to the capital.

But this lifeline lacked several links. Philadelphia presented one gap. The bridgeless Susquehanna River introduced another. Baltimore posed a third barrier to Washington-bound passengers who had to change from the PW&B to the B&O. This final fissure caused the most trouble for late antebellum passengers, including members of the military. Six days after Union troops surrendered Fort Sumpter, the 6th Regiment Massachusetts Volunteer Militia arrived in Baltimore's President Street Station. The Minute Men were the first to answer Lincoln's call for reinforcements. Their coaches were decoupled from their locomotive, hitched to horse teams, then towed streetcar style, one by one, to the B&O's Camden Station.

Baltimoreans lined the route: unionists, secessionists, copperheads, and centrists who simply wanted war to avoid them. The crowd watched carriage after carriage of Union troops roll through Baltimore toward the southern front. Someone hurled a brick at one of the cars. More bricks followed. Confederate sympathizers blocked the rails by dumping sand on Pratt Street. Others flung ship anchors on the tracks. The Massachusetts volunteers disembarked and marched toward Camden Station. Rocks rained down on them. Someone fired a gun. The troops returned fire. Twelve people died in a skirmish known as the Pratt Street Riots. The Civil War's first blood spilled in a corridor gap.

One face along Pratt Street belonged to Isaac Ridgeway Trimble. Since working on Canton Viaduct, Trimble had trekked the country in search of rail projects. His career included stints with the Boston & Providence, the Baltimore & Susquehanna, the Philadelphia & Baltimore Central, and the Baltimore & Potomac. In Cuba, Trimble helped track gangs slog through tropical heat to connect Santiago with Havana.[73] He made pilgrimage to England and met steam locomotive pioneer George Stephenson. In 1842 the PW&B promoted Trimble to chief engineer and superintendent.

The former cadet dazzled his colleagues. When the winter of 1852 froze the Susquehanna River solid, sidelining the PW&B's ferry steamers, Trimble orchestrated an ingenious effort to spike tracks across the ice. Workers pulleyed train cars from bank to bank on makeshift track. The "natural bridge" carried over 10,000 tons of cargo before a February thaw melted the right-of-way, and ferries resumed.[74] Just one year after this wintry triumph, however, Trimble was accused of misappropriating "large quantities" of lumber, nails, iron, and paint.[75] He denied the charges but resigned in disgrace, bearing a lifelong grudge against PW&B President Samuel Morse Felton.

Maryland's strife gave Trimble a chance to take revenge on his old employer. After the Pratt Street Riots, mayor George Brown and governor Thomas Holliday Hicks begged Abraham Lincoln to reroute troop trains around Baltimore. The president, one month removed from his own humiliating passage through Baltimore, sympathized with Brown but stressed the "absolute, irresistible necessity of having a transit through the State for such troops as might be necessary for the protection of the Federal Capital."[76] When Mayor Brown learned that more Union soldiers were departing south from Philadelphia, he ordered Trimble to shut down the PW&B.

Trimble's raid party arrived at President Street Station near midnight. The former chief engineer knew the terminal well, having supervised construction of its arch-roofed headhouse and Greek relief columns.[77] Trimble strode through the train shed and onto a locomotive hauling the night mail from Philadelphia. Trimble aimed a pistol at the driver and ordered him to steam north. The hijacked train chugged out of Baltimore along the Patapsco River. Every so often Trimble had the engineer stop so that his men could clip iron telegraph wires, douse bridges with turpentine, and set blazes.

The sortie left only minor damage. The telegraph wires were restrung. The bridges were scorched but intact, owing to their tenders, who sprinkled salt on the spans to keep engine sparks from igniting. Lincoln dispatched general-in-chief of the army Winfield Scott to guard the PW&B against further assaults. He ordered Scott to suspend habeas corpus, the writ that presented detainees before judges, around Maryland's tracks. Preserving communication between Philadelphia and Washington was so crucial, Lincoln claimed, that it justified suspending civil liberties. The needs of corridor war freight eclipsed constitutional rights. "Are all laws but one to go unexecuted, and the Government itself go to pieces lest that one be violated?" the president asked.[78]

War returned to the PW&B in 1864 when Confederate general Jubal Early's corps swept through Maryland. On July 11 a detachment led by major Harry Gilmor reached Magnolia Station, beside a picnic grove where day-tripping Baltimoreans enjoyed the "beauties of nature, and pleasure of social intercourse."[79] Gilmor's troops arrested the depot telegrapher. They stopped a passing train, removed its riders, then set the coaches on fire. Gilmor's raiders then halted a second train, evacuated the carriages, and ignited them. They backed the flaming coaches onto the Gunpowder River trestle, a portion of which collapsed. The "appearance of the tilted stack of the engine above the wreck of the bridge is still strong in my memory," recounted Buffalo nurse Marie Noye.[80]

Beside occasional attacks, PW&B passengers endured cars "crammed to suffocation" and prone to delay.[81] Legislators accused carriers of price gouging. Massachusetts senator Charles Sumner blamed the C&A for fraud "hardly less flagrant and pernicious than those which ripened in bloody rebellion."[82] Calling New Jersey the Union's "valley of humiliation," Sumner proposed chartering a new "air line" from New York to Washington—a geometrically perfect route that circumvented "local impediments."[83] Northerners questioned whether their parochial tangle of railways could handle the rigors of war. Not for the last time, they dreamed of starting over to get the great chain right.

President Felton shot back that the "present route . . . is the most direct line practicable."[84] He boasted that the PW&B had added a second track between Philadelphia and Baltimore and promised future improvements. "Agitation for the Air Line," claims historian Albert Churella, prodded railroads "into closer cooperation with each other."[85] The fruits of these partnerships would include a permanent bridge across the Susquehanna River, a connecting railway between Frankford Junction and West Philadelphia, and tunnels under Baltimore. By 1872 trains rolled continuously from the Hudson

River to Washington courtesy of the United New Jersey Railroad (formed from the C&A's 1867 absorption of the NJRR), the P&T, the PW&B, and the B&O. Sumner surmised that the northeast had become coterminous with the railroad "by which the Union itself is bound together."[86]

Isaac Trimble, who had forged and sundered segments of that rail, enlisted in the Volunteer Forces of Virginia and rose through the Confederate ranks to become a major general. Trimble was shot in the leg at the Second Battle of Bull Run, then lost that limb while leading a division of Pickett's Charge at Gettysburg. When Union troops imprisoned Trimble on an island in Lake Erie, the battle-worn amputee conspired to escape with other Confederate POWs.[87] One plot entailed climbing over the prison's stockade walls and skittering across the frozen lake to Canada, a scheme that recalled Trimble's triumph over the solid Susquehanna twelve years earlier.[88]

Before he could act, Trimble was transferred to Fort Warren, a garrison perched atop a glacial drumlin in Boston Harbor.[89] The fort took its name from Dr. Joseph Warren, the man who dispatched Paul Revere on his midnight run and after whom Revere named his son, the future Canton coppersmith. Trimble waited for the war to end eight miles from the B&P depot, which sent trains to Rhode Island over the viaduct he helped engineer.

Trimble returned to Baltimore in 1865, where he busied himself in municipal projects, like the Druid Lake Reservoir, and hosted former Confederate president Jefferson Davis in his home.[90] Trimble died in 1888 and was buried in Baltimore's Green Mount Cemetery. Today, the graveyard's southern wall abuts Hoffman Avenue. Beneath Hoffman Avenue is a tunnel through which Amtrak and MARC commuter trains pass several times an hour. Trimble the builder, the saboteur, the Maryland Confederate rests eternally beside the northeast corridor track.

II. POWER

· 4 ·

A TALE OF
TWO EMPIRES

Dalmatian-spotted woods,
snow patches and leaf patches spin by, wooden stakes
poke like bad teeth from mudflats, the silken,
pearl-gray kimono of sky is draped over Long Island Sound.
ROSANNA WARREN[1]

In 2013 Metro-North decided to build the corridor's newest station atop a Bridgeport brownfield. The proposed depot would slot between the Remington Arms Munitions Factory and a chickweed meadow where Connecticut's first public housing project once stood.[2] When the projects opened in 1940, they boasted electric refrigerators and copper awnings.[3] Some units overlooked the Yellow Mill Channel, where anglers reeled in striped bass and spotted fluke. Tenants walked out their front doors to assembly lines at the rifle plant, the cartridge mill, the brass works, the Frisbie Pie Company, and the Singer Sewing Machine factory.[4] Their community took its name from a local Slovakian priest, Stephen Panik, who said, "no sermon is more effective than to take poor people out of dirt and filth and place them into sunshine."[5]

By 2013, nothing remained of Father Panik Village except the acres of sunshine-filled emptiness that follow the bulldozers of urban renewal. Gone was the courtyard where kids chased balls and addicts stripped awnings. Gone, too, was Remington. The seventy-three-acre plant that pumped out a million guns for Czar Nicholas II left only its brick shell and the shot tower where musket balls were formed by dribbling lead down a ten-story shaft.[6] Outside, students of the New England Tractor Trailer Training School coaxed empty rigs around orange cones. The school leased offices in a warehouse that advertised itself as "Just 22 Minutes from Norwalk . . . Half the Rent!"[7]

City officials vowed to bring back East Bridgeport. They promised to cleanse the brownfield and fix up its buildings. They promised to repeople the asphalt prairie after draining its underground oil plume. They spoke of seeding pocket gardens, upgrading retail, and restoring shore access through the charred ruins of Pleasure Beach amusement park. And they pledged to partner with the railroad that bisected the neighborhood on a blackened granite embankment. Together they would put East Bridgeport back on the map by penciling it into Metro-North timetables. Their act of transit-oriented dreaming was called Barnum Station.

Who better to brighten Bridgeport's debris than Phineas Taylor Barnum? The circus king and gimmick warden raised his onion-domed pavilion, Iranistan, on Bridgeport's western border in 1848. "I wished to reside within a few hours of New York," Barnum reminisced. "Bridgeport seemed to be about the proper distance from the great metropolis. It is pleasantly situated at the terminus of two railroads which traverse the fertile valleys of the Naugatuck and Housatonic Rivers. The New York and New Haven Railroad runs through the city, and there is also daily steamboat communication with New York."[8]

The New Haven Railroad reached only Fairfield in 1848, but Barnum could picture the full route unspooling in his mind's eye. Locomotives would soon chug the length of Long Island Sound through harbor hamlets and cottonwood groves, over clam-studded flats and brackish creeks crowned with wild rice. Barnum imagined coasting beside the dawn-colored water, blasting through the forests where Sarah Kemble Knight blundered along the Pequot Path, careening around the Bronx's Bear Swamp, trestling over the savanna of Upper

Manhattan, and ramrodding through the Bowery to the pentagonal park that became City Hall.

Others could see it too. The finished line would convert Manhattan residents into Connecticut commuters. Station agents distributed a free pamphlet, *Homes on the Sound for New York Business Men*, to tantalize readers "cooped up within the brick walls of the city" with visions of "forests and groves, lakelets and rivers with stretches of blue sea."[9] Each station received a profile ("New Canaan: 39 Miles; 5 trains daily. Time, 1 hour 40 min."), accentuating its singular pleasantness with historical lure and ink sketches. Would you rather live in Greenwich, where an "air of neatness and thrift" prevailed, or tonier Stamford, home to the state's "most elegant private residences"?[10] Either fantasy entailed a lot of train travel.

In the "great commercial center of Bridgeport," two hours from New York, Barnum watched train after train parade past his estate.[11] He sent an elephant from his "Great Asiatic Caravan" to a trackside corn field accompanied by a keeper "whom I dressed in oriental costume" and "furnished with a timetable of the road."[12] Whenever a train approached, the keeper made the elephant drag a plough through the dirt, seeming to till it. When curious riders inquired into the merits of pachyderm agriculture, Barnum referred them to his American Museum, just blocks from the line's terminus.

The New York & New Haven Railroad received its charter a full decade after passengers began riding across Massachusetts on the Boston & Albany and down the Boston & Providence to Stonington, where paddle steamers delivered them to the Long Island Railroad station in Greenport. The New Haven lacked its own entrance into Manhattan and had to settle for leasing an easement over the tracks of the Harlem Railroad.[13] In 1854 the New Haven almost collapsed when its first president, Robert Schuyler, issued 19,540 counterfeit stock certificates, "a fraud so significant and of such magnitude [it] would shake modern Wall Street," wrote Clarence Deming for the *Railroad Gazette* in 1904.[14]

Despite its struggles, the New Haven tapped a surging market of northeasterners who, like Barnum, wanted to live the "proper distance from the great metropolis." The seaside railroad conveyed commuters over tidal flats on plank boardwalks and through cities atop stone embankments. The New Haven entered Boston by leasing the Old Colony Railroad (which already leased the old B&P). In 1889 the New Haven opened a drawbridge over the Thames River in New London, spiking the final rail between Boston and New York.[15] In Manhattan, the New Haven partnered with the New York Central, successor to the Harlem Railroad, to raise Grand Central Depot, a Beaux Arts edifice that canopied twenty-one acres—the country's largest interior space.

Part wharf, part masonry, part palace, the New Haven Railroad was not merely another link in the antebellum "great chain." Its concentration of humanity in motion instead represented what historian John Stilgoe calls a "conglomeration of new spaces and forms seen too quickly for study."[16] With its commuter droves, showpiece terminal, and chockablock timetables, the New Haven had grown into a "metropolitan corridor," attesting the "power of the new, expert builder, the engineer, the architect, and the landscape architect."[17] The railroad had become a place unto itself—a place promising other places, and, as commuters would soon learn, a place governed by people elsewhere.

Born on Wall Street, the New Haven obeyed its shareholders to the detriment of riders. "Such persons as chose thus to remove from a neighboring state and bring their families and capital without our borders should have the right to pass over the railroad on the terms fixed at the time by the president and directors," proclaimed P. T. Barnum before the Connecticut assembly in 1865.[18] The carnival tycoon turned country squire turned state representative had sniffed out a New Haven plot to raise commuter fares 20 percent and now urged his colleagues to ban railroad employees from sitting on Connecticut's rate commission. "The interests of the State as well as commuters, demand this law," Barnum carried forth, unfazed even as he learned midspeech that his American Museum had burned to the ground. The bill passed "almost with a hurrah."[19]

Barnum foiled the fare hike but could not slow the New Haven's ascent. By 1900 the railroad's majority shareholder personified an even more rapacious commercial order. John Pierpont Morgan stood six feet without his top hat. He possessed a fraying mustache and smelled of Cuban tobacco. To meet his eyes, recalled photographer Edward Steichen, was to stare down the "headlights of an express train."[20] Morgan built an empire of coal, electricity, telegraphy, farm machinery, dry goods, and railroads. But before he cemented his status as legendary financier and imperious titan—before he grew into a glowering, potbellied caricature of Gilded Age excess—the Hartford native turned his attention to the New Haven Railroad. Morgan saw in his hometown carrier a chance to dominate New England transportation.

Morgan delegated the New Haven's day-to-day affairs to Charles Sanger Mellen, a sharp-elbowed industry veteran whom contemporaries found arrogant, combative, and proudly unversed in the soft power of public relations. The Railway Age Gazette opined that Mellen "should have been born a pope or a czar," noting that his "curt manners and arbitrary methods have made him numerous enemies."[21] As Morgan's deputy, Mellen epitomized Wall Street's control of Yankee enterprise, rankling New Englanders whose ancestors laid rails to keep their goods off the Erie Canal. The New Haven further antagonized commuters by buying out anything it construed as competition: railroads, trolleys, steamships, and bus lines. As local companies vanished into merger, the New Haven's snooty cursive foot blazed everywhere from Waterbury to Provincetown.

Mellen's conquests outstripped his revenues. By 1903 the New Haven owned only 438 of its 2,037 miles of track, paying nearly five million dollars a year to rent the rest of its sprawling network.[22] Handcuffed by lease payments and annual debt interest outlays that eventually topped a quarter billion dollars, the New Haven made for a shabby empire.[23] Instead of upgrading the lines it annexed, the railroad rolled profits into dividends. Riders needled by Mellen's brusque personality were incensed by the New Haven's antiquated equipment—especially its flammable wooden carriages that rolled

on long after other carriers upgraded to steel.[24] The New Haven's
Wall Street underwriters showed little interest in the everyday work
of running a railroad.

Wrecks occurred often on the New Haven, which critics took as
proof of the company's negligence. The railroad entered the annals of
train catastrophe in 1853 when a Boston express charged off an open
drawbridge into Norwalk Harbor, crushing or drowning forty-eight
passengers. The New Haven's affluent, literate, and connected riders
drew outsized attention to accidents, which invariably received coverage in the *New York Times*.[25] A rash of derailments between 1911 and
1913 led cartoonists to depict New Haven locomotives as skulls and
engineers as grim reapers ready to open "the summer slaughtering
at Stamford."[26] When asked to justify the New Haven's safety record
in a congressional hearing, the reliably guileless Mellen attributed
wrecks to "the same thing I do the rain and the sunshine . . . they are
incomprehensible to me."[27]

But some accidents were too egregious to shrug off. In the early
hours of July 12, 1911, the Federal Express thundered over Bridgeport's
viaduct. The Federal's slumbering passengers included the St. Louis
Cardinals, enroute to a doubleheader against the Boston Rustlers.[28]
While the Cardinals slept, New Haven engineer Arthur Curtis
worked frantically to wrench his late train back on schedule. Curtis hit
a crossover switch at sixty miles per hour—forty-five miles per hour
over the limit—and derailed. The engine and coaches tumbled off
the Fairfield Avenue overpass. Fourteen people died. They included
Curtis, two other crew members, and eleven passengers. Men in straw
hats and women with parasols gathered to gape at the "tangled iron
and splintered timbers which once composed six sleeping coaches."[29]
The Cardinals (who all survived) posed for photographs atop their
overturned Pullman.

New Haven executives blamed Curtis for the crash. But when Fairfield County's coroner found the railroad "criminally negligent" for its
excessively sharp switch, the *New York Times* talked of a "Bridgeport
Massacre."[30] Breathless wreck reports filled headlines from Kenne-
bec to Laramie, raising new questions about the public obligations

of what Louis Brandeis called the "be-bankered railroad."[31] What did the New Haven owe to Connecticut and to those passing through it? What did it owe to the burgeoning metropolis of New York, the maritime hub of Boston, and all the Bridgeports that lay between their bright lights? Could a J. P. Morgan holding be trusted with the infrastructure that it built? And who would decide?

While the New Haven grew into a Gilded Age black sheep, the Pennsylvania Railroad (PRR) basked in the glow of a favored son. Chartered in 1846 the PRR replaced the lethargic barges and creaky inclines of the Main Line of Public Works. Too big for Wall Street to claim as its satellite, the railroad expressed the enduring clout of Philadelphia, which had surrendered the seat of federal power to Washington, the mantle of mercantile leadership to New York, and the state capital to Harrisburg. Philadelphian Christopher Morley described his home as a "surprisingly large town . . . surrounded by cricket teams, fox hunters, beagle packs, and the Pennsylvania Railroad."[32]

The PRR maintained the aura of a public work that seemed to float above the greed and graft that characterized other carriers. In 1891 British tourist Thomas Fitzpatrick observed that "Americans are very proud of the Pennsylvania Railroad, which enjoys an acknowledged pre-eminence for its able management, the immense extent of its operations, the speed of its express trains, the excellence of the road, and its comparative freedom from accidents. It bears in fact an irreproachable character, which no one would think of contesting."[33] By 1900 the PRR had parlayed its staid managerial hierarchy, lawn tennis executive culture, and sterling reputation to become the largest corporation in history and the "standard railroad of the world."[34]

The reverence persists today. Rail fans still call the PRR "Pennsy," as if the long-dead company were an old school chum. They model Pennsy railscapes in scaled dioramas and photoshop its gold and Tuscan paint scheme onto modern locomotives, a fantasy tantamount to imagining that mastodons trod the earth.[35] Shirts, hats, and coffee mugs sport the PRR's keystone emblem. In Altoona, tourists picnic on a grass crescent inside Horseshoe Curve, where locomotives wheeze toward the Allegheny summit. Today, when state-run passenger trains linger like anemic ghosts of railroads past, nostalgia retains the PRR's full-blooded glory.

The railroad played a heavy hand in cultivating this mystique. While the New Haven scarcely bothered to explain why the St. Louis Cardinals crashed into Bridgeport and New York Central president William Henry Vanderbilt hissed, "the public be damned," the PRR commissioned multivolume histories of its achievements, compiled photo albums of scenic routes, and released cinematic documentaries detailing its modern operations and expert staff.[36] In 1912 the PRR hired Ivy Ledbetter Lee, the public relations wizard credited with inventing press releases. The railroad grasped the value of telling its story.

In 2012 historian Albert Churella tore through the Pennsy's mythic shroud with his corporate biography, *The Pennsylvania Railroad*. To those who admired the PRR as a guardian of common men, Churella recounted how the railroad ran its laborers raw and suppressed their calls for higher pay and safer working conditions. To those who esteemed the PRR as a "bastion of free enterprise" exemplifying the virtues of no-frills capitalism, Churella reminded readers of times when the railroad behaved "like a creature of public policy," shaped no less "by government as by the marketplace."[37] To anyone fooled by the PRR's facade of serene prosperity and "automatic railroad men," Churella pulled back the curtains on an executive stress factory rife with strokes, heart attacks, and nervous disorders.[38]

Before the Civil War, the PRR's trunk lines followed the westward procession of internal improvement through Pittsburgh, Cleveland, Columbus, Indianapolis, and Chicago. But as postbellum traffic increased between industrializing ocean ports, a maturing District of Columbia, and a rebuilding South, the PRR branched out along the seaboard. In 1871 it leased the United Company, a conglomeration of the Camden & Amboy, New Jersey, and Philadelphia & Trenton

Railroads, to access New York Harbor. A decade later the PRR cut the largest check in history—$14,949,052.20—to acquire the Philadelphia, Wilmington, & Baltimore Railroad, thereby extending its reach into the Chesapeake.[39]

In the 1870s the PRR upgraded its New York division to handle the crowds flocking to Philadelphia's International Exhibition of Arts, Manufactures, and Products of the Soil and Mines—better known as the Centennial Exposition. The railroad added tracks between Philadelphia and Newark, replaced iron rails with steel ones, and installed new signals to convert a ragtag assemblage of antebellum railways into the mid-Atlantic's own metropolitan corridor.[40] Over two million visitors stepped off trains into the Centennial's tradeshow, where they spoke into Alexander Graham Bell's telephone, rode Roy Stone's A-frame monorail, sipped from soda fountains, and scarfed popcorn.[41] Mighty Bridgeport's industrialists displayed a smorgasbord of wares: Read's reversable carpets, Armstrong's ventilated garters, Ives's mechanical toys, Union Metallic Cartridge bullets, Hotchkiss pruning shears, Smith & Egge padlocks, and Jerome B. Secor's "automaton singing birds in cages and vases."[42]

After delivering America to the Centennial, the PRR began plotting a permanent exhibition to its own greatness in the heart of Philadelphia. Broad Street Station began life as a polite Gothic confection prepared by the Wilson Brothers firm for the PW&B. Less imposing than New York's Grand Central Depot or Boston's South Station, the first Broad Street Station would have looked at home on a college quadrangle. By opening day, however, the PRR had absorbed the PW&B and began converting the quaint hall into the hemisphere's largest train station. The railroad hired Frank Furness, the exuberant Victorian architect behind the Pennsylvania Academy of Fine Arts. Furness gave the station several new stories, an office tower, and room for eight more tracks.

The Wilson Brothers were rehired to raise a glass and iron shed over the platforms where the PRR's lines of longitude and latitude knotted together in a smoky bedlam of whistle shrieks, baggage smashers, shoe shiners, and refrains of "All aboard!" The enclosure

FIGURE 4.1 Pennsylvania Railroad's Broad Street Station looms over downtown Philadelphia. Courtesy of the Special Collections Research Center, Temple University Libraries.

reminded some riders of the Centennial's Machinery Hall, which the Wilson Brothers had designed to house the Corliss steam engine that powered the fair. With its gingerbread portico and iron-plated annex, Broad Street Station loomed beside Philadelphia's City Hall—twin symbols of a potent commonwealth that New York dare not invade.

The PRR decked Broad Street's interior with triumphal allegory. A mural mapped the railroad's growing national network. Fireplace tiles depicted scenes from Walter Scott novels. One wall of the waiting room displayed Karl Bitter's relief, *The Spirit of Transportation*, which carved in glistening plaster the story of human mobility from ox-drawn carts to steam locomotives to a toy airship alluding to the hypothetical possibilities of flight. The terminal extended the PRR's perpetual public relations campaign through plastic arts and decorative stone.

Trains entered Broad Street over a granite rampart that split Center City. Pedestrians despised this so-called Chinese Wall, one of several barriers left by the PRR's "traffic free steel boulevard."[43] In

New Brunswick, residents fought the PRR's plans to sink its tracks into a downtown canyon. When the railroad agreed to build a viaduct instead, only neighborhood protests prevented it from walling off Townsend Street.[44] In Elizabeth, citizens fought the PRR's attempt to seize Railroad Avenue to add a fourth track to its line. When the PRR raised a viaduct in Jersey City, the structure sunk into reclaimed swamp triggering a landslide. Trackside residents woke in "tilted houses; ground swells lifted backyards up against the bedroom windows."[45]

Such acts of creative destruction were orchestrated from PRR headquarters on the second floor of Broad Street Station. Of the many leaders who strolled through Broad Street's oak-beam boardroom, none shaped the modern corridor more than a cautious Pittsburgher named Alexander Cassatt. The railroad's seventh president rose through the industry ranks, from surveyor on the Georgia Railroad to assistant engineer on Philadelphia's Connecting Railway project to vice president of the PRR and finally, after a brief retirement, to the top job in 1899. Cassatt, who studied at Germany's Darmstadt University and the Rensselaer Polytechnic Institute, brought worldliness to the brutal business of railroading. His bohemian sister, Mary, became a renowned impressionist painter who rivaled fellow Parisian ex-pat and railroad son James McNeill Whistler.

Alexander appeared as comfortable inspecting Altoona classification yards as he did strolling galleries in Berlin or walking the turf at Monmouth Downs, where his thoroughbreds raced.[46] Cassatt's "facility in the actual details of the work gave him faculty in the big affairs," wrote one journalist.[47] Mary painted her brother as sympathetic, handsome, a furrowed forehead and penetrating eyes above an auburn mustache. With his Rittenhouse Square townhouse and Chesterbrook horse farm, Cassatt was every ounce a fin de siècle aristocrat—a Henry James protagonist come to life. "He believed in spending his evenings in the company of people worth talking to, or of a book worth reading," prattled a 1906 magazine profile. "He wanted to do big things in life, yet to get some natural pleasure out of existence as he went along."[48]

Cassatt wanted nothing more than to make the PRR the greatest railroad of all time, an ambition to which the coastal line proved integral. Cassatt invested millions of dollars in the railroad's "glittering steel pathway."[49] He extended the centennial-era embankment work through Newark, Rahway, Bristol, and Philadelphia. In Wilmington, the PRR raised its tracks onto Clearfield sandstone and Kittanning brick arches that conveyed the solemn durability of a Roman aqueduct. Cassatt oversaw the construction of new masonry bridges across the Delaware and Raritan Rivers that look as gloomily eternal today as they did in the first decade of the twentieth century.

In 1900 the PRR acquired the Long Island Railroad, raising speculation as to what the company might attempt next.[50] Attention turned to the PRR's cramped Jersey City station, where millions of passengers shuffled off trains onto wave-tossed ferries. A century after Franklin's fateful boat ride across New York Harbor, the water around Manhattan still stymied travel. Even PRR admirer Thomas Fitzpatrick bemoaned that his favorite carrier "does not possess a station in New York, and that its terminus is situated in Jersey City, on the opposite shore of the Hudson River."[51] To minds as ambitious as Cassatt's, this river presented an irresistible challenge—the sort of trial that capped careers and bred legends. But for the time being, New York lay beyond the Pennsylvania's grasp, as did tracks of the New Haven Railroad, and New England beyond.

Five years after he moved to Connecticut, and ten years before he entered its general assembly, P. T. Barnum surveyed a "beautiful plateau" overlooking the Pequannock River.[52] The bluff facing downtown Bridgeport charmed everyone from Yale University President Timothy Dwight, who claimed that a "more cheerful and elegant piece of ground can scarcely be imagined," to historian Samuel Orcutt, who deemed it one the "loveliest pieces of country."[53] Barnum was enchanted by the land's rustic splendor and commercial potential. He partnered with attorney William H. Noble to acquire several hundred acres, which he proclaimed the "nucleus of a new city."[54]

Houses, churches, schools, and factories sprung from the hillside. People moved in. Businesses opened. "New Pasture Lots" became East Bridgeport.[55] Barnum took out an advertisement in the *Republican Farmer*, boasting that his community had no "mud holes, or grog shops or nuisances; a new Church is now in course of erection, and one of the largest and best School-Houses in the state is to be built forthwith. Gas and water are soon to be introduced through the New City, and no inducements are lacking for respectable families to secure lots thereon."[56] Like Father Stephen Panik, who wanted to set bedaubed Bridgeporters in sunshine, Barnum conceived his city as a project of charitable and topographical uplift. Moral sobriety would follow civil engineering to the high ground.

Barnum's East Bridgeport remains largely intact today thanks to its 1979 entry onto the National Register of Historic Places. You can still walk from the bandstand at the center of Washington Park through concentric rings of residential architecture: clapboard Italianates and gabled Queen Annes for nineteenth-century captains of industry, brick row homes and triple-decker tenements for their employees. Power lines and chain-link fences now clutter the streetscape. Some of the houses retain wistful plum siding and rookwood-green trim, but the lead paint peels, and the asbestos shingles are chipped.

One wedding cake white Victorian has become a church, Casa de Restauracion y Avivamiento a las Naciones. Around the corner is Iglesia de Dios Pentecostal, Funeraria Luz de Paz, Tazi Notary, and El Cochinito restaurant. East Bridgeporters of Puerto Rican descent have turned Barnum's moral experiment into a center for Hispanophone life and Caribbean culture. These Bridgeporters live among shuttered factories that once embossed ivory buttons and dim warehouses that packed ice. They are remaking an old neighborhood to which the Connecticut Center for Economic Analysis attributes some of the worst quality of life in the state's poorest city.[57]

The epic of East Bridgeport plays out beside the corridor tracks.

FIGURE 4.2 Proposed site of Metro-North's Barnum Station. It remained vacant in October 2022. Photograph by author.

Since 2013, when Metro-North announced its Barnum Station project, the chickweed ruins of Panik Village became a mixed income development called Crescent Crossings. With its sunny townhomes clad in panels of blue, lemon, and cream siding, Crescent Crossings cuts a sharp contrast with the boarded-up projects it replaced. When the development opened in 2017, units for low-income residents filled immediately. A waiting list opened, then closed due to "overwhelming demand."[58] The complex's market-rate units, which rent for up to $1,500 a month, offer the accoutrements of leased affluence: pendant fixtures, granite counters, and stainless steel appliances.

Crescent Crossings advertises itself as one mile from Bridgeport's Amtrak station, and "walking distance to the PROPOSED Barnum Station."[59] As of 2023 the station remains "proposed," its site a reedy lot where people pitch tarp tents and ditch rusted cars. In 2019, the Connecticut Department of Transportation decided not to build the park and ride stop.[60] Some officials blamed Barnum's cancellation on budget. Others wondered whether East Bridgeport needed a station at all. Why, people asked, should Metro-North slow schedules to serve a divested community with few passengers? Why should East Bridgeport delay corridor riders from getting elsewhere? To locals, Barnum Station was another unfulfilled promise named after a man who issued his share of them.

Station or no station, the next new East Bridgeport is already forming in Crescent Crossings. It has found another foothold in the warehouse that contains the offices of the New England Tractor Trailer Training School. Now rebranded SingerCt (after the sewing machine manufacturer that once occupied 480 Barnum Avenue), the complex leases space to companies that sell luxury doughnuts, vegan cookies, orangery greenhouses, garden speakers, and hand-sawed blanket chests. Bridgeport is making things again, but what these ventures will make of Bridgeport remains unclear. As city planner Lynn Haig said in 2016, "we expect eyes will refocus on the train station area."[61] Another trackside spectacle is brewing in this corridor town. Step right up.

· 5 ·

TERMINAL ZONES

There were people who thought there would one day be a tunnel under the Hudson through which the trains of the Pennsylvania railway would run straight into New York. They were of the brotherhood of visionaries who likewise predicted the building of ships that would cross the Atlantic in five days, the invention of flying machines, lighting by electricity, telephonic communication without wires, and other Arabian Nights Marvels.

EDITH WHARTON[1]

Amtrak trains serve over five hundred stations, from the clapboard visitor center in Brunswick, Maine, to the cross-gabled Great Northern depot in Sandpoint, Idaho. Of these five hundred plus stations, just two stops account for a quarter of the system's ridership.[2] More passengers board or alight Amtrak trains in Washington's Union Station than they do in Los Angeles, Chicago, Houston, and San Antonio combined. Two hundred and twenty-five miles up the corridor, Manhattan's Penn Station generates more ridership than the entire South, the whole of New England, or any other Amtrak destination by a factor of two.

In September 2019 Amtrak debuted nonstop Acela Express service between New York and Washington. Publicists touted the 155-minute ride as an "ideal solution" for the region's supercommuters.[3] But despite blitzing past Baltimore, Philadelphia, and Newark, the new express shaved just fifteen minutes off ordinary Acela schedules, a quarter hour easily frittered on coffee lines and cab cues. Timetables

could not explain the nonstop's allure: neither the streamlined pleasure of a straight shot nor the vanity of skipping everywhere else.

In 1900 the journey from New York to Washington took most of
a day. Passengers began on Manhattan's docks, where wind whipped
the tan Hudson into whitecaps and fog imperiled ferry crossings.
Trains left Jersey City's Exchange Place Station, the continent's most
gruesome transit choke point, and arrived in Washington, where
whistles shrieked through the halls of Congress and engines shunted
back and forth over rails engraved in 6th Street.

As the twentieth century dawned the Pennsylvania Railroad
needed new stations in New York and Washington—not claustro-
phobic sheds but dignified portals to modern cities. PRR executives
had a few models in mind. South Station unified Boston's spaghetti
wad of track into what Mayor Josiah Quincy called a "wide and spacious gateway of unrestricted freedom."[4] Providence's yellow brick
and sandstone trim Union Station handled three hundred trains a
day, many of them bound for another architectural jewel, New York's
Grand Central Depot.[5]

From the second floor of Broad Street Station, Philadelphia's own
bastion of artisanal pride, Alexander Cassatt plotted a Washington
terminal worthy of the capital's gravity and an entrance to Manhattan
befitting the "standard railroad of the world." These projects would
fuse New England to the mid-Atlantic to the South. They inaugurated
dramas of development and displacement that define the northeast
today. In New York, the corridor knit Gotham's water-parted bor-
oughs to the wider seaboard. In Washington, the line's gracious retreat made way for the modern National Mall.

The District of Columbia was never a congested ocean port or smoking factory town. Washington's breezy marble monument park considers sightlines and shade patterns. Its shrines leave space for lawn
and sky. Nothing blemishes or protrudes in the "city of magnificent
distances," which draws its geometry from the Constitution's call for

a "district (not exceeding ten Miles square) as may, by Cession of particular States, and Acceptance of Congress, become the Seat of Government of the United States."[6]

In 1787 politicians wanted to build a capital manifesting their classical pretensions and Enlightenment ideals. But they could not decide where. Northerners planned federal cities beside the Hudson River and Trenton Falls. Virginia offered Williamsburg as one potential site. Maryland proposed Annapolis as another. In 1790 Alexander Hamilton convinced the Virginians Thomas Jefferson and James Madison to sponsor the federal government's assumption of state war debts in return for platting the District of Columbia beside the Potomac River.

President George Washington hired Parisian painter and Revolutionary War veteran Pierre Charles L'Enfant to convert a scrabble of tobacco fields and whitewashed cabins into metropolitan art. L'Enfant imagined America's capital on a grand scale. His plan embellished Philadelphia's grid iron pattern with radial avenues, traffic circles, and a boulevard from Jenkins Heights, site of the Congress House, to Washington's monument, an equestrian statue south of the presidential palace. His Columbia combined the rigidity of graphing paper with the sinuousness of a spiderweb.

L'Enfant worried little about budgets or mosquitos, the shoreline mud or the sun that baked it into dust. He was, however, tormented by the fear that speculators would find his blueprints and jump on prime real estate. L'Enfant grew paranoid, secretive, slow. Washington grew impatient. He fired the Frenchman and hired surveyor Andrew Ellicott to scale back his predecessor's grandiosity. Among his most striking revisions, Ellicott turned L'Enfant's Champs-Élysées to the Potomac into a tree-lined promenade, or "mall."

In 1800 legislators left Philadelphia for a vainglorious shantytown. Charles Dickens called Washington a "monument of a deceased project."[7] Actor Tyrone Power likened the District's "gloomy and unimproved" landscape to the "prairies of Arkansas."[8] The District had "no university, no classes of students in science or literature, no philosophical societies, no people who seem to have any leisure," lamented London geologist Charles Lyell.[9] L'Enfant had created not a city but its shell. There was no reconciling his ambitious plan with its empty reality, what Henry Adams called "the immensity of the task and the paucity of means."[10]

Nowhere did Washington's stifled potential appear starker than on the National Mall, a tattered commons where residents planted crops and grazed cows.[11] To the mall's north oozed Washington Canal, a remnant of Madison-era infrastructural enthusiasm that now sloshed excrement into the Potomac. To the mall's south stood brick pens from which manacled slaves were driven to auctions at Lafayette Square. "The voices of patriotic representatives boasting of freedom and equality, and the rattling of the poor slave's chains, almost commingled," recalled Solomon Northrup, a freeborn New York musician imprisoned at what is now 1800 Independence Avenue.[12]

After the Civil War, B Street paved over the putrid canal. Coffles no longer trudged past Congress. The Mall became many things at once: an evergreen arboretum, a botanical garden, a cattle depot, and an experimental farm where the Department of Agriculture tested strains of sorghum and rye.[13] In 1851 landscape designer Andrew Downing planted trees around the Smithsonian's Norman castle headquarters. Where L'Enfant imposed Cartesian order on the Potomac backwoods, Downing injected wilderness back into the capital, smearing L'Enfant's right angles with brush strokes of the picturesque.[14]

The mall then became a rail yard. Trains arrived in Washington in 1835 when the Baltimore & Ohio converted a Pennsylvania Avenue tailor's shop into the district's first station.[15] The B&O's monopoly lasted until 1859, when a PRR subsidiary, the Baltimore & Potomac, built a branch off its Pope's Creek line to the National Mall's southern edge. This "branch" effectively extended the PRR from Baltimore to the capital. United States Marshal of the District of Columbia, Frederick Douglass, rejoiced that his city was "no longer isolated from the outside world and dependent on a single railroad."[16]

No sooner had the B&P entered Washington than it lobbied Congress for permission to lay tracks across the mall to the city's business district. The proposal divided Congress. Some legislators championed the extension as an overdue act of progress. "If you want to make Washington a *pleasant* place, make it a *useful place*," reasoned Connecticut representative Henry Starkweather.[17] Others condemned the terminal scheme as a desecration of sacred greensward. "By no consent of Congress," chided Charles Sumner, "would I allow any business interest or disturbing railroad company to fasten itself upon this inclosure."[18] Sumner continued, "there is a place for all things, and this I know, the place for a railway-station is not a public park."[19]

The B&P got its way. By 1873 trains rolled across the mall to a black iron shed that jutted through Downing's garden and L'Enfant's parade ground. Citizens complained about the tracks and the carriages parked on them, about the coal lumps scattered pell-mell, the hissing valves and clanging bells, and the smoke spoiling Washington's measured vistas. The new B&P station not only diminished Columbia's beauty but exposed its seedy underbody: arriving passengers now deboarded on the edge of "Murder Bay," a ferocious red light district steps from the mall.[20]

Before Congress approved the B&P extension, forty-year-old Ohio representative James Garfield pondered Washington's busy tracks and haphazard terminals. Garfield foresaw more carriers converging on the capital, more passengers disembarking wherever those carriers could acquire land, more chaos. On March 26, 1872, he asked his colleagues to dedicate "some place in this city for a Union Depot building, which will accommodate all railroads, and to which all railroads shall come."[21] While Congress fought over a single strip of the mall, Garfield wanted to concentrate all Washington train activity within one square of L'Enfant's grid. His suggestion died on the floor.

Nine years later, President Garfield marched through the B&P station he once thought redundant. He was leaving Washington to convalesce with the first lady, Lucretia, who contracted malaria in the sweltering Potomac summer and was recovering at the Jersey Shore. As Garfield passed, a spurned spoils seeker named Charles Guiteau sprang from the women's waiting room, pulled an ivory-handled British Bulldog revolver, and fired twice. One bullet glanced off Garfield's arm.

FIGURE 5.1 Trains cross Washington's National Mall along 6th Street on a winter day in the early 1900s. Miller-Gillette *Washington Seen* photograph collection, DC History Center.

Another stuck in his abdomen. Garfield survived the attack but not the doctors who plunged their unsanitized hands through his wounds. The president grew febrile as his blood festered.

The "excessively hot" night of September 5th gave Garfield fits.[22] His temperature spiked. His pulse raced. A guarded entourage carried the president onto a train bound for New Jersey, where doctors hoped the salt air would slow his infection. The train eased out of Washington through a tunnel beneath the jail cell where Guiteau awaited trial.[23] It thundered over the tracks of the B&P, PW&B, and PRR, which diverted all other trains onto sidings.[24] Garfield arrived at the seaside village of Elberon, New Jersey, where workers laid temporary rails to the front door of Charles Francklyn's mansion. To prevent "any unnecessary jar or shock," workers pushed the bedridden president's car by hand the final feet across Francklyn's lawn.[25] Garfield died seventeen days later.

Washington would not consider a serious terminal solution until

December 1900, when the American Institute of Architects (AIA) held its annual meeting at the Arlington Hotel. The visiting architects bemoaned their down-at-heel surroundings. Everywhere they saw L'Enfant's vision betrayed. In his opening remarks, AIA president Robert Peabody pledged to "make our Government architecture more worthy of the greatness and intelligence of the Republic."[26] Conversation turned to the railroaded mall. Frederick Law Olmsted urged his colleagues to treat the B&P tracks as a border marking the "terminus of one unit of the plan."[27] Others favored ripping up the rails, flattening their eyesore berm, and reclaiming the park for pedestrians. All agreed that a committee of architects, landscapers, and artists should develop a plan to revive the capital.

American Institute of Architects members may have revered L'Enfant's Columbia, but they drew more direct inspiration from another city. In 1893 Chicago celebrated its arrival as the country's second largest metropolis by hosting a world's fair. The Columbian Exposition hailed a new era in urban planning. With its genteel parks and stately boulevards, the City Beautiful movement imagined civic space as an aesthetic display and moral teaching aid. Its proponents claimed that attractive streetscapes could uplift city dwellers. To the AIA, Chicago's architectural pantheon offered a glorious example of how L'Enfant's blueprints might rematerialize. The former maze of stockyards and hovels offered hope that Washington could still become a "magnificent and consistent work of art."[28]

In March 1901 the Senate put Michigander James McMillan in charge of Washington's resurrection. McMillan assembled a commission that included the Columbia Exposition's mastermind Daniel Burnham and his associates Charles Follen McKim, Frederick Law Olmsted, and the Beaux-Arts sculptor Augustus Saint-Gaudens. Several commissioners toured Europe, combing Rome, Vienna, Versailles, London, and Frankfurt for artifacts of Old World design they could bring back to the Potomac.

Their final report called for winding parkways, regal memorials, a Federal Triangle office complex to bury Murder Bay's brothels, and the revitalization of the national mall as a "monumental core." The commissioners concluded that a "dignified approach to the Capitol" required the "exclusion of the Baltimore and Potomac Railroad from Public grounds."[29] Washington's trains, they reasoned, should share a single station. Garfield's union depot concept returned to life, now grandly reconceived as a transportation temple "superior to any structure erected for railways purposes."[30]

At the end of his European fact-finding mission, Burnham pitched his scheme to PRR chief Alexander Cassatt, then vacationing in London. The patriotic Cassatt quickly squared capital beautification with his railroad's interest. Ever since the PRR had gained a controlling share of its former rival the B&O, a combined terminal made economic sense. In return for vacating the mall, the PRR received federal money to dig a tunnel beneath Capitol Hill for trains running south to Virginia. The District reclaimed its signature park. Senator McMillan credited Cassatt for treating the terminal project as a "national matter."[31]

In keeping with City Beautiful ideals, planners located the new station atop a slum called Swampoodle. Swampoodle was everything that offended L'Enfant, Downing, and McMillan: a quagmire where flimsy shacks teetered over Tiber Creek and free-range goats browsed on garbage. The neighborhood took its name from its abundance of puddles, "solvent of the miscellaneous foulness of which they are made the receptacles and the resort."[32] Residents included famine-ravished Irish immigrants and "contrabands," Black Americans who escaped from plantation slavery to Washington. Southern writers detailed Swampoodle's foulness to justify slavery.[33] Lurid journalists peppered their reports with brawling mobs and cutthroat gangs.

If Swampoodle exposed Congress's negligence, Union Station gave legislators a chance to bury their shame. Before construction could begin, millions of cubic tons of rocky fill were dumped on the slum as if to sop up its pervasive dampness.[34] Over this base rose the largest train terminal in the world. The commission naturally went to Burnham's firm, which borrowed its floorplan from the Baths of Diocletian, a public thermae and gymnasium that accommodated up to three thousand recreating Romans in the third century. Colossal Union Station would welcome Americans to their own forum.

Passengers entered from Massachusetts Avenue through ionic colonnades adorned with statues sculpted by Louis Saint-Gaudens (brother of commissioner Augustus Saint-Gaudens) and a carved inscription from Samuel Johnson. They waited in a barrel-vaulted hall guarded by statues of imperial soldiers backlit by geometric window traceries. Riders departed through a cavernous shed to the platforms. The Diocletian baths drew fresh water from the Aniene River via the Marcia aqueduct. Union Station received trains over the new Magruder Branch, an ostensible branch of a branch of the old Pope's Creek line that became the corridor's southernmost trackage.

Though Union Station buried Swampoodle like Pompeii, it retained the old neighborhood's function as a waystation. During the twentieth century's Great Migration, millions of African Americans passed through Union Station enroute to new lives in Washington, Philadelphia, and New York. For Black southerners who crossed the Potomac, then rumbled under Capitol Hill on trains that sent vibrations shivering through the Library of Congress, Washington's Romanesque terminal marked what Isabel Wilkerson calls "the start of the north."[35]

When Union Station opened in 1908, President Theodore Roosevelt ordered the demolition of the vacant B&P terminal so that work could begin on McMillan's mall. The site sat empty for years while people debated what to do with it. Those ruins eventually became the National Gallery of Art. Today, the gallery's west wing displays American masterpieces, including several Mary Cassatt oil paintings. In the same air where brother Alexander's locomotives sooted the mall and where a president crumpled over in gunfire now hang portraits of children wearing straw hats and a girl lounging on a blue armchair, a man rowing a lime rowboat across an azure lake, and a single woman holding a perfect red zinnia.[36]

In May 1909 the PRR issued an orange booklet containing schedules for "Fast Express Trains Between New York, Philadelphia, Baltimore, and Washington."[37] Despite the timetable's title, no train drew closer to New York than Jersey City. The tracks ended at Exchange Place Station on Paulus Hook, where Manhattan-bound passengers completed their journeys on ferries that plied the same busy water as Albany steamers, Cunard ocean liners, and the Cuba Mail.

Riders traveling to New England remained in their seats. Their coaches rolled onto rails pinned to the decks of the steamboat *Maryland*. The *Maryland* once carried PW&B carriages across the Susquehanna River and later paddled Union troops around Chesapeake Bay during the Civil War.[38] It now provided a floating bridge between the PRR's Jersey headland and the New Haven's South Bronx terminal. For all its improvements, the last link in the great chain from Washington to Boston was still a boat.

On a December night in 1888, the *Maryland* chugged up the Harlem River. Fire broke out in the galley kitchen. The captain throttled toward Mott Haven, reaching the wharf as flames consumed his vessel. A conductor evacuated passengers from coach seats and sleeping berths while the double-decker ship sank. Sunrise revealed a "collapsed smokestack, some blackened stanchions, twisted iron, and two charred sides which rose from the Harlem River."[39]

The wreck underscored the PRR's need for a true rail link into Manhattan. The company consulted with Viennese engineer Gustav Lindenthal, who proposed a suspension bridge to carry trains between Castle Point Terrace and Canal Street. When the Army Corps of Engineers nixed this structure for fear its sixty-story anchor piers would block ship traffic, Lindenthal dreamed further crossings. One intended span from Hoboken to Chelsea received a groundbreaking ceremony in 1885 before financial panic scuttled the project.[40] This unbuilt bridge's foundation stone today rests in a mulch bed on the campus of Stevens Institute of Technology.

While Lindenthal tried to lift trains through the sky, others envisioned them burrowing under the river floor. The first person to imagine a submarine connection between New Jersey and Manhattan was resort developer and steam pioneer John Stevens, who in 1806 recorded his plan to sink brick tubes to the bottom of the Hudson

River and then pump out the water to permit dry passage.[41] The first practical attempt at an interstate bore came seventy-three years later when the Hudson Tunnel Railroad Company began laying subway tracks beneath the river.

Men in mud-spattered overalls descended to compression locks beneath Morton Street, where they shoveled silt by candlelight. The darkness strained their eyes. The weight of overhanging water put nitrogen in their blood. Whirring compressors pressurized the atmosphere until July 21, 1880, when the river burst in. Twenty workers drowned. It took the Hudson Company months to retrieve their bodies through caissons. The project was abandoned, revived, abandoned, then finally completed when engineers used a boring shield and cast-iron rings to finish off the shaft. Port Authority Transit Hudson (PATH) trains clatter through this former crypt today.

While the PRR pondered its Manhattan entrance, two emerging technologies gave tunnels an edge over bridges. Hydraulic shields accelerated underground boring. These three-story metallic cylinders used jacks to push their lamprey-shaped mouths through sopping earth. Whenever the shield got stuck, workers opened muck chutes to let silt plop into the tunnel like playdough through a press. Hydraulic boring coincided with the rise of electric traction, which propelled smokeless trains through confined spaces. The installation of direct current "third rails" on the London Underground in 1890 and beneath Paris's Gare D'Orsay in 1900 proved that trains could function underground.

On December 11, 1901, Alexander Cassatt unveiled the PRR's New York terminal zone project. It included a new branch between Newark and Weehawken and a new station, Manhattan Transfer, where steam locomotives swapped out for electric engines.[42] These engines shuttled passengers over the meadows, through Bergen Hill, beneath Hoboken, under the Hudson River, then up through layers of glittery Manhattan schist. Another iron bore pierced the East River's clay bed. The tracks resurfaced in Queens, climbed over Astoria, and crossed Hell Gate. At Woodlawn Junction, trains dropped their electric engines and returned to steam power.

In 1902 the PRR's Base Line Measuring Corps scaled Bergen Hill.[43] The nine white men in starched shirts, suspenders, bowties, bowlers, and fedoras gazed through theodolites and penciled measurements. The North Jersey landscape that appeared through their lenses remained rugged. To the west, jagged gullies and plank cabins overlooked the infinite meadows. To the east were the Erie Railroad's stockyards, a parquet of boxcars, a sepia band of river, and Manhattan's first skyscrapers thrusting through gauze. In a July photograph, corps members grin and smirk. They project confidence in themselves, their instruments, and the grand design that drew them up the Palisades.

The men who laid the tracks shared none of the surveying corps' tranquility. Italian, Slavic, and African Americans toiled in muck-covered boots, sweaty skin glinting under light bulbs dangling from cords looped over crossbeams. Camera flashes turned their eyes into white coins. Long exposures made their bodies a blur of gross motor movement. One worker lifts a massive iron wrench. Another clutches a pipe. Another hunches over a spade. One stands beside an excavation car glued to its tracks by mud. As the periodical *Scientific American* cheerfully intoned, the PRR terminal project required a thousand tons of iron and steel, a quarter million barrels of cement, and the "energy and enthusiasm" of hundreds of laborers who acquired the nickname "sandhogs."[44]

Even with hydraulic shields, train tunneling remained hazardous work. Diggers found that the drone of compression engines and the buzz of nitrogenated blood dulled their concentration, an effect PRR managers addressed by serving coffee.[45] No one knew when the shield might puncture a pocket of quicksand or when the compressors would conk out. In June 1906 a tunnel blowout made the East River surface foam like a geyser. In November 1906 the "bravest of tunnel men," African American New Yorker Lee Stribling, drowned under a torrent of liquefied sand.[46] In Manhattan Austrian tunnelers who had braved the Alps grappled with a rhizomatic mess of pipes, ducts, and foundations. In December they cut into an underground stream, ripping open a sinkhole on 33rd Street.[47]

Twenty-two years after the steamer *Maryland* sunk in the Harlem River, PRR trains rolled through the underworld between New Jersey and Queens. The tunnels were a "permanent monument to the mastery of science over the greatest barriers in nature" and a memorial to those who drowned in seawater and writhed from the bends.[48] But their achievement vanished into the darkness it opened. The dim sameness of tunnel riding made it hard for passengers to contemplate what had been done for them. Few gave thought to the flounder wriggling over their heads, the crabs clattering over rocks, or anything other than the pressure building in their ear drums. As E. B. White observed, the typical rider "calmly plays bridge while buried in mud at the bottom of the East River."[49]

In Manhattan the PRR tunneled under a Midtown slum of laundry-line tenements and triple-decker brownstones, Saturday matinees, Sunday morning masses, all-night dance parties, and backroom poker games. Bakers, butchers, and pastors shared blocks with pimps, hustlers, and cutpurses. Legend holds that the district took its name from the readiness of Tammany cops to overlook "Satan's Circus" for bribes.[50] Upon his promotion to the precinct, Captain Alexander "Clubber" Williams quipped that he had long settled for ground chuck (or some other cheap cut of cow in the tale's infinite retellings) but thanks to his new czaristic powers of extortion, planned to "eat Tenderloin."[51]

Like Swampoodle, the Tenderloin received African American migrants from the South. The newcomers lived in close quarters with Irish cooks, porters, carpenters, cops, and construction workers. In August 1900 race riots followed the stabbing of James Thorpe, a white undercover police officer, by Arthur Harris, a twenty-one-year-old Black Virginian. White mobs chased African Americans down streets, dragged them from diner counters, and pulled them off the trolleys swishing down Eighth Avenue.[52] Cops "stood idly by for the most part," observed the *New York Times*, "except when they joined savagely in the sport."[53] Police blamed the violence on Black southerners harboring "very peculiar ideas as to freedom of action."[54]

The Tenderloin bristled until 1902, when it burned out like a broken light bulb. Overnight, it seemed, the burlesque became a dead zone. "There is a 'Deserted Village' in the heart of the Borough of Manhattan," proclaimed the *Times* in 1902.[55] The desertion that felt so sudden had begun a year earlier when agents from a mysterious holding company canvassed the Tenderloin, knocking on doors and offering residents cash for their homes. No one had heard of the Stuyvesant Real Estate Company, though its allusion to New York's Dutch origins had a suitably generic ring to it. Enough to seem like it had always been there. Enough that no one questioned why its agents were buying up the neighborhood.

The Deserted Village stood until 1903, when wrecking crews reduced the Tenderloin to brick shards and grout. Suspendered men shoveled Gomorrah's remnants into carts hitched to chestnut draft horses. A few tree trunks held out, as did some fence palings and a bar, temporarily preserved to revive tired crews.[56] The three-block void between Seventh and Ninth Avenues resembled a National Mall by bomb blast. At the western edge, trains darted over the Interborough Rapid Transit Company's elevated railway. At the eastern edge shone the red star logo of the new dry goods emporium, Macy's.

The ruinous prairie then became a pit, an excavation of sparkling mica schist so yawning that people likened it to the biggest hole they could imagine: the unfinished Panama Canal. From this crater came the bright clang of metal on rock and the click-clack of mining hoppers shunting spoils over trestles. Voices echoed up as if from Hades. Ashcan artist George Bellows pitched an easel beside the hole and painted it four times. His most sublime composition captures the work on a winter night. Lamps shine against ice-caked rock. Orange flames quiver deep within the crevice like ladled steel. Candlelight burns dismally from the windows of pitside tenements.

The hole expelled dust and smoke over the streets of Midtown.

Sometimes it vomited solid matter. In November 1904 a dislodged gneiss fragment shattered the window of Johanna Verstein's candy store.[57] Another shard of bedrock entered Joseph Lonzo's seafood shop, crushed a plate of fried crabs, and sent Mr. Lonzo scampering beneath "fish and pans and grease."[58] Another stone smashed the Macy's toy department window display, nearly decapitating a window washer. Yet another errant blast rained rock down on Erlen Bell's saloon, rupturing a jug of "very old port wine."[59]

When blasting stopped, masons lined the pit with concrete. Steel beams stretched from each side like yarn on a loom. Bar by bar, a corrugated skeleton rose over the base, a modest five stories on Seventh Avenue that vaulted skyward at Eighth. Wind whistled through the frame. Over eleven hundred gondolas of Milford granite arrived from Massachusetts and were snapped into place.[60] The sheets sparkled pink with potash salts, lime feldspar, and quartz. The finished hall had the brooding air of a public library or science museum. Its stony sobriety seemed like penance for the Tenderloin sin circus.

One felt their smallness passing through the Seventh Avenue colonnade decked with granite eagles, marble goddesses, and a roman numeral clock. To enter was to fall into what Langston Hughes called a "vast basilica of old."[61] For all its lofty grandeur, Washington's Union Station routed passengers horizontally from portico to platform. Pennsylvania Station, as this landmark was called, plunged travelers four stories into the earth.[62] Stairs dropped from street level to a foyer of Corinthian columns, an allusion to Jupiter's temples and testament to the hidden steel holding this classicism aloft.

An arcade lined with florists, tobacconists, and soda fountains led to more stairs, which descended to another room decked in marble, travertine, and concrete mixed to look like travertine.[63] Lamps sprouted from the floor, their globular bulbs like glowing fruit. Semicircle windows gave the polished chamber a "mellowness of tone."[64] An alcove carved from one wall contained a ghost: a bronze statue of Alexander Cassatt in buttoned topcoat and bow tie clutching a

FIGURE 5.2 Pennsylvania Station's illuminated interior just before its 1910 opening. Library of Congress Prints and Photographs Division.

bowler hat and cane. In 1905 PRR assistant chief engineer Joseph Richards worried that the president was pouring over terminal plans when "he was on his vacation at Bar Harbor and supposed to be resting."[65] By 1907 Cassatt was dead of heart failure. A placard honored the man "whose foresight, courage, and ability achieved the extension of the Pennsylvania Railroad System into New York City" but who never got to see it.

Behind a final set of doors, the Roman bath gave way to a greenhouse that scissored the sky into ovaloid swaths. The stone station turned crystalline. A final staircase brought passengers to the pit floor. Here, forty-five feet beneath the trolleys and milk trucks and hawkers and pickpockets that made Manhattan Earth's most encumbered ground, gleamed train tracks. Over these tracks lisped electric trains. They came and went through tunnels that howled like elevator shafts. Through the west portal was the Hudson's silt bed, the Jersey

Meadows, Philadelphia, Washington, Chicago, California. Through
the east shaft lay everything else.

If Pennsylvania Station were a shimmering granite proem, Queens
was where the terminal zone showed its scratchwork. Trains leaving
Midtown rolled under the East River to Long Island City, where
they surfaced in a former Huguenot farm. Turn-of-the-century photographs depict Sunnyside Hill as a dust bowl of shotgun shacks and
cow pasture. On a meadow four thousand feet from Manhattan, PRR
engineers scooped another pit. In it they laid fifty-three miles of track
in forty-five rows that fanned off the main like the veins of a palm
frond.[66] Crews installed repair shops, inspection offices, commissar-
ies, lavatories, smith sheds, and signal cabins. Sunnyside Hill became
Earth's largest coach yard.

From a passing train, Sunnyside Yard surpassed comprehension —
like someone had shaken out the contents of a million model railroad
kits. The yard employed PRR mechanics and Pullman personnel who
scrubbed windows, hosed down wheel wells, restocked dining cars,
and heaved ice slabs into air conditioner bays. An eight-woman team
of bedding inspectors cleansed 110,000 pieces of linen every twenty-
four hours.[67] Their storeroom was nicknamed "widow's haven"
according to a Pullman employee newsletter, which marveled that
all but two of the twenty-five women had survived their husbands
"and have dependent on them 64 children — more than the ordinary
complement of a country school house."[68]

Queens filled in around the yard like a healing wound. Borough
residents moved to courtyard apartments and shaded townhouses
close to rail work. A model community, Sunnyside Gardens, sprouted
south of the tracks. Social critic and Sunnyside resident Lewis Mumford championed his greenbelt neighborhood, which became known
as the "maternity ward of Greenwich Village."[69] Manufacturers
clustered north of the tracks around freight access. The placards of

Sunshine Biscuits, Swingline Staples, Steinway Piano, and Chicklets Chewing Gum rose over the yard.[70]

Trains bound for New England swung past Sunnyside onto the New York Connecting Railroad, which fused the tracks of the PRR to those of the New Haven. The railbed climbed over Astoria's backyards on rusting girders and ivy-bearded concrete to the edge of Queens, where they met the tidal strait that seventeenth-century Dutch trader Adriaen Block called "Hellegat."[71] Mariners feared this channel's roiling currents and treacherous shoals, which they named Diamond Reef, Frying-Pan Rock, Pot Rock, and Flood Rock. The outcroppings sunk ships until October 1885, when the Army Corps of Engineers dynamited Flood Rock before two hundred thousand spectators.[72]

The PRR hired Gustav Lindenthal to build a bridge across Hell Gate, a consolation prize for the Hudson spans he never finished. Lindenthal worked with Philadelphian engineer Alfred Pancoast Boller, who had designed a "graceful and pleasing" Whipple double intersection truss swing bridge over Connecticut's Thames River.[73] For Hell Gate, Boller conceived a dramatic cantilever bow stretching between granite turrets on each riverbank.[74] Hell Gate Bridge slapped an elegant signature on the unified corridor. The iconic epoxy red arch publicized the new one-seat ride from Yankeedom to the Chesapeake. It was the northeast's closest thing to a golden spike.

To complete Boller's arch, Lindenthal recruited bridge builders unfazed by heights. Among those who came to Queens was an ironworker from Quebec's Kahnawake Reservation named John Diabo. Diabo worked as a bucker-up, capping rivets for an Irish gang whose foreman called him "Indian Joe."[75] Other Canadian Haudenosaunee joined Diabo until there were enough men to form an all-Indigenous crew. At night they came down from the bridge and slept in a section of Boerum Hill, Brooklyn, which they called "Downtown Kahnawake."[76]

Centuries after the Lenape were driven from Manhattan to Ontario, Wisconsin, Kansas, and Oklahoma, "Mohawk Skywalkers"

FIGURE 5.3 Hell Gate Bridge under construction in 1915. Library of Congress Prints and Photographs Division.

entranced megalopolitans. Haudenosaunee riveters, sheeters, heaters, and buckers-up worked on Rockefeller Center and the George Washington Bridge. One journalist referred to the West Side Highway and Pulaski Skyway as "modern Iroquois trails" in recognition of their Indigenous builders.[77] Diabo saw little of the phenomenon he launched. One day, while working on the Hell Gate scaffold, he stepped into the air and plunged to the East River. No one could explain his death. A crew member speculated, "it must've been one of those cases, he got in the way of himself."[78]

On April Fool's Day 1917, the Federal Express steamed out of Union Station over the remnants of Swampoodle, then crossed Maryland, Delaware, Pennsylvania, and New Jersey. The train paused on the Passaic flats to change engines at Manhattan Transfer, a station that had neither entrances nor exits, that "served no town, no village," yet sat in clear view of New York's incandescence. "It's funny this waiting in the wilds of New Jersey this way," remarks a character in the 1925 novel that John Dos Passos named after the interchange.

Hitched to an electric engine, the Federal shot across the new

Hackensack Cutoff, through the North River Tunnels, and arrived at Penn Station after midnight. Five minutes later, it slipped under the East River, passed the floodlit fray of Sunnyside Yard, and ascended over sleeping Queens. Around one in the morning, the Federal crossed the dark turbulence of Hell Gate and merged with the New Haven's tracks to Boston.[79] A few moments later, a Washington-bound train crossed the same track heading south. After eighty-four years, the great chain had become an unbroken ride. The corridor was complete.

WIRING
THE COAST

They know that without hands or feet, without horses, without steam, so
far as they can see, they are transported from place to place, and that there
is nothing to account for it except the witch-broomstick and the iron or
copper cobweb which they see stretched above them. What do they know
or care about this last revelation of the omnipresent spirit of the material
universe?

OLIVER WENDELL HOLMES[1]

Metropark, New Jersey, beckons riders to a white-collar enclave
twenty-four track miles from Manhattan. "Metro" comes from Metroliner, a stainless steel bullet train that once served the station. "Park"
means office park, a collection of jigsawed ponds, mulch islands, and
solar atria hoisting the flags of Fortune 500 capital. "Park" also hints at
the station's chief draw: parking. Daily parking. Permit parking. Overnight parking. Alternate parking. When it opened in 1971, Metropark
parked 820 cars.[2] Today, the station's multideck garage absorbs three
thousand. So convenient is Metropark's parking that Staten Islanders
drive over the Outerbridge to use it, some crossing state lines to commute from one New York borough to another.

Joel Garreau classifies Metropark as an "edge city," a point on the
urban perimeter where office workers stare at one another "from re-
spectful distances through panes of glass that mirror the sun in blue
or silver or green or gold."[3] Edge cities feel imperviously modern,
as if engineered to forget they had a past. But nick any northeastern

surface hard enough and history will flood through. Most of Metro-park belongs to Woodbridge Township. Woodbridge's 1669 charter claims for King Charles II the land beneath the corporate campus, the junior executive apartments, and half the dosa joints lining Oak Tree Road's "Little India."[4] Redcoats trooped through Woodbridge on a King's Highway now graced by dialysis labs and gas stations. George Washington slept here at an inn behind the 7-Eleven.

Among its stealth landmarks, Metropark claims one of the most important sites in transit history. From the train station, cross Route 27 (a motorized swath of Assunpink Trail) and turn right on Christie Street. The lane leads away from the corridor tracks through regal oaks and shipshape lawns. At Middlesex Avenue, a bed of marigolds and morning glories surrounds a wooden sign. The sign reports that in May 1880, on this precise patch of suburban earth, Thomas Edison released seventy-five amps of direct current through his experimental electric railway. The tracks ran three miles from Christie Street to "Pumptown," a streamside shack at what is today the fifteenth hole of the Metuchen Golf and Country Club.

Power crackled from the twin columns of "Long-legged Mary Ann" steam generators through wires soldered to the tracks. The engine, a cross between a lawnmower and a StairMaster, brushed current from the rails to its driving axel. Edison challenged his creation with sharp grades, hairpin turns, and a splendidly pointless trestle. He piled rid-ers onto two miniature cars and shrugged off wrecks with laughter. Tourists who learned about the electromagnetic train in the pages of *Scientific American* or *New York Graphic* made pilgrimage to Menlo Park. "At the word go the machine shot off like a bullet," recalled a *New York Herald* reporter. "The riding was very enjoyable for the first five hundred yards or so when suddenly a most horrible curve was reached, round which the motor, with its car attached, spun at a rather uncomfortable gate."[5]

Ever since the Danish chemist Hans Christian Oersted spun a compass needle with charged wire in 1820, inventors had dreamed of moving things with electricity.[6] Steam power reigned supreme on American railroads, but the technology was reaching its limits.

FIGURE 6.1 Thomas Edison's electric railroad, Menlo Park, New Jersey. Originally published in William H. Meadowcroft's *The Boy's Life of Edison*, Harper & Brothers, 1911.

A locomotive could go only as fast as the vapor it produced. High velocities required mounds of coal, ponds of water, tenders, tanks, and boilers. All this weight sapped speed. By offboarding power generation, electric engines did not need to lug around their fuel. "The more power our stationary engine gives the more rapidly we go," Edison deduced. "I could drive the car along at 180 miles an hour if I wanted to."[7]

Edison was not the first person to invent an electric train. In 1879 Werner Von Siemens's *elektrische Lokomotive* towed visitors through the Berlin Industrial Exposition.[8] Three decades before that, Congress gave twenty thousand dollars to a shovel-bearded patent officer, Charles Grafton Page, to find a "general substitute for the dangerous agency of steam."[9] In 1849 Page took his galvanic battery train for a test-drive. The trolley reached nineteen miles an hour on the Baltimore & Ohio tracks. People waved handkerchiefs at the machine. Enslaved tobacco pickers watched in "utter astonishment" at the eleven-ton car, "propelled by some invisible giant, by which his silence was as impressive as his noisy predecessor."[10] Page's glory evaporated when the ceramic battery cells ruptured. His car slowed, jerked, then doddered back to Washington under a cloud of nitrous fumes.[11]

Electric traction achieved commercial success forty years later on streetcar systems. In 1888 Menlo Park alumnus Frank Sprague wired the Richmond Union Passenger Railway, the first tram to replace horse-drawn carriages. Electrified trolleys spread across the seaboard. Wires canopied the major thoroughfares of every coastal city. Residents savored the distinctly modern pleasure of seeing streetscapes jammed with hack carts, jitneys, omnibuses, and their attending manure heaps plug into a clean and nearly noiseless grid.

Railroads harnessed electricity to power underground operations. In 1894 the B&O strung wire to the ceiling of Baltimore's smoke-choked Howard Street Tunnel. In England, the City and South London lined its tubes with strips of five-hundred-volt "third rail," a demonstration that inspired the Pennsylvania Railroad to employ direct current in its terminal zone project. But electricity remained a fix to ventless tunnels rather than a viable competitor to steam. Edison's own patent suggested his electric railway would best serve "regions where the traffic is too light for ordinary steam railways, or where the main bulk of the traffic is limited to certain seasons, or where the difficulties or expense of grading render ordinary steam-roads impractical."[12]

Electric railroading's ascent began on a foggy Manhattan morning in 1902. The mist draped tree branches and clung to fire escapes. It enveloped ferries puffing between Jersey City and Desbrosses Street. It dabbed the sandstone townhouses on Park Avenue and wafted down to the tracks beneath Park Avenue's pavement. The sunken rails formed the final approach to Grand Central Depot, terminus for New Haven and New York Central trains. A passing steam engine fumigated the rock cuts and brick tunnels every forty-five seconds. Trains moved timidly through paper air.

Fifty-two miles away, a New Haven Express highballed out of Danbury, Connecticut. The Express switched onto the Shore Line at Norwalk and clipped along the gray bank of Long Island Sound. At New Rochelle, the train's last car received a stenographer, a florist, a salesman, a veterinary surgeon, an optician's secretary, a stock trader, a carriage builder, and a teacher.[13] The express rolled through the Bronx, over the Harlem River, and into the Park Avenue cut. At 8:17, it paused at a stop signal one thousand yards from Grand Central.

That same morning, another commuter-laden train chugged out of White Plains. Its engineer was thirty-seven-year-old John Wisker, whom colleagues characterized as "sober" but "ambitious and impatient of delay."[14] The stalled Danbury train caused a green "caution" semaphore to drop before Wisker at 63rd Street. He throttled past it without slowing. At 59th Street, a red "stop" blade fell. Wisker barreled forward, unresponsive as his fireman screamed the colors: "Green! Green! Red! Red!"[15]

Up ahead, the Danbury Express sat motionless. New Haven flagman Frederick Barnum dropped to the tracks and fastened a small dynamite charge to one of the rails behind the last car. The charge, or "torpedo," would alert an oncoming train that another train lay ahead. Barnum gazed through the ash. The pinprick of Wisker's headlight glimmered down the tracks. But which track? Nine pairs of rails mazed together at 56th Street. Barnum watched the pinprick fatten into an oval, then sharpen into a silhouette. The silhouette ripped through the shroud, its pistons and drive shafts charging forward on what was now unmistakably the Danbury Express's track. Barnum swung his lantern against the locomotive like champagne on a yacht's bow.

Meanwhile, the Danbury Express received a clear signal. The train rolled a few feet before the White Plains local caught it. Wisker's engine entered the Express's last carriage like a missile. Its cylindrical boiler burst. White vapor scalded the New Rochelle commuters. From the carriage came shrieks and groans and the sound of escaping steam like a whistling tea kettle. Survivors leapt from the geyserous wreck and crawled along a track bed littered with glass, rags, and chunks of seat cushion. They climbed to the street through escape hatches with smoke-stung eyes, burned scalps, blistered limbs, cracked ribs. Fifteen passengers died.

Wisker survived. He appeared in court gaunt and trembling.

His pale face seemed to hold the morning fog in it. Facing second-degree manslaughter charges, Wisker testified that tunnel smog smudged out the signal blades. The clamor kept him from hearing the torpedo, an emergency gong, his fireman. He had done his best. The jury believed him. They blamed the Park Avenue wreck not on a fallible human but on his employer's indefensible dependence on steam. Wisker walked free. The Albany legislature banned coal engines from Manhattan, suggesting that trains could run "by electricity, or by compressed air, or by any motive power other than steam."[16]

The New York Central complied by laying a third rail of the sort that British engineers installed in the London Underground. The Central's new, nearly emissionless electric trains did not require a hulking shed, so down came Grand Central Depot and up sprung a new terminal hewn from Indiana limestone and crowned by the Roman God Mercury carved in contrapposto. The station buried trains in its basement but lifted passengers into the cosmos by scattering stars across the ticket hall's cerulean vault. From the fateful foggy morning of January 1902 came the modern Grand Central Terminal.

The New York Central's electrification compelled its guest, the New Haven, to figure out how to power its Manhattan trains. The simplest solution would have been to extend the Central's wire work up the Sound. But when the New Haven installed ground-level conductors on its Berlin-Hartford branch in 1897, neighbors protested the bristling bars, which menaced children and livestock. Some feared that the conductors discharged venomous fluid into the air. A string of grisly electrocutions led the Connecticut Superior Court to prohibit third rail.[17]

The banning of steam in Manhattan and third rails in Connecticut left the New Haven with two options: it could operate steam trains to the Harlem River, then ferry passengers into Grand Central on electric shuttles. Or it could build an overhead power distribution system, then design new trains that worked with suspended wires and the Central's low-voltage third rail. Long maligned for its stinginess, the New Haven for once refused a cheap fix. It instead undertook one of the country's greatest public works. The New Haven launched the first main line electrification in American history.

"There was so much more to electrifying the New Haven than just the salary," reflected William Spencer Murray, a Boston consulting engineer who gave up half his income to work for the railroad.[18] Murray saw the Shore Line's electrification as holy work that would evangelize the "most potent factor in modern advancement" and settle a schism over the imperceptible movements of subatomic particles.[19] For years, Edison's direct current (DC) technology dominated the field. But by 1890 the rival standard of alternating current (AC) had made inroads. According to its proponents, who included former Edison employee Nikolas Tesla, railway brake inventor George Westinghouse, and Murray himself, AC conveyed more power over greater distance with less leakage than DC.

Alternating current scored a series of high-profile victories over its counterpart, culminating in the 1893 Chicago Columbian Exposition, where AC lit the White City's fair. Edison griped against the upstart technology and even tried to terrify consumers by conspiring to have the first electric chair employ alternating current. But in time, even the General Electric Company founded by Edison began marketing AC gear. The so-called War of the Currents seemed all but over in 1902. Then, the New York Central announced that its state-mandated system would employ DC technology. This decision reignited debates over the safest and cheapest method to propel trains as the New Haven grappled with its electrification mandate.

In what historians have called a fit of "vast technological hubris," the New Haven decided to power its Shore Line with alternating current conveyed through a wire strung above the tracks.[20] Thus began the railroad's "great experiment" with catenary, a Latin word for the shape of a chain hanging between two fixed points.[21] Catenary's geometric form beguiled observers. Thomas Jefferson admired its "perfect equilibrium."[22] Victorian art critic John Ruskin called cat-

enary one of the "most beautifully gradated natural curves."[23] The
Catalan architect Antoni Gaudí incorporated red porphyry catenary
arches—catenary curves flipped upside down—into Barcelona's
Sagrada Família Cathedral.[24]

Murray needed his catenary to "remain in true line and level."[25]
The wire could not droop sensuously or swing in the wind like trolley
string looped over telephone poles. Electric trains required constant
tension, which Murray achieved by raising H-shaped steel bridges
every three hundred feet of track. Each bridge gripped the electrical
wires like the headstock of a guitar. The taut spans formed a tunnel of
zigzagging steel that receded into the distance like one mirror turned
on another. Some residents complained that the right-angled girders
spoiled the supple coast. Others treated the structure like a land art
installation. Yale graduate and Olympic pole vaulter Alfred Carlton
Gilbert claimed the wire supports inspired him to invent the erector
set.[26]

The New Haven's catenary received eleven thousand volts of alternating current from a power plant on Greenwich's Studwell Point,
where John Wilkes Booth's tragedian brother, Edwin, once owned a
cottage. When it opened in 1907, the Cos Cob Power Station consolidated the discharge of hundreds of steam locomotives under
one red tile roof. Coal arrived by barge on the Mianus River, was
crushed to bits, then fed into one of fourteen boilers that spun a bank
of turbogenerators. Workers fussed over walls of gauges, valves, and
wheels. They wore vests and ties even though the turbine hall grew
hot enough to melt shoes.[27] The New Haven planted rhododendrons
in a sad attempt to harmonize its Spanish Revival electric factory with
the picturesque peninsula.

Shore Line trains collected current through hinged rooftop pans
called pantographs. The pans skimmed along the catenary like sleigh
ruts on snow, touching just enough to create a circuit. At Woodlawn
Junction the engineers of inbound trains pushed a button to retract
the pantograph and deploy a pickup shoe that clutched the New
York Central's third rail. Their motors now ran on direct current.
Outbound trains made the opposite conversion, pulling up shoes and

FIGURE 6.2 Cos Cob Power Station in Greenwich, Connecticut. Library of Congress Prints and Photographs Division.

releasing pans to the New Haven's wire. With scarcely a dimming of coach lights, New Haven trains switched sides in the war of the currents.[28]

The first electric train arrived in Stamford in 1907, an event that the *Times* described as the "beginning of the last stage of the greatest enterprise in electrical railroading yet attempted."[29] By 1914 the wires stretched to New Haven. Murray boasted that his catenary provided "a cleaner and more reliable ride for the public" and greater profits for their carrier.[30] Electric motors contained fewer parts than steam locomotives, which meant they could clock more miles between maintenance sessions. Electric trains accelerated faster than coal engines, which required the ponderous buildup of steam pressure. The new machines practically scooted. Electric traction let the New Haven pack more trains on the same length of track, increasing capacity. In 1922 the railroad carried sixteen million passengers.[31]

And yet, Murray observed, "instituting electric service was not exactly laid over a bed of roses."[32] The catenary that seemed so perfect on drafting paper was prone to kinking in New England's salty air. Pantographs sparked. Frigid weather caused lightning arcs to pop from pans. Bending contact wires around embanked curves took months of trial and error before a suitable support system was devised. Trackside residents complained that high-tension AC wires made static sizzle through their phone lines.[33] Many considered the macrame of wires and trusses a blight. For all its Spanish Mission gables and pink-flowered hedgerows, Cos Cob showered Greenwich with soot and pumped fly ash onto the sound.

What Murray called the "most potent force in modern advancement" dealt gruesome injuries to steam-era railroaders. In May 1907 an electrician slipping off his platform car instinctively grabbed hold of a feed wire, which caused his body to swell to "almost twice its natural size."[34] One month later, a contact wire grazed the back of a brakeman working on top of a boxcar. It burned him "to a crisp . . . the feet and the hands were gone."[35] That October, engineer Charles Phillips accidentally touched the catenary, sending "12,000 volts through his body, 10,000 more than are used to put a murderer to death at Sing Sing Prison," but somehow survived.[36]

With a shrug of Mellenesque apathy, Murray attributed these gruesome injuries to "carelessness or violation of instructions."[37] He hoped that the "future will be free from this most regrettable feature."[38] Scorched bodies would not detract from his "great experiment," or, he believed, from the incontestable triumph of alternating current on the modern Shore Line.

After toiling fifteen years under the wires, Murray traveled to Colorado, where the snowcapped Rockies whetted his vantage on "problems that had been faced too closely in the daily routine."[39] Vistas known to coax romantic poetry from some tourists stirred in the engineer a prosaic hope for the "better use, through orderly co-ordination, of the great forces used in the electric utility field."[40] The New Haven project confronted Murray with America's poor management of power.[41] "We have been building fast and building well, but not always in co-ordination," he lamented.[42] This patchwork approach could no longer meet the country's growing appetite for energy—a gap exposed when World War I's industrial ramp-up sent blackouts rolling through the Midwest.

In the glow of purple mountains' majesty, Murray envisioned large networks linking the country's coal mines, dams, and generating plants to power-hungry customers. Like an Albert Gallatin of the electrical age, he wanted superregional circuits to integrate local utilities. United States Department of Interior Secretary Franklin Lane invited Murray to organize his thoughts in a report focusing on the North Atlantic seaboard, where an "active market for manufactured products automatically creates a maximum demand for power."[43] In 1921 Murray submitted 261 pages of numeral-laden prose, graphs, charts, and maps titled "Professional Paper 123," or "A Superpower System for the Region between Boston and Washington."

Superpower found that the "finishing shop of American industry" relied on 315 separate utilities.[44] Steeped in a New Haven corporate culture that relished top-down consolidation, Murray advised the federal government to connect these siloed systems with the same zeal that J. P. Morgan once annexed competitors. Nothing should stop this project: not municipal borders or gubernatorial edicts, not the profit motives of plant owners or what Murray derided as the "un-American" demands of organized labor.[45] *Superpower* imagined the northeast as a formal political entity, an electric free-trade zone carved from the thickets of domestic wire.

The Superpower region that stretched from the Atlantic Ocean to Pennsylvania's anthracite fields centered on the New Haven and PRR tracks. Murray observed that transmission lines strung atop catenary towers could conduct surplus electricity to wherever it was needed. A right-of-way that conveyed train passengers and telegraph pulses could also distribute energy. The great chain of 1832 seemed destined to become 1921's power strip in a region configured around logistical infrastructure. Secretary of Commerce and licensed civil engineer Herbert Hoover commended Murray's plan, noting that "no one has yet been able to kick a hole in it," and established the Northeast Superpower Commission to implement his ideas.[46]

Despite its technical elegance, Superpower garnered little industry support. Local power suppliers feared federal regulation.[47] The coal lobby worried that better transmission networks would reduce demand for fossil fuel. When a Department of Interior study showed that electrifying railroad trunk lines would decrease coke consumption by nineteen million tons a year, mine owners attacked Murray's plan.[48] A chartered Superpower Corporation never materialized. Just as confederated interests defeated internal improvements in the early nineteenth century, the federal dream of a seaboard grid languished, leaving private companies to do as they pleased with the promise of superpower.

Nine years after Murray returned from the mountains like Moses laden with tablets, his ideas came back to life in a conference room cluttered with binders, blueprints, and line charts. Maps plastered wainscoted walls. Multicolor pins stabbed through power plants, rail lines, neighborhoods, and factories.[49] Whoever generated this paper seemed acquainted with the future and authorized to shape it. But this oracular bastion held no formal planning authority. It was neither a federal office nor a Wall Street suite nor some statutory conclave of superpower. It was the second floor of Broad Street Station.

The Pennsylvania Railroad already operated electric trains in its New York tunnels and on several commuter lines around Philadelphia. The social science of demography now compelled these efforts to accelerate. Where the New Haven responded to legal mandates, the PRR anticipated a coming day when its seaboard main line would serve thirty million passengers. In 1928 the railroad announced it would electrify its New York–Washington line, a project that historian Michael Bezilla characterizes as the "largest capital improvement program undertaken by an American railroad up to the that time."[50]

"Yes, it is a new era in railroading, though the new will not supplant the old, but supplement and extend it," explained PRR president William Wallace Atterbury, a former brigadier general who built military railroads in France during the Great War.[51] Like his gifted predecessors Alexander Cassatt, Samuel Rea, and James McCrea,

Atterbury recognized that the PRR could either adapt or atrophy in the face of new competition. News of the electrification project broke one week after Newark Airport opened. The *Times* coverage of Atterbury's plans ran beside advertisements for the Reo Motor Car Company, Socony Special Gasoline, and the Capitol Bus Terminal, which invited readers to "see America from an armchair."[52]

The PRR chose the same alternating current system that Murray pioneered. The railroad would buy its energy from the Philadelphia Electric Company, which funneled the Susquehanna River through its seven turbine Conowingo Dam.[53] The dam sat eight miles upstream from the PRR's main line bridge, which meant that passengers could see out their windows the mazy flow that powered their ride. Atterbury's railroad made way for wires through herculean feats of civil engineering: a canal was raised in Trenton, a tunnel relined in Baltimore, and new stations erected in Philadelphia and Newark. The project proceeded with trademark Pennsylvanian inevitability. In March 1929 Atterbury predicted "uniformly good times" on a seaboard where industry hummed along at 95 percent capacity.[54]

One winter later, PRR employees were not presiding over "good times." They were chopping rail ties into firewood to warm the freezing poor of Elizabeth.[55] When the stock market collapsed in October 1929, Atterbury assured shareholders that electrification would proceed "without any slackening, retrenchment, or postponement."[56] He reminded investors that the PRR had weathered panics before, that its stock certificates commanded the respect of currency, and that its bonds found buyers everywhere from London to San Francisco. But when the Depression deepened, equity markets tanked. The railroad turned to President Herbert Hoover, the former superpower advocate, who created the Reconstruction Finance Corporation (RFC) to brace America's wobbling economy.[57] The PRR requested a fifty-million-dollar RFC loan. The RFC offered the railroad twenty-seven million dollars at 6 percent interest.[58]

By the time New York governor Franklin Delano Roosevelt succeeded Hoover in 1933, the PRR had chosen to repay its RFC loan and pause electrification. Unlike Hoover, Roosevelt grasped that laissez-faire tweaks would no longer suffice. During his first summer in office, Roosevelt expanded the RFC and created a new agency, the Public Works Administration, which summarized its mission in a leather-bound Keynesian parable titled *America Builds*: "Here was a country with a great and growing need for more schools, more highways, more bridges, more waterworks, more services of all kinds. Here was an army of men willing and able to build them. Here was an industry hungry for orders for the needed materials. The idea was to bring all of them together. The job would have to be some time, why not now?"[59]

The PWA poured most of its money into roads, "major arteries for the Nation's commerce and for the national defense."[60] But it also recognized that the "mightiest industries are spiked to the cross ties" and reserved two hundred million dollars to help railroads "catch up."[61] A seventy-seven-million-dollar infusion from the PWA helped the PRR string wires to Washington. Conceived in Broad Street's palace of corporate sovereignty, the tax-funded power project wound up demonstrating a form of hothouse capitalism.

The corridor became a federal public work. Electrification generated forty-five million labor hours for Depression-era workers.[62] The project busied people beyond the tracks by stimulating the production of raw materials. The PRR converted fifty-five million pounds of copper into catenary, transformers, substations, and locomotives.[63] One hundred thousand tons of steel became catenary bridges and the Passaic River lift bridge.[64] By August 1934 the railroad had poured 6,650 tons of cement into catenary pole supports.[65]

Like a small-scale Tennessee Valley Authority, the PRR's electrification used the "most potent force in modern advancement" to galvanize an immiserated region. Despite its uplifting imagery, the work remained grueling and dangerous. Rubber-gloved workers hung from span wires. They strung copper in continuous shifts through sun and snow, risking their lives clamping high-voltage wire over tracks as steam engines blasted them with smoke from below. In 1933 the PRR distributed a booklet to workers in electrified territory that addressed topics like "Resuscitation from Electric Shock and Apparent Death" and included such insights as "accidental electric

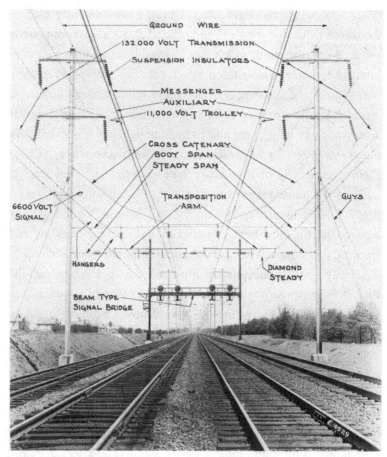

FIGURE 6.3 Pennsylvania Railroad's new catenary, Hackensack, New Jersey, 1936. Audio-visual Collections and Digital Initiatives Department, Hagley Museum and Library.

shock does not always kill; it may only stun the victim and stop his breathing for a while."[66]

When the first electric train left Washington in 1935, Interior Secretary Harold Ickes claimed that the project "demonstrates what actually had been accomplished under PWA when private initiative aids the Administration in carrying out its re-employment plans."[67] The PRR drew from the darkest depths of the Depression one of the country's most enduring acts of infrastructure. But in so doing, the railroad had been reduced to "aid," auxiliary help to a federal design, even a human resources contractor. Ickes relegated the PRR to a time when states chartered railways to serve the people. His remarks also foretold a future when war, recession, and demographic shifts would again blur the line between private and public interest.

The PRR now wanted a vehicle worthy of its circuitry. The early days of electric railroading had produced some ungainly machines. Engines stood stiffly upright with rods, springs, lamps, and handlebars jutting everywhere. Some sported cowcatchers even though the days of free-ranging northeastern cattle were long gone. The DD1, a direct current workhorse built in 1910, resembled two cabins coupled together atop enormous wheels and jackshafts. The P5 of 1931 bore the stubby heft of a power plant. In search of something more elegant, the PRR turned to a consortium that included Westinghouse, General Electric, and Gibbs Hill.[68]

Westinghouse had recently launched its art-in-engineering division under the direction of Donald Dohner, an Indianan with a trapezoidal mustache and wire frame glasses. Dohner studied landscape painting at the Art Institute of Chicago and later developed the world's first industrial design curriculum at the Carnegie Institute for Technology.[69] At Westinghouse, Dohner designed everything from plastic vacuum cleaners to Micarta serving trays to locomotives. He began the PRR job with a knife and gypsum lump, peeling strand upon strand of plaster to reach the engine inside. Dohner was, in the most literal sense, *streamlining*, a word that signified both the reduction of an object's wind resistance and a poetics of simplification. His finished mold was a feat of aerodynamic optimization and exquisite art.

Westinghouse and General Electric converted Dohner's gypsum mold into a full-size prototype at the Baldwin Locomotive Works in Eddystone, Pennsylvania.[70] The builders struggled to match Dohner's supple knife work with bolts and shells. The prototype, which retained Dohner's signature steeplechase cab and symmetrical tapered ends, performed beautifully in tests. It mustered 8,500 horsepower (necessary for freight) and topped one hundred miles per hour (vital for passengers). The PRR ordered 139 of the engines to be manufactured at General Electric's Erie plant and the railroad's own locomotive shops in Altoona. They classified the new motor GG1.

One week before the engine entered production, the PRR paid an external consultant five thousand dollars to "enhance the GG-1's esthetics."[71] This consultant was a Parisian combat veteran who inhaled mustard gas at the Battle of Reims and later dressed windows for Macy's. As a teenager, Raymond Loewy designed rubber band airplanes. At twenty-four, he lost both parents to the 1918 global influenza outbreak. He claimed his first kiss possessed "helicoidal characteristics with accelerating progression in depth" and tasted like "Parma violets in April."[72] When conscripted in the French army, he furnished his trench with floral wallpaper, drapes, and tufted pillows.[73]

Loewy haunted rail yards throughout his adolescence, lamenting that "my irresistible craving to sketch and dream locomotives led to my complete oblivion as a dancing partner."[74] Upon immigrating to New York, Loewy made it his goal to work for the Standard Railroad of the World. The flamboyantly individualistic Parisian may have seemed like a poor fit with the PRR's starchy corporatism, but he shared with Atterbury, the railroad's Great War veteran president, a faith in progress through innovation. The persistent Frenchman received a commission to redesign terminal trash cans.

Impressed by the receptacles, PRR executives showed Loewy photographs of the GG1 prototype. "It had a disconnected look," Loewy recalled. "Component parts did not seem to blend together, and its steel shell was a patchwork of riveted sections. It looked unfinished and clumsy."[75] Loewy proposed replacing the rivets with a welded body, restoring the smooth surface that Dohner had cut from clay. He also suggested a Brunswick green paint scheme accented by five golden pinstripes, a curvilinear flourish that tied the composition together. Loewy visited the PRR car shops at Wilmington, climbed a ladder, flung off his overcoat, and began marking up the prototype with tape and chalk. "I could feel that my audience was convinced. The corrections were obvious improvements and all realized that I knew what I was doing."[76]

FIGURE 6.4 Raymond Loewy posing before one of the GG1 engines he stylized in 1934. Audiovisual Collections and Digital Initiatives Department, Hagley Museum and Library, and Estate of Raymond Loewy.

The GG1 became an instant art deco icon: lithe, sensuous, perfected. Its streamlined body symbolized a metropolitan northeast in postage stamps, paintings, and photographs set against the Manhattan skyline, the Philadelphia Museum of Art, and the Washington Capitol. The GG1 cameoed in Hollywood films, including *Broadway Limited* (1941), *Bright Victory* (1962), *Blast of Silence* (1961), and *The Manchurian Candidate* (1962). It towed kings, actors, ball clubs, and presidents (campaigning, sitting, retired, dead). Loewy received most of the acclaim. By the time GG1s purred along the corridor, Westinghouse had fired Dohner, after learning that his art-in-engineering division spent over seventy-five thousand dollars a year.[77] Dohner taught at Brooklyn's Pratt Institute until he died of carbon monoxide poisoning on Christmas Eve 1943.[78]

Dohner's death left Loewy the GG1's exclusive spokesman, poet, and theorist, a role he parlayed into a twenty-thousand-dollar annual consulting contract with the PRR and eventual pop stardom.[79] Loewy would apply the GG1's fluid contours to Coke bottles, Studebakers, KitchenAid mixers, Le Creuset saucepans, and NASA's Skylab. An equally prolific graphical artist, Loewy sketched the logos of the Coast Guard, the Postal Service, Exxon, and Shell Petroleum. In 1962 he watched a "rather gaudy" orange military plane carry John F. Kennedy into Palm Springs and pictured the "luminous ultramarine blue" livery that graces Air Force One today.[80] The electrification project that sped corridor trains and returned Depression-era northeasterners to work launched one of the greatest design careers in history.

Once quintessentially novel, electric traction has grown old enough to leave ruin. Vines wrap around catenary poles. Rusted signs from the 1920s scream, "DANGER LIVE WIRE, 11,000 VOLTS." The New Haven's Cos Cob Power Station closed in 1986 after decades of violating federal air-quality laws. While rail fans usually associate the middle twentieth century with steam power's last stand, electric trains continued to collect steam-generated current until 1979, when engineers replaced Cos Cob's turbines with oil burners.[81]

The flower-girted plant was one of the few places where corridor infrastructure disturbed the lives of affluent northeasterners, a predicament encapsulated by a Greenwich resident who sent her white poodle into the yard each morning "and got a black one back each night."[82] A playground now sits atop the corridor's first source of alternating current. An Astroturf soccer field offers beautiful views of the harbor and of corridor trains whipping over the Mianus River.

Thomas Edison closed his Menlo Park Laboratory in 1887 to open a larger campus in West Orange. The woods reclaimed his electrical railway. Today it's nearly impossible to trace the line, save for a potential telltale gap between old growth trees, a sidewalk claiming the old track bed, an orphaned gully, and the historical placard on Christie Street explaining what once was. Tract housing has buried Edison's experiment. On a late fall afternoon, crickets chirp, birds call, mowers drone, and the Garden State Parkway murmurs in the distance. The oak leaves are just starting to brown. Every few moments an electric train whispers through Metropark.

III. RUST

· 7 ·

RUNAWAY

I stand at the window of a railway carriage which is travelling uniformly, and drop a stone on the embankment, without throwing it. Then, disregarding the influence of the air resistance, I see the stone descend in a straight line. A pedestrian who observes the misdeed from the footpath notices that the stone falls to earth in a parabolic curve. I now ask: Do the "positions" traversed by the stone lie "in reality" on a straight line or on a parabola?

ALBERT EINSTEIN[1]

When Albert Einstein fled Germany in 1933, he bounced between Belgium, Britain, and Pasadena before settling in the black-and-white pattern book cottage at 112 Mercer Street, Princeton. As a Jewish refugee, Einstein treasured the safe haven of North America while fascism stormed across Europe. As an academic, Einstein cherished his fellowship at the Institute for Advanced Study, where he chased a unified field theory without the burden of teaching students or appeasing deans.

But Einstein bristled at his small-town surroundings. He called Princeton both a "wonderful piece of earth" and a "ceremonial backwater."[2] New Jersey's imitation Oxford "could not be better or more harmonious," except when it soured with the scholastic bloviations of "demigods on stilts."[3] On sunnier days, Princeton reminded Einstein of an "unsmoked pipe, so fresh, so young," a budding center for natural inquiry fed by industrial philanthropists.[4] At other times, this intellectual promise wilted in the musty trappings of a suburban country club.

When Einstein needed to escape pompous professors and gar-
goyled facades, he walked past Princeton Theological Seminary to
the train station. Beside the Gothic revival depot gasped a black
steam engine waiting to haul its log-filled tender and single carriage
to West Windsor, where passengers connected to trains for New York
and Philadelphia. The corridor once cut right through Princeton. But
when the Camden & Amboy straightened its Trenton line during
the Civil War, it cast the college town into wilderness. The railroad
appeased local riders by laying a branch track from campus to the
realigned corridor at a new station called Princeton Junction.[5]

A one-car train, nicknamed "dinky," shuttled Princetonians between the university's arcadia and the junction's clamor. It departed
from the grass apron before Blair Hall, past the rippling brown water
of Carnegie Lake, over the old Raritan Canal and the older New
Brunswick Turnpike, before easing into the junction. In less time
than it took to read a feature or pray the rosary, passengers left what
Princeton dropout F. Scott Fitzgerald called the "peacocks and deer
parks" of rural New Jersey for the "ugliest country in the world. Sor-
did Trenton sweats and festers a few miles south; northward are Elizabeth and the Erie Railroad and the suburban slums of New York."[6]

The dinky became a Princeton ritual. Professor emeritus Woodrow
Wilson departed for his 1913 presidential inauguration on the train.[7]
Someone once spotted macroeconomist John Maynard Keynes
aboard the same car as the Wicked Witch of the West, Margaret
Hamilton.[8] Toni Morrison, Brooke Shields, and Bill Bradley were
dinky riders. Before his 2015 death, the mathematician and *Beautiful
Mind* subject John Nash haunted the Princeton Branch, riding back
and forth in Converse high-tops and a rumpled raincoat. "I just like
trains," he explained.[9]

Einstein also liked trains. For years he schlepped through Europe's
gares, Bahnhofen, and *staziones ferroviaria* enroute to teaching posts.
He later sketched a stormy railscape to illustrate relativity, showing
how the world not only looks but becomes different to those click-
clacking through it. Einstein's thirteen-year-old son Hans Albert fashioned a model railroad out of cardboard and, owing to the wartime

coal shortage, planned to "make the train electric."[10] At Princeton Junction, Einstein was known to stand trackside watching whatever came past: fidgety locals depositing Wall Street traders; Pullman sleepers from Akron, Savannah, and St. Louis; endless freights brimming with the harvest of garden state factories.[11]

Three miles from campus, Einstein discovered the modern corridor. This bustling realm shone in polished rail and signal glare. It whispered wordlessly through sine waves of alternating current. It gathered in the doppler pileup of an approaching whistle. Princeton Junction displayed a landscape wired for speed, what writer Al Kalmbach called a "tremendous integrated machine" pressing people into relative motion and physics into flesh.[12] Where Einstein thought Princeton a tabernacle of pretense, he found clarity at West Windsor, a junction where American railroading achieved its zenith.

Einstein had lived in Princeton for two years when the Pennsylvania Railroad finished electrifying its New York–Washington line. Copper catenary now draped 301 miles of track from downtown New Haven to the foot of Capitol Hill. For a time, the wires spooled south into Virginia through a tunnel bored beneath the basements of the House Office Building and Library of Congress. In 1933 the railroad opened Philadelphia's 30th Street Station, an Alabama limestone jewel box that let trains bypass the opulent but aging Broad Street Station. Newark opened its own neoclassical hearth in 1935, outfitted with terrazzo floors and frosted globe chandeliers orbited by bronze zodiacs.

These transit cathedrals cemented the PRR's status as a civic fixture that not only survived the Depression but enhanced itself with New Deal relief. "Do not think of the Pennsylvania Railroad as a business enterprise," urged a 1936 article in *Fortune Magazine*. "Think of it as a nation. It is a bigger nation than Turkey or Uruguay. Its boundaries are wider and it has larger revenues and a larger public debt than they. Corporately also it behaves like a nation; it blankets the lives of its 100,000 citizens like a nation, it requires an allegiance as single as a

patriot's."[13] To Christopher Morley, the PRR represented an industrial age Vatican where "nothing was so holy as the local to Paoli."[14]

The New Haven still foundered. J. P. Morgan died in 1913, three
weeks after Princeton political scientist Woodrow Wilson became
president. Wilson's Department of Justice accused the railroad of
violating the Sherman Antitrust Act. In 1916 the New Haven's most
dogged critic, Louis Brandeis, joined the Supreme Court. Depression swept the carrier into bankruptcy. Despite its woes, the New
Haven debuted a strikingly modern train in 1935. Funded by the
PWA, sculpted by Donald Dohner, manufactured by the Goodyear-
Zeppelin Corporation, and tested in a wind tunnel at the Daniel
Guggenheim Airship Institute, the diesel-electric Comet hit 110 miles
per hour on the old Boston & Providence line.[15] The three-car train
was too short to handle the demand it stoked, but its sleek aluminum
profile streaked through magazines and postcards, projecting better
days for beleaguered New England riders.[16]

The eternal power of trains took center stage at the 1939 World's
Fair in New York, which converted the ash dumps of Flushing into
a flea market and theme park. Like earlier expositions in Chicago
and Philadelphia, World's Fair exhibitors teased the future with trin-
kets of a bright and brave tomorrow: punch card calculators, nylon
stockings, Smell-O-Vision. A sarcastic robot named Elektro smoked
cigarettes and insulted guests. Cows spun around a milking merry-
go-round called the rotolactor. Billy Rose's *Aquacade* spectacular
treated audiences to synchronized splashing by Johnny Weissmuller,
Eleanor Holm, and a supporting cast of "fetching mermaids and vir-
ile mermen."[17] Salvador Dalí contributed an erotic funhouse where
topless models pretended to be pianos.

If these marvels portended "a new day," the Eastern Railroad Presidents Conference tried to turn back the clock. Its seventeen-acre
exhibit contained over four thousand feet of track. Inside the adobe
brick Hall of Railroads, visitors studied the original John Bull locomotive that puffed through Amboy's orchards and watched model
trains jitter through miniaturized prairie. In the Court of Railroads,
fairgoers toured the cabs of a PRR GG1 and New Haven EP4, the

same engines that brought many of them to New York. These domestic workhorses sat by the Elettro Treno Rapido 200, an Italian train that topped 125 miles per hour outside Rome. Mussolini paid to ship the ETR to Queens, using the fair to showcase fascist industry.

There was even a pageant choreographed by modern dance composer William Matons featuring actors, singers, horses, oxen, and actual trains that rolled back and forth on rails grooved in the stage.[18] "Railroads on Parade" blended wistful sentimentality with madcap abandon. Hoopskirted pioneers scampered onto carriages. Mourners knelt inches from Lincoln's funeral special. A highballing locomotive led a pantomime of westward expansion.

New York Times critic John Martin applauded the "Iron Horse Opera," which "boasts not a single bathing beauty or dove dancer, yet succeeds in being exciting entertainment."[19] Composer Kurt Weill called his show a "fantasia on rail transport."[20] Despite its avant-garde creators and talented young cast, the show also gave the impression of a lifetime achievement award, a "downright touching" but compulsory tour of old triumphs suggesting that trains had passed their pinnacle. Promoters leaned into nostalgia by promising to show the "glamorous past" of American railroading and a "future *no less* significant."[21]

Audiences exited into a plaza decked with corporate emblems of a new order: Firestone, Goodrich, Ford, Chrysler, General Motors. General Motors's "Highways and Horizons" pavilion hosted the fair's smash-hit attraction: a ride that took guests on a bird's eye tour of a model city filled with beveled skyscrapers, topiary-dotted malls, and freeways knotted into parabolic cloverleaves. E. B. White felt soothed by the narrator's voice of "utmost respect, of complete religious faith in the eternal benefaction of faster travel."[22] Compared to the vaudevillian racket of trains, this tomorrow actually felt new. Designer Norman Bel Geddes called it Futurama.

Beyond the fair gates of futurity, the corridor still performed its own daily pageant: Albert Einstein pads past Princeton Junction's luggage carts as Duke Ellington rides south to a Philadelphia gig. Leopold Stokowski shuffles through sheet music on another train enroute to guest conduct the New York Philharmonic while Marianne

Moore broods over her "scintillating diamond arabesques, my dark blue cape... (in the train to N. Brunswick)."[23] Their coaches arrive at the same Penn Station where Holden Caulfield considers calling his sister in J. D. Salinger's *The Catcher in the Rye*, where homeless men carry "with them the smell of the snow falling" in William Faulkner's short story, and where a hungover Nick Carraway wakes "in the cold lower level... staring at the morning *Tribune* and waiting for the four o'clock train" in Fitzgerald's *Great Gatsby*.[24]

The same corridor that staged these literary transits inspired musical odysseys. The Chattanooga Choo-Choo in Glenn Miller's 1941 big band homage to Appalachia departs track 29 in Penn Station.[25] New Haven passenger George Gershwin recalled that "it was on the train with its steely rhythms, its rattle-ty bang that I suddenly heard— and even saw on paper—the complete construction of Rhapsody [in Blue] from beginning to end."[26] John Coltrane saw, heard, and most certainly felt those same percussive tracks, which ran directly behind his Philadelphia home at 1511 North 33rd Street.

The corridor moved minds to music and bodies to Stamford. It conveyed metrical art through machine sounds and political power in the conclaves of smoking cars. It was not a garden-walled exposition of some far-off future but life lived in the vibrant color of the present—a present nearing its end.

When the World's Fair returned in 1940, its triumphal Lagoon of Nations had lost two tenants. Hitler's conquest of Warsaw forced Poland to shutter its exhibit, which featured a tower made of bronze shields and a restaurant that served caramelized calf brain and honey wine. Across the water, Czechoslovakia's beer garden closed after Germany invaded the Sudetenland and installed a pro-Nazi regime in Prague. Both pavilions eventually reopened following charity drives, but their boarded-up silence on opening day spoke to a world on fire.[27]

As Europe sprinted back to war, Franklin Roosevelt shunned corridor travel for fear of sabotage. The president cloaked his movements by boarding a bulletproof car on concealed spurs beneath Manhattan's Waldorf Astoria Hotel and the Federal Bureau of Engraving. Though the United States initially espoused neutrality, many saw war coming to America: to the fairgrounds of Queens, to Princeton's leafy solitude, and to the tracks connecting them. Where Einstein had emigrated to escape the Third Reich, railroads now reminded him that his adopted home was retooling itself into "an arsenal of democracy."[28]

When the United States declared war on the Axis Powers in December 1941, the eastern seaboard joined the Atlantic Theater. The corridor became a military machine. The fight for Europe flooded the PRR and New Haven tracks with shipments of mortars, bombs, linens, canned fruit, and powdered milk bound for American troops and their British, French, and Soviet allies. Flatbed cars conveyed obvious instruments of war, like Sherman tanks and camouflaged jeeps. Petroleum tankers and coal hoppers bore the fuel that propelled Allied ships through U-boat infested waters. Boxcars clanked past, carrying anyone's best guess.

Troop trains delivered soldiers to ocean convoys. Thousands of war-bound GIs laid over at Camp Kilmer, a base built outside New Brunswick, where the corridor tracks crossed branches of the Reading and Lehigh Valley Railroads. The Kilmer yards, which held fifteen trains at a time, became a staging ground and last call for soldiers "on their way" to ships in Newark Bay and New York Harbor. When the PRR ran out of passenger cars to accommodate everyone shipping out, it jury-rigged new carriages by sawing window holes out of boxcars.[29]

No one rode alone on the wartime corridor. Trains filled with troops, prisoners of war, and civilian motorists stifled by new driving restrictions. When Japan invaded Malay in 1941, America lost its chief rubber source. The Office of Defense Transportation tried to extend tire life by reducing the national speed limit to thirty-five miles per hour.[30] Pumping twelve gallons of gas required three #7 coupons from the ration books and the correct windshield sticker. Scarcity put Futurama's freeway utopia on hold—and drivers back onto trains. These begrudging passengers slept on station floors and rode standing in the aisles, reminded by posters that "first things must come first."[31] Gone were the sumptuous parlor cars where passengers smoked, drank, gambled, and flirted. Every chair, every bench, every inch of Pullman sofa now held human freight.

Wartime controls increased train ridership while conscription thinned employee rosters. The New Haven and PRR searched abroad to replace enlisted staff, hiring hundreds of Mexican guest workers from Zacatecas, Jalisco, Guanajuato, Durango, and Mexico City. The so-called braceros completed the most backbreaking labors: uprooting old ties with tongs and claw bars, sledgehammering new rails into place, spreading layer upon layer of limestone ballast over track beds.[32] Promised "hygienic lodgings adequate to climate conditions in the region," some migrant workers received decent barracks in North Haven, Guilford, and East Greenwich, but others shivered through the winter in drafty trackside huts and boxcar camps.[33]

The labor shortage opened opportunities to domestic railroaders previously denied posts by virtue of their race and sex. The PRR was already the nation's largest employer of African Americans before war broke out.[34] Sunnyside Yard had become an intergenerational hub for Black railroaders, many of whom arrived in New York by train during the Great Migration. But the white men who ran the railroad excluded African American porters, redcaps, and mechanics from promotion. Now short-staffed by conscription and compelled by FDR's Fair Employment Practices Committee, the PRR considered Black waiters "for steward jobs on an equal basis with other applicants" and opened "ten new skilled occupations in the mechanical equipment department" to African American candidates.[35]

The PRR welcomed twenty-three thousand women to "fill the breach left by their fighting brothers-in-arms."[36] Some left clerical posts to join train crews. Others became public address announcers, their voices piercing the murmurous din of waiting halls. Male reaction ranged from gratitude to anger. Union boss A. F. Whitney assailed the PRR for hiring "coupon clippers" who might depress wages.[37] For its part the railroad venerated women's contributions in visual propaganda. A 1944 advertisement in *Life Magazine* depicted a "Molly Pitcher" of the rails crouched in overalls, poised to throw a switch. The steel-eyed and muscular Molly was modeled on photographs of an actual teenager, Ruth Hilger Hoffman, who pulled night shifts in a Philadelphia yard during the war. "Often I worked four o'clock in the afternoon to eight o'clock the next morning," Hoffman recalled in 2013. "I was young."[38]

The mobilizing northeast drew notice in Berlin, where Nazi intelligence officers plotted how to sabotage the coast's salt plants, oil refineries, cryolite factories—and the railroad synchronizing their production. U-boats already hounded the seaboard, torpedoing ships in sight of the Jersey Shore, forcing the US to convey petroleum by train instead of tanker (just as Britain's 1812 naval blockade diverted maritime cargo onto roads). In 1942 Hitler's Abwehr hatched Operation Pastorius. Named for Daniel Pastorius, the seventeenth-century Frankfurter who led Pennsylvania's first German settlement, the scheme recruited undercover agents to strap dynamite to various sites, including Hell Gate Bridge and Newark Penn Station. The saboteurs trained at a lake chateau in Brandenburg, where they received instructions, fake birth certificates, and cash.[39]

On a foggy June night, four of them climbed through the hatch of submarine U-202. They pontooned ashore and buried their explosives in a dune. A Coast Guard officer approached through the mist. "Who are you?" he asked.[40] The Germans claimed to be fishermen, then clammers, then offered twenty-one-year-old "sand pounder" John Cullen three hundred dollars to get lost. Cullen sprinted back to the Coast Guard Station and told his commander.[41] The Germans fled inland. A train track led them to Amagansett. When the village depot opened, they bought seats on the Long Island Railroad's 6:57 inbound express and rode in silence behind newspapers to Jamaica.[42]

"On the train I felt safe. At least there was no longer the danger that someone would take a shot at me," recalled George Dasch, the plot's ringleader.[43] Dasch and an accomplice went shopping for new shoes in Queens, then caught another train through the East River tunnels to Penn Station. They checked into room 1414 of the Governor Clinton Hotel.[44] The Germans proceeded to play tourist for the next few days, feasting on coconut pie ("my weakness," confessed Dasch), patronizing jazz clubs and brothels, and engaging in all-night pinochle games.[45] They planned (but never took) an outing to Palisades Park, where visitors bobbed in wave pools and rode the Cyclone roller coaster.[46] One could picture them at the World's Fair.

Dasch, it turned out, never planned to execute any attacks. A declassified federal report speculates that he had "every intention of giving himself up to the American authorities and compromising the whole expedition."[47] This double cross was as vainglorious as its plotter. Born in the Rhineland, Dasch stowed away to Philadelphia at age twenty. He enlisted in the army twice and married two American women at once with the help of an alias. When Dasch returned to Germany in 1942, Nazis imagined the disgruntled English speaker as an ideal secret agent. Now he frolicked about Gotham on Hitler's dime.

At last Dasch shuffled off to Madison Avenue and dialed the FBI from a hotel lobby payphone. "When the man answered, I told him I would like to make a statement. I told him I believed my case was so big that only Washington would be the place to spring it. In my own little mind the only person who should hear it first would be John Edgar Hoover."[48] Dasch hung up. The next morning he bought a suit from Macy's and a seat on the 2:30 train to Washington. He paced through Penn Station's glass atrium, a greenhouse of train fumes and summer heat where sweating riders milled under a sagging "V" banner.

Once aboard, Dasch experienced the ordinary aggravations of American rail travel in 1942. "The train was an uncomfortable one. It was jam-packed like most trains in wartime and I was lucky to get a seat."[49] Dasch's train called at Newark, the glimmering art deco station he had trained to blow up, then ran express through Princeton Junction, where newsstands cheered Allied progress in the Mediterranean: "US-British Fliers Cripple Italian Navy, Sink Big Cruiser, Set 2 Battleships Afire."[50] Dasch's train passed the Martin Aircraft plant in Maryland where "the large number of planes pleased my spirits, which had become more and more depressed, got a new lift."[51]

In Washington, he caught a taxi from Union Station to the Mayflower, a Connecticut Avenue hotel later famous for hosting presidents, diplomatic summits, and the tryst that brought down Eliot Spitzer's New York governorship. Dasch again called the FBI to request an audience with Hoover. This time, the FBI came to Dasch. Agents knocked on the door of room 351 and escorted him out. It must have dawned on Dasch at some point over the coming days that he would not be talking to Hoover. Perhaps this realization arrived when he was flung into a jail cell, or when the interrogators kept grilling him after he gave up his New York accomplices and another Nazi sleeper cell in Miami—certainly by the time his capital charges were read.

The FBI used Dasch's intelligence to round up the remaining German spies, some of whom actually intended to detonate the northeast corridor. Six died in the District of Columbia's leather-strapped electric chair. Their bodies were dumped in nameless numbered graves in a potter's field beside Washington's Blue Plains Advanced Wastewater Treatment Plant. Dasch and his closest accomplice received commuted sentences for their cooperation. In 1948 they were deported to the American Occupation Zone in Germany.

The United States had been at war for twenty months on Labor Day Weekend 1943 when Army Chief of Staff George Marshall declared, "the end is not yet clearly in sight, but victory is certain."[52] Italy had surrendered. Allied troops would liberate Paris within the year. In Washington, the PRR's Congressional Limited departed Union Station running heavy, its manifest brimming with holiday crowds and troops trickling back from Europe. The weight of sixteen coaches scarcely taxed GG1 locomotive 4930 as it sped past fattening corn and humming factories.

The Limited, nicknamed "Congo," reached eighty miles per hour on its nonstop run to Newark.[53] The express banked through Philadelphia ahead of schedule. At C Street Switching Yard, on the Kensington border, an employee saw flames shooting from the under-carriage of coach 1860. He told the yard attendant, who phoned Shore Tower. By the time the tower operator picked up, the front axle of 1860 had snapped. Its broken rods dangled down and jammed into the track, pole-vaulting the coach through a signal bridge. The roof sheared off. Bodies pelted the tracks. "There were no signs of panic but there was quite a lot of crying," recalled one passenger, Corporal Otis Tellis. "I had no idea how many people were killed or injured. I started to go to the aid of the injured, but I could not stand the sight of the blood all about, and I had to leave."[54]

Kensingtoners enjoying their last moments of summer on front stoops ran to the tracks. Ambulances blared toward Frankford Junc-tion. Surgeons steeled themselves to perform amputations. Forty priests prepared to administer last rites.[55] Crews sifted through charred metal under the lunar glow of flood lamps. Welders from a nearby shipyard used blow torches to reach survivors and retrieve remains.[56] The Congo's streamlined "fleet of modernism" splayed across the tracks like disjointed vertebrae. Loose threads of catenary dangled menacingly. The damaged gantry drooped to one side of the tracks, but its signal still flashed a horizontal row of bulbs: "stop."

Seventy-nine people died. The Interstate Commerce Commission blamed the wreck on an overheated journal box, the same metal-on-metal friction that toppled John Quincy Adams's train a century earlier.[57] The sheared journal glowed cherry red at 1,400°F.[58] Pennsyl-vania Railroad officials claimed the box had been "carefully checked at Washington by an experienced oiler," but workaday employees confided that the war had placed "too great a strain on the nation's railroads."[59] Years of vigilance, improvisations, and deferred main-tenance had exacted an inevitable toll. Brakes squealed. Contacts shorted out. Toilets clogged. Burnout glared through the bloodshot eyes of engineers, conductors, track crews, and dispatchers. Having blistered through the ultramarathon of war, the railroad had no an-swer for peace.

During the war, American railroads demonstrated what filmmaker

Carl Dudley called "productive capacity in the hands of a free and de-termined nation."[60] For a brief moment, this power appeared limitless after the Axis surrender. In July 1946, passengers could descend into the bustling depths of Penn Station and emerge a few days later in the sunshine of Los Angeles, Miami, or Mexico City. Streamlined luxury sleepers ran daily to Chicago. Most trains had air conditioning and some even featured onboard phones. The PRR discussed lengthening corridor station platforms to handle twenty-car Clockers.

Such optimism curdled with the return of cheap gasoline and plentiful rubber. In 1948, Thornton Wilder's *The Happy Journey to Trenton and Camden* debuted on Broadway. The play follows the Kirby family on a car trip through New Jersey towns long linked by rails: Newark, Elizabeth, New Brunswick, Trenton, and Camden. Trains are a ghostly presence in the vehicularized landscape of bill-boards and gas pumps, mentioned only when a bored child, apropos of nothing, sings "I've Been Working on the Railroad."[61]

The ascent of private automobiles that Wilder dramatized coincided with the collapse of the northeast coal industry, a stal-wart freight customer whom the railroads undercut by replacing anthracite-burning steam engines with electric and diesel-electric locomotives. By 1950, turnpike commissions in Pennsylvania, New Jersey, New York, and Connecticut were drawing new routes on survey maps. Flush with toll revenue, the New York Port Authority opened a "functional and businesslike, yet comfortable and pleasant" bus terminal in the former Tenderloin.[62] The new Idlewild Airport on the edge of Jamaica Bay offered direct flights to Boston and Wash-ington at speeds no train could match.

The PRR tried to gin up investor confidence by issuing dividends in lean years—a gesture that came at the cost of equipment repairs and track maintenance.[63] While executives blustered on about past glory and "clear track ahead," a conductor's manual painted a more realistic operational portrait. Acknowledging that "competition on the highways and in the air will be keener," the booklet urges PRR staff to impress existing riders to "build for the protection of our own future."[64] "It is within the power of all of us," the guide continued, "to show our patrons that we sincerely desire to please."[65]

It had been a grim week on the PRR when the sun rose on January 15, 1953. A freight derailment in Morrisville, Pennsylvania, closed the corridor for ten hours.[66] Turnpike Commissioner Paul Troast filed papers to run for governor of New Jersey. The Radio City concert violinist Isidore Gralnick slipped off a Penn Station platform and was crushed to death by a Long Island Railroad train.[67] Down the line in Maryland, Henry Brower, engineer for the PRR's Federal Express, had no reason to be thinking of any of these things when he applied the brakes to his GG1 and nothing happened.

Brower lived in a tidy brick rowhome in West Philadelphia. He had worked seventeen of his sixty-six years as an engineer for the PRR.[68] A model employee, Brower piloted the inaugural Morning Congressional in 1952. A photograph from the day's festivities shows him in thick spectacles and denim overalls, smiling next to the fur-coated Elizabeth Jane Barkley, second lady of the United States. When interviewed about the new train, Brower commended its "amazing new safety device" that would read trackside signals and automatically regulate speed.[69]

On January 15, 1953, GG1 4876 had no functional brakes, automatic or otherwise. Brower slammed his engine into an emergency stop. He threw it into reverse. He dropped sand under the wheels. Nothing worked. What Brower did not know—could not know—was that the fourth coach's air brake had shut, and nothing would restore pressure. "When I came under New York Avenue, I started to blow the horn on the engine to notify the people that we couldn't hold the train, or to scare them away from the platform," he later testified at a Senate committee hearing.[70]

The Federal Express had offered a rare ray of hope in the dismal world of postwar railroading. The popular overnight train, a joint production of the New Haven and PRR, departed Boston's South Station

FIGURE 7.1 Wreckage from the runaway Federal Express that crashed into Union Station on January 15, 1953. Raymond Gallagher Photograph Collection, DC History Center.

at 11 p.m. and arrived in Washington the next morning. On January 15, riders rousing themselves from sleep and polishing off continental breakfasts realized something was wrong. The train hurtled past Ivy City Coach Yard, C Tower, K Tower—the landmarks that told passengers when to pull their suitcases down from luggage racks. "We were going too fast when all of a sudden the motion became jerky," recalled Eleanor Johnson, a reporter for the *Baltimore Evening Sun*.[71] Seconds later, the Federal ran out of track.

Engine fireman John William Moyer estimated that the train was going "around 35, maybe 40" miles per hour, when it whipped past Union Station's platforms and crashed through the bumper at the end of track 16.[72] The Federal plowed through a newsstand, entered the station, and skidded over the concourse's Vermont marble floor. The GG1 slid just far enough to shine its headlight into the main waiting room where passengers scattered beneath the eternal gaze of Louis Saint-Gaudens's centurion statues. Then the floor gave way. The 215-ton engine plunged into the basement mail room. Its pantograph reached into empty air. The New Haven coaches piled up like strewn toys.[73]

The station master called for fire engines and morphine. But no fire erupted. And no one died, not even Brower, who remained at his controls the whole time, tugging his whistle until the engine outran its power. Doctors treated injured riders. Workers threw plywood boards over the gashed concourse floor and heaped sacks of quick-drying asphalt over the planks. Dwight D. Eisenhower would become president in five days. An intact Union Station was needed to handle the inaugural crowds. Crews chopped apart GG1 4876 and shipped its salvageable parts to Altoona for reassembly.

By 1953 Albert Einstein had spent twenty years in Princeton: twenty years of sauntering through the Institute's dogwood groves with John von Neumann and Robert Oppenheimer, twenty years of fruitless slogging toward a unified theory, twenty years of watching the tracks. Einstein still boarded the Princeton shuttle a few blocks from his home, though its weatherworn coaches rattled on rough roadbed. Colonial homes mushroomed beside the right-of-way. Brunswick Pike bulged into Route 1, four lanes of diesel-smelling pavement festooned with car dealerships and motor lodges.

Einstein was sixty-four years old when the Congressional Limited derailed at Frankford Junction. He was seventy-two when the Federal Express burst through Union Station. And he was seventy-three the following December when Princeton Junction's waiting room, site of so many contemplative afternoons, burned to the ground. Stationmaster Virginia Worrilow woke at 4 a.m. on December 27 to the sound of "mice gnawing."[74] Smoke billowed from behind the walls. Worrilow escaped through a window onto the platform awning where riders helped her down. Firefighters arrived but then "stood by, fearful of spraying water on high voltage wires." The station house collapsed. Worrilow's dog died in the blaze.[75]

The *New York Times* blamed "hungry pyromaniacal mice."[76] Worrilow told reporters that this was not the first time that vermin "tres-passed on company property and had caused a short circuit nibbling wires."[77] Despite this terrifying ordeal and tragic loss of a pet, the *Times* report ended on a jaunty note of collegiate nostalgia: "Although older generations of Princeton men may brush a furtive tear for the loss of the station, from which they often took the five-mile [*sic*] spur to school, the present generation probably will have a ticket window, waiting room and roof before the Christmas holidays are ended."[78]

Just as the Pennsylvania planked over a train wreck to keep up appearances in Washington, railroad officials talked around their mounting troubles. They needed to convince themselves that American railroading would enjoy a "future no less significant" than its storied past. No executive seemed willing to acknowledge how fast their lines had deteriorated or face up to new threats—not Nazi saboteurs this time, but Plymouths, Greyhounds, and Boeing 707s. No one was willing to consider the possibility that northeasterners no longer needed trains.

FLAGGING
THROUGH
SPRAWL

Nothing was more up-to-date when it was built, or is more obsolete today,
than the railroad station.

ADA LOUISE HUXTABLE[1]

They came by the thousands to a former broccoli patch beside Bristol
Pike and the corridor tracks. Car upon car pulled into the parking lot.
Couple after couple emerged under cement skies and a light drizzle
that beaded on their camel peacoats and velour fedoras. December
1951 blew warm and wet through the northeast. Manhattan broke
sixty-five degrees. Puzzled azaleas burst with pink petals by the on-
ramps to the George Washington Bridge.[2] Roses bloomed in Washington's record-breaking balminess. Humidity mildewed clothes and
dampened armpits.

They kept coming to this soggy patch of Pennsylvania despite
the rain, the lines, the country roads jammed with sedans back to
Philadelphia city limits, and the public address announcer telling late-
comers to come back another day.[3] They milled over the same earth
where Quaker farmers plucked broccoli florets and spinach leaves,
where Philadelphia & Trenton track crews dug gravel to ballast their
horse tram. They waited their turn in Bucks County, three miles from
William Penn's summer estate, to enter the office of Levitt & Sons.

The arriving hordes wanted homes—newer and better homes
than the ones they had. They flocked from the rowhouse river wards

of Kensington and Bridesburg; from coal camps on the outskirts of Scranton; from Texas, Missouri, and Canada. Some locals drove in from New Jersey's factory belt or down Oxford Valley Road from Fairless Hills, the company town of slab and bolt "magic homes" that U.S. Steel assembled for workers at its new mill. All came for the chance to buy a fractional acre of what the Levitts proclaimed the "most perfectly planned community in America."[4]

Buyers paraded through sample homes. They toured "wonder kitchens" of streamlined steel cabinets and an open living room where the upholstered ottoman and Danish coffee table projected casual urbanity. One could almost hear ice crack in a cocktail shaker or smell the floral wraith of pipe smoke wafting behind a dog-eared novel. Or imagine gazing out the picture windows onto rye grass lawns dotted with pines, willows, poplars, and the single apple, pear, and peach tree allotted to each plot. Matico tile floors shimmered with wax. Cream and emerald paint gave rockboard walls a Plextone sheen.[5] Even curmudgeonly Lewis Mumford, the Sunnyside Gardens historian who ridiculed suburbs as an "asylum for the preservation of illusion," conceded the Levitt home's "superior interior design."[6]

Levittown would eventually contain seventeen thousand homes more or less like this one (though none so radiant as the sample). Having cut their teeth raising the first Levittown from Long Island potato fields, Levitt & Sons took their mass production methods to Pennsylvania. "Levitt carpenters never touch a hand saw," marveled one reporter, who watched assembly line crews bulldoze crops, grade roads, bed drainage creeks, pour concrete bases, and assemble houses from plywood frames, gypsum board, asbestos siding, and cedar shingles.[7] They had domesticity down to an algorithm.

Each house belonged to a subdivision of alphabetized lanes that resembled intestines but sounded like poetry: Cobalt Ridge, Vermilion Hill, Forsythia Gate, Elderberry Pond, Orangewood. Builders dug a pit to quarry sand and gravel for road paving. When finished, they let the quarry fill with rain, then had the Pennsylvania Fish and Boat Commission stock "Levittown Lake" with rainbow trout.[8] Their earthwork approached alchemy.

The northeast became a testbed for suburbia in the nineteenth century, when the New Haven Railroad plied city dwellers with fantasies of seaside life and the Philadelphia, Wilmington, & Baltimore commissioned landscape architect Robert Morris Copeland to design the Victorian borough of Ridley Park. Neither of these experiments approached the scale of Levittown, a "planning type and state of mind" engineered to offer everything midcentury consumers craved: a surefire repository for GI housing stipends and federally backed mortgages, a warren for the brisk coupling that gave America its baby boom, an exurban resort, a utopia, a fruit orchard.[9]

William Levitt envisioned homes "so well designed, nicely landscaped and soundly built that people of low incomes will not want to turn to public housing projects."[10] He defied unions. He turned away African Americans. When a Black family bought a home from existing residents at the corner of Deepgreen and Daffodil Lanes, neighbors hurled rocks through their picture window and a bamboo cross blazed in front of Walt Disney Elementary School.[11]

In Levittown, "everybody lives on the same side of the tracks," proclaimed a *Saturday Evening Post* columnist in 1954.[12] The claim bore a shred of literal truth insomuch as Levittown unfurled west of the corridor's tracks like the world's most repetitious miniature train diorama. The Levitts plopped their model homes before PRR passengers clattering by under New Deal catenary towers. The nation's largest residential development bloomed beside its busiest rail line.

The PRR hired Levitt & Sons to build them a new station on Bristol Pike across from the Shop-O-Rama strip mall. During construction, the railroad enticed motorists with a sign that foretold "Parking for 1000 Cars."[13] The depot's squat box shape and fieldstone facade reflected its suburban environs. Its platform awning resembled a carport. William Levitt proclaimed it the "most modern suburban station in America."[14] On April 26, 1953, Levittown appeared on PRR timetables sandwiched between Trenton and Bristol, communities with four hundred more years of combined history.[15]

Despite plugging into the corridor, Levittown never behaved

FIGURE 8.1 Commuters boarding the Pennsylvania Railroad's Silverliner Train at the Levittown-Tullytown Station in 1965. Audiovisual Collections and Digital Initiatives Department, Hagley Museum and Library.

like one of the Gilded Age Connecticut villages that the New Haven strung together like beads. In traditional suburbia, John Stilgoe writes, "one drives along the old parkway, along the former streetcar route leading out to the commuter station. Always one drives toward the railroad-right-of-way, the energizing spine of the corridor."[16] Levittown had no spine. It was a jellyfish. It wriggled with the passive aggression of people keeping a polite distance from one another. In its backyards and easy chairs, arterial parkways and curvilinear lanes, Levittown embodied a demand for mass privacy—a demand trains were ill equipped to meet.

Levittown pitched its patio fantasies against the dirty and dangerous city. Levitt's advertisements depicted white families driving luggage-laden station wagons away from gray skylines to "suburbia straight ahead."[17] Levittown promised an escape from high taxes, corrupt politicians, cramped quarters, and nonwhite neighbors. Its open-road ethos also implied a potential solution to the problems of mass transit.

In the 1950s urban dysfunction followed the corridor tracks. The Federal Express plowed through Union Station one year after a PRR commuter train caught fire under the Hudson River.[18] In January 1955 a pipe bomb exploded in a Penn Station parcel locker. Another bomb detonated that March.[19] In 1956 crews dynamiting the path of the Connecticut Turnpike accidentally sent a buckshot blast of rubble through the New Haven's catenary, shredding William Murray's wire weave.[20] Six months later, another bomb exploded in a Penn Station toilet, driving porcelain shards into the leg of seventy-four-year-old porter Lloyd Hill. Hill spent two months recovering in St. Vincent's Hospital but held no "ill feeling" toward the perpetrator, disgruntled Con Edison employee turned "mad bomber" George Metesky.[21]

In February 1958 northeastern temperatures plunged to single digits, and winds whipped to sixty miles an hour. An iceberg floated past the Jersey Shore for the first time in anyone's memory.[22] Diamond-shaped snowflakes showered the region. The arctic flakes were so fine that they shot right through the GG1's French linen air intake filters, then melted on its traction motors. The entire fleet shorted out. The PRR's most reliable machine could not do its job. Delays mounted.[23] A New Jersey rider reported that his train's door had frozen open, and ice lined the aisles. A New Haven commuter claimed that crews abandoned her train in a "freezing nowhere."[24]

As northeasterners fled urban cores and temperamental trains, downtown terminals began to look like vulgar follies. Levittown Station rose from its Bucks County sod in 1952 while wrecking crews dismembered Broad Street Station twenty miles away. Frank Furness's masterpiece lost its shed to a 1923 fire. In 1930 it surrendered commuter trains to a subterranean station beneath an office tower next door. In 1933 Broad Street relinquished most of its intercity traffic to 30th Street Station. Christopher Morley saw Furness's temple as proof of a time when "trains were really trains," but the station now had little reason to exist.[25]

"Many of us will dislike seeing it go," acknowledged the "Broad Street Station Closing Program" issued to PRR employees, "but remember—it is being replaced by one of the most modern, practical, and beautiful passenger terminals in the world."[26] Riders packed the waiting room one last time that April. Some bought souvenir farewell tickets. The Philadelphia Orchestra's brass section played "Auld Lang Syne" from the final train's rear vestibule as it pulled away into darkness.[27] Demolition crews got to work hours later. They took two years to finish the job. Broad Street's remains were dumped in the Delaware River to form the base of piers 122 and 124 in Philadelphia's Greenwich shipyard—where the rubble rests today.

Broad Street Station's empty footprint inspired various schemes to redevelop downtown Philadelphia. Architects Vincent Kling and Louis Kahn vied for the chance to sculpt the station parcel into a modern "Penn Center." Raymond Loewy presented his own proposal in the form of a colorful plastic terrarium that resembled a pinball game. Executive director of the City Planning Commission Edmund Bacon wanted Penn Center to express the "dignity of Philadelphia as the center of a growing metropolitan region."[28] Sketches showed a Rockefeller Center–style ice-skating rink ringed with two floors of upscale shops and the then-ubiquitous Savarin Restaurant. A three-dimensional model followed at the 1947 Better Philadelphia Exhibit in Gimbel's Department Store.[29]

Penn Center looked best in plastic. At human scale, Bacon's concept shook out to bland pickets of international style office towers linked by barren plazas that reeked of urine or bleach. At night, commuters dropped from office towers to dank tunnels, then trudged over to the cellar terminal that the PRR had already named for the place they were going: Suburban Station.

Having decapitated one terminal in Philadelphia, the PRR contemplated another execution in New York. Penn Station had always been a swan song. Just two years after it opened, Wabash Railroad president Frederic Delano proclaimed it the last of the big terminals, which were too grand to justify their cost.[30] Unlike Philadelphia's Suburban Station, which occupied the basement of a twenty-two-story skyscraper, low-slung Penn Station left the sky above it untouched. These nine acres of unclaimed real estate grew conspicuous as Midtown Manhattan built up around them.

The station's interior, meanwhile, grew shabby and confused. The granite lost its sparkle. The greenhouse dimmed from grime and wartime blackout paint. Efforts to modernize the somber hall backfired in what Lewis Mumford called a "symposium of errors" that included a sacrilegious digital clock, tacky kiosks, cars on pedestals, and a scalloped airport-style ticket counter made of Formica, steel, and fluorescent plastic.[31] "No one entering Penn Station for the first time could, without clairvoyance, imagine how good it used to be," Mumford stewed.[32]

One could still squint past the ill-conceived updates and penny-ante profiteering to imagine Penn Station as a gateway to the world. Fidel Castro—jet-black beard, olive shirt, brass buttons, and all—sauntered through the waiting room in April 1959 thronged by Cuban American supporters. That fall, a beaming Nikita Khrushchev passed through Penn Station from a chartered train to the United Nations, where he rapped a loafer against his desk.[33] But no amount of ceremony could stem the tidal pull of Manhattan property markets. And no one could any longer ignore the developable air imprisoned by the railroad's faux classical hall.

In 1954 William Zeckendorf proposed replacing Penn Station with a "Palace of Progress" containing a textile mart, world trade center, and "permanent world's fair"—all overseen by former World's Fair Aquacade hustler Billy Rose.[34] When engineers deemed the palace architecturally unsound, Zeckendorf proposed an even vaster "Atomic City" that included a 1,750-foot-tall "Freedom Tower."[35] Zeckendorf savored the prospect of demolishing Penn Station. "When great cities have rotted at the core, civilizations have perished," he lectured, extolling the same progressive faith that levelled the Black and Irish Tenderloin sixty years earlier.[36]

FIGURE 8.2 Cuban leader Fidel Castro stepping off a train in New Haven, Connecticut, during his 1959 visit to the United States. Charles Gunn Papers, Archives & Special Collections, University of Connecticut Library.

So brazenly ultramodern were Zeckendorf's ideas that when Irving Felt proposed Penn Station as the site of a new Madison Square Garden, the idea carried some comfort of tradition. The MSG moniker had floated around Manhattan ever since P. T. Barnum raced "Shetland ponies ridden by monkeys" in a hippodrome over the ruins of the Harlem Railroad's Madison Avenue depot.[37] A second Garden, by architect Stanford White (who would go on to codesign Penn Station), evoked the Cathedral of Seville through a soaring minaret. The third Garden, a "monument to the charley horse and cauliflower ear," opened north of Times Square in 1925.[38] This event warehouse creaked under the weight of cigar-smoking crowds who cheered the Knicks, Rangers, Billy Graham, and Sugar Ray Robinson. A roomier Garden, Felt hoped, would grow from the rubble of Penn Station.

The arena scheme outraged architects and antiquarians, who marched along Seventh Avenue in August 1962, their suits, scarves, and pearls crisp against Penn Station's blackened facade.[39] The picketers included Jane Jacobs, whose recent polemic, *The Death and Life of Great American Cities*, assailed the academic groupthink that foisted renewal projects on city dwellers. Of Philadelphia's Penn Center, Jacobs opined, "it would be hard to think of a more expeditious way to dampen downtown than to shove its liveliest activities and brightest lights underground."[40] Jacobs joined other members of the Action Group for Better Architecture in New York (AGBANY) toting signs ("Be a Penn Pal," "Renovate Don't Amputate"), buttonholing passersby with petitions and otherwise raising a polite ruckus. Penn Station, they claimed, was not a glaring anachronism or impediment to progress but New York's birthright.

Behind the scenes, AGBANY lobbied the Port Authority to acquire the station and nurse it back to health. Group cofounder Norval White conceded that the PRR should not suffer for the "current bad economics of this structure" but also reasoned that "the citizenry of our city should not be made to suffer from the economic exploitation of an important monument and symbol."[41] The Port Authority saw no reason to save a piece of transit architecture from its creators.[42] Pennsylvania Railroad officer Allen Greenough found absurd the notion that tax dollars should preserve anything "merely as a 'monument' when it no longer serves the utilitarian needs for which it was erected."[43]

In October 1963 the Lauria Brothers Company arrived on Seventh Avenue for "just another job."[44] Its workers pried apart Penn Station with sledges and jackhammers. They unwrapped the steel beams that bore the travertine walls. They crated off the marble statues and granite eagles. Madison Square Garden grew within the rubble like a creature cracking through an egg. Passengers watched from the inside out through dust clouds and welding sparks until drop cloths censored the carnage like an offstage murder. By the time wrecking balls pummeled what remained of the hall, riders were encased by a concrete floor. They navigated the same concourse that Mumford found cluttered with "fevered illuminations of the soft-drink machines" and looked up at Styrofoam.[45]

No piece of passenger architecture felt safe after 1963. In Massachusetts, where track beds filled with trash, the Boston Terminal Corporation tried to offload its ornate but overbuilt South Station. "The City of Boston taxes us to the Queen's taste," complained New Haven president George Alpert.[46] Alpert noted that the terminal—once the world's busiest—was assessed at over twelve million dollars even though the railroad had been "trying for three years to get somebody to buy it for four million."[47] Like the PRR, the New Haven saw its future in suburban ridership. A 1962 brochure encouraged passengers to drive to its new Route 128 Station in Dedham, "park free, then take the train!"[48]

The Boston Redevelopment Authority eventually bought South Station for $6.9 million plus back taxes. It considered replacing the terminal with a parking garage, a world trade center, and an arena to succeed the un-air-conditioned Boston Garden.[49] When Fenway Park gate revenue plummeted in 1966, a study proposed South Station as the site of a new stadium for the ninth-place Red Sox—a relocation that would have razed 130 years of architectural history at once.[50]

In 1972 the Redevelopment Authority settled on the partial conversion of South Station into a postal annex, parking garage, and bus terminal. The structure that Mayor Josiah Quincy hailed in 1898 as a "wide and spacious gateway of unrestricted freedom" lost its tan brick wing abutting Atlantic Avenue and almost two-thirds of its tracks.[51] The station's Catholic chapel, Our Lady of the Railroads, shuttered, as did its candlepin bowling alley. Only the original granite headhouse and a "much smaller and more modern" boarding area survived.[52]

At the opposite end of the corridor, Union Station also slid into limbo. The PRR could not maintain the deteriorating Roman palace it co-owned with the Baltimore & Ohio. The railroad proposed removing passenger operations to a smaller station on the district outskirts. Executives met Smithsonian officials to talk about turning

Union Station into a transportation museum.[53] Congress later voted to convert the terminal waiting room into a bicentennial welcome center. The center received murals and a slideshow theater, derisively nicknamed "the pit," that plunged straight through the marble floor.[54] Trains parked out back in a "replacement station."[55]

The National Park Service proved no better at stewarding Union Station than private railroads. Its critically panned visitor center closed in 1978. Two years later, *Washington Post* reporter Blaine Harden found a vacant station that "smells of rot. In its abandoned corridors, toadstools grow on soggy maple floors and fetid rainwater drips from light bulbs long since gone dark. In the evacuated offices and hallways upstairs, roaches the size of mice and rats the size of telephones flit amid shards of peeled paint and puddles of mud."[56]

New Yorker editor and train aficionado Rogers E. M. Whitaker seethed during a visit to the replacement station, which he found at the end of a quarter mile of plywood rampart. "It is so ugly. Everything about it is ugly. The station looks like a bad small town bus terminal. God, what a depressing place!"[57]

The corridor's sickness originated outside the northeast. The New York–Washington line was just a fraction of the PRR's national network, which crisscrossed Pennsylvania, Ohio, Michigan, Indiana, and beyond. Pennsylvania Railroad tracks embroidered Ohio, the fruitful plain that inspired Jacksonian visionaries to build roads, canals, and other monuments to Erie Fever. The "old west" once used its proximity to Lake Superior's Iron Range and Appalachia's coal fields to become a steel belt. By 1910 the industrializing Lake Erie Watershed contained three of the country's ten largest cities: Cleveland, Detroit, and Buffalo.[58]

For half a century the Midwest filled flatbed cars with slabs, beams, and wire. But by the late 1950s, high interest rates and Japanese competition ravaged American steel. A region where railroads once made hay languished into the Rust Belt. This decline coincided with the arrival of competing modes of freight transport. Routes 80 and 90 of the new Eisenhower interstate system sent trucks rumbling coast to coast at fifty-five miles per hour. In 1959 the St. Lawrence Seaway effectively turned the upper Midwest into an ocean port. While rigs and container ships siphoned cargo from trains, jets swiped the railroad's priority parcel and certified mail business.

Despite slumping manufactures and rising competition, the Interstate Commerce Commission regulated railroads like the imperious Gilded Age monoliths they once were. Commissioners forbid carriers from cutting unprofitable routes, enforcing regulations drafted to curb the Morgans, Mellens, and Vanderbilts. Now in a period of infirmity, railroads were made to pay for the sins of their youth.[59] "As a public utility, we expect regulation," said PRR vice president David Bevan, "but it should be modern regulation that takes into account today's competitive facts."[60]

Former rivals clung to one another for survival. Mergers followed. Unlike the adventures in domination that characterized nineteenth-century railroading, twentieth-century creations like the Erie Lackawanna and Norfolk & Western were marriages of last resort. Desperate to raise revenue, cut staff, and discharge old facilities, the PRR pursued a match with the New York Central (NYC) over the protests of passengers, freight customers, unions, legislators, and Interstate Commerce Commission (ICC) officials. The ICC blessed the union only after the PRR agreed to make the insolvent New Haven part of the new company.

At 10:18 a.m. on January 15, 1968, a message flashed across the Dow Jones ticker: "THE SUPREME COURT TOLD THE PENNSYLVANIA AND NEW YORK CENTRAL RAILROADS TO PROCEED WITH THEIR MERGER."[61] The Penn Central Corporation lurched to life at midnight, February 1, in the dour catacombs of Philadelphia's Suburban Station. The super railroad took custody of the New Haven eleven months later. For the first time, the corridor had a single owner—an owner valued at $4.5 billion.[62]

The Penn Central's size had no precedent. Its car fleet could have stretched from "New York to Laramie," journalist Rush Loving calculated, and its track would have reached "all the way around the world and then some."[63] Penn Central executives hoped that economies of scale would resolve issues that confounded their predecessors. Interstate Commerce Commission officials expected the merger to "accelerate investments in transportation property and continually modernize plant and equipment."[64] Pennsylvania Railroad CEO Stuart Saunders and NYC president Alfred Perlman promised to combine the "talent and experience of the officers of both railroads."[65]

Others worried that sheer magnitude would only amplify problems. Allen Greenough likened the Penn Central to a "big dog with a lot of fleas. We'll be scratching for a long time."[66] The corporation first had to figure out what to do with its redundant assets. The PRR and NYC had been rivals. Their lines chased one another west, tangling up in towns like Toledo and Terre Haute where traffic was now evaporating. All of these superfluous tracks, stations, yards, and warehouses required regular maintenance and bore local property taxes. Historian George Drury compared the Penn Central to a "late-in-life marriage to which each partner brings a house, a summer cottage, two cars, and several complete sets of china and glassware—plus car payments and mortgages on the houses."[67]

The Penn Central marriage proved wasteful and acrimonious. While the company projected a seamless face to the public through its new logo—a letter *C* entwined with a letter *P*—no amount of graphic design could paper over its internal fissures. Divided into "red" (PRR) and "green" (NYC) teams, executives scrapped for corporate turf in boardroom battles twenty stories above the Suburban Station tracks. Green partisans, led by progressive NYC president Alfred Perlman, wanted to invest in electronic classification yards and cybernetic automation systems. They were stifled by their red counterparts, who rewarded "loyalty and conformity to the established corporate culture."[68] In one emblematic episode, the Penn Central needed months to develop a computer system that reconciled the NYC's punch cards and the PRR's Fridden Flexowriter tape.[69]

The Penn Central dropped orders, misrouted trains, and stonewalled customers. Every week, flanged wheels slid off the rails of some desolate spur or rust bucket yard. The merger gave legacy employees little time to familiarize themselves with the combined operations. Freight trains left terminals without their waybills (the list of goods they carried) and had to park in yards until someone sorted through the mess. Those yards filled with so many paperless gondolas and boxcars that frantic dispatchers started sending cars away—anywhere—just to free up tracks. Such cascading screwups famously culminated in the Syracuse division losing a one-hundred-hopper coal train.[70] It took the company ten days to recover its fugitive freight.[71]

Penn Central leaders distracted themselves by toying with investments in trucking companies, oil pipelines, executive jets, Texas industrial parks, Florida resorts, California condos, and Six Flags Amusement Parks. Former PRR president William Wallace Atterbury heralded diversification in 1929 by insisting "we are no longer railroads alone; we are transportation companies."[72] But the Penn Central took this proposition to a ridiculous extreme. Indeed, some saw its overbrimming portfolio (held by an independent parent company) as evidence that executives were pursuing side hustles not to improve the core business but to wriggle out of being a railroad.[73] "Trailers, pipelines, real estate, amusement parks, progressive railroading, that's Penn Central," explained a 1968 promotional film, "or part of it at least."[74]

In February 1968 Bob Hope looked out at nineteen thousand faces from the center of a boxing ring. "It's a wonderful thing to be here for the opening of Astrodome East," he quipped.[75] "Isn't this a beautiful sight and a beautiful ceiling?" He gestured to the beige sound dampeners suspended overhead and to the lighting ring that shone like a "diamond tiara."[76] The National Broadcasting Company's cameras followed Hope's cues, alighting on every angle and surface of Madison Square Garden. The arena looked that much sharper for its state-of-the-art air filtration system, which sucked up cigar smoke.

Hope shambled across the canvas ring where he would later "box"

Rocky Marciano. He reeled off one-liners about senators and tow-away zones, Mayor Lindsay and the garbage strike before spinning around on wing-tipped toes: "I'm going to tell you one thing: they sure have a crazy set of trains in the basement." A second passed before spectators caught it. Laughter rumbled, slow, tentative, then swallowed by a rip current of applause. Mirth and sorrow mingled in the smokeless air. New Yorkers who came to christen the fourth Madison Square Garden with a man named "hope" now remembered what they had shoved to the basement. The old comedian felt that melancholy and led others to it.

"This place is built over the Pennsylvania Station, and I wish they told me," Hope continued, though he knew the terminal well, having once mugged in the basement from the cab of a GG1 and snuggled with sidekick Jerry Colonna on some rucksacks piled on the platforms during the war. "This morning I walked into the wrong dressing room and wound up in Jersey City." The crowd laughed again, this time from their stomach pits. Hope beamed. His joke landed on the miraculous power of train stations to put people elsewhere. Penn Station still performed this daily magic, even in labyrinthine form, even under the drab banner of the Penn Central.

Most of the station was now elsewhere, strewn across a tract of Jersey meadow at 2800 Secaucus Road.[77] Fractured columns, marble torsos, and granite rubble bleached in the sun beside the corridor tracks. Riders saw these relics as their trains raced north toward Manhattan's new Garden and south in the direction of Levittown's laminate ascendance. The stone sat there for years. The owners of 2800 Secaucus Road planned to use it to harden marsh beneath a planned industrial park. The hallowed rock seemed destined to return to the earth from which Italians and New Englanders had quarried it a century earlier. When asked whether it was appropriate to use Penn Station as infill, demolition chief Morris Lipsett shot back, "If anybody seriously considered it art, they would have put up some money to save it."[78]

· 9 ·

THE
GREAT SOCIETY
DERAILS

Although not our geographical heartland, it certainly is our intellectual, financial, governmental and manufacturing heartland.

CLAIBORNE PELL[1]

On the broiling afternoon of June 8, 1968, a twenty-one-car Penn Central train slalomed through Elizabeth. The tracks bend here and always have. They form a flattened S that the Central inherited from its predecessors: the Pennsylvania, the United Company, and the New Jersey Railroad, which strapped iron to the Essex & Middlesex Turnpike in 1836. The turnpike made the same double swoop as it followed the course of an older road from Stone Bridge to Newark.[2] The modern corridor traces a colonial lane that jogged between apple orchards, kitchen gardens, a Presbyterian parsonage, and the Nag's Head Tavern.

The long train buckled through Elizabeth like an arthritic snake. Two solid black GG1s came first. Behind them stretched a quarter mile of freshly washed silver coaches. Last came a Tuscan observation car draped with black bunting and ivy.[3] Inside the car, chairs propped up a coffin containing the remains of Robert F. Kennedy. Kennedy had been New York's junior senator two days earlier when he won the California Democratic presidential primary and then was gunned down in Los Angeles. He left a pregnant wife, ten children, and 393 delegates.

People lined the tracks to salute the slain candidate on his way to Arlington National Cemetery, just as their parents watched FDR's funeral train and Walt Whitman extended his "sprig of lilac" toward Lincoln's steam cortege.[4] The Elizabeth Firing Squad stood stiffly at attention in tucked brown shirts.[5] Dads hoisted children on shoulders. Mourners toed the platform edge, then spilled onto the tracks to better see the flag-draped casket, the beautiful family, the festive grief of a "rolling Irish wake."[6]

No one saw the Admiral, an overnight train from Chicago, lumbering north. The engineer tugged on his airhorn whistle, but the S curve concealed his approach. Helicopter blades swallowed the blares. Elizabeth mayor Thomas Dunn begged his citizens to get off the tracks when the Admiral's headlamp swung around the bend. They scrambled back to the platform, but not all in time. Antoinette Severini flung her granddaughter to a stranger before falling under the engine wheels. John Curia grabbed her hand and was dragged under too. Police covered their bodies with blankets. The three-year-old child went "spinning like a top" but survived.[7]

No one told the Kennedys. The Penn Central canceled New York–bound corridor trains to prevent further tragedy upon tragedy. The funeral special rolled the rest of the way to Washington under thirty miles an hour. Scenery that normally streaked past in watercolors clicked into photographic clarity: a woman in a floral blouse at Princeton Junction, a Levittown man in camp shirt and Bermuda shorts, rosary-clad nuns in North Philadelphia, uniformed Little Leaguers in Baltimore, kids barefoot in Chesapeake honeysuckle. They clutched homemade signs and pressed hands on hearts. They perched on car hoods and dangled legs from coal hoppers, or stood still, unsure what to do.

Northeasterners brought their sorrow to the corridor. The line reflected their sadness. Warped rails rested on cracked wooden ties. Catenary bridges rusted. Ivy roots clawed apart embankments. Pigeons roosted in the white-splattered eaves of platform awnings. Litter sprinkled the ballast. People had taken to leaving tires in the path

FIGURE 9.1 Mourners watch the funeral train of Robert F. Kennedy pass through North Philadelphia. Courtesy of the Special Collections Research Center, Temple University Libraries.

of trains and pelting engines with bricks. In 1971 the Penn Central replaced glass windows with lexan polycarbonate, a thermoplastic that could withstand stonings and, it was advertised, bullets.[8] The New Haven installed metal grills on locomotive windshields, which engineers called "ghetto grates."

Trackside factories emitted black smoke and rotten egg stench or sat quietly behind broken suncatcher windows. Miles of brick and stucco rowhomes filled out innercities where African Americans replaced whites driving their station wagons to "suburbia straight ahead." On the corridor's rural fringes, family farms went to seed, devoured "by recent forest growth, like vestiges of disappeared civilizations."[9] As RFK's funeral train rumbled over a weed-fringed, oil-soaked track bed, it struck one onlooker as "the train to the end of the era."[10]

"There is the decay of the centers and the despoiling of the suburbs," President Lyndon Johnson told the University of Michigan's graduating class of 1964.[11] "There is not enough housing for our people or transportation for our traffic. Open land is vanishing, and old landmarks are violated," he continued. And yet, Johnson proclaimed in another speech at Ohio University, "We will build the Great Society, a society where no child will go unfed, and no youngster will go unschooled, where no man who wants work will fail to find it, where no citizen will be barred from any door because of his birthplace or his color or his church. Where peace and security is common among neighbors and possible among nations."[12]

Over the next two years, Johnson would sign some of the most progressive legislation in US history. Kennedy's 1968 train trundled through communities where people obtained groceries with food stamps and paid doctors with Medicare and Medicaid. It rolled by Job Corps Centers and public housing projects. Its engine whistle carried across the quadrangles of Rutgers, Princeton, Drexel, the University of Pennsylvania, the University of Delaware, and Catholic University, where undergraduates paid tuition with federal grants and loans. It clacked through the countryside, where farmers received crop subsidies and borrowed from the Office of Special Programs to Combat Rural Poverty.

Johnson promised to lift city, suburb, and country together through the rehabilitation of public transit. "Our Constitution empowered Congress to provide for post roads," Johnson declared at his 1964 signing of the Urban Mass Transportation Act, weighing in on the great Jefferson-era debate over the legality of internal improvements.[13] "All of us recognize that the curses of congestion in commuting cannot be wiped away with the single stroke of a pen," he acknowledged, "but we do know that this legislation that we are coming to grips with faces the realities of American life and attempts to put in motion a movement to do something about it."[14]

A year later, Johnson signed another bill, this one addressing the future of passenger trains. The High-Speed Ground Transportation Act would bring the "revolutionary advances of tomorrow" to a battered corridor. It promised to make the old line a "better servant of our people."[15]

Trains seemed an unlikely vehicle for progress in midcentury America. When the World's Fair returned to Flushing in 1964, there was no Hall of Railroads, no cavalcade of engines, no pageant. Trains no longer paraded through the Transportation Zone but were banished to an outpost across the Grand Central Parkway, where they chuffed around a canvas tent enticing visitors to "come on in . . . See Long Island."[16] The carnival ride paled in comparison to the American Machine Foundry's suspended monorail, the Port Authority's helipad, and the new General Motors pavilion, where "Futurama II" simulated life on the lunar surface and ocean floor.

The railroad's demotion to sideshow coincided with Robert Moses's tenure as fair boss. The imperious bureaucrat was running out of power in 1964, having surrendered all titles save for his chairmanship of the Triborough Bridge and Tunnel Authority and control over the fair. Moses had built his reputation as a maestro of urban space in the 1930s by sinking Manhattan's West Side Freight Line below a widened Riverside Park. He amassed power within city and state government by directing New Deal grants to shovel-ready pools, playgrounds, roads, and tunnels. Moses befriended Futurama creator Norman Bel Geddes at the 1939 World's Fair and came to see New York as his own motorized diorama.

The great builder had little use for trains. Moses stonewalled the Second Avenue Subway and scoffed at calls to extend mass transit to Idlewild and LaGuardia airports. Tracks came nowhere near Moses's most acclaimed recreation areas, including the barrier island state park Jones Beach. Moses refused to widen the Long Island Expressway's grass medians so that the Long Island Railroad (LIRR) could lay tracks there.[17] Moses's famously damning biographer, Robert Caro, suggests that the power broker wanted the LIRR weak, preferring to deal with a "rickety 'Toonerville Trolley' line" than contend with a railroad that could defy him.[18]

As American trains sputtered toward obscurity, passenger railroads elsewhere experienced an astounding revival. In October 1964 Japanese National Railways christened its Tokaido Shinkansen High Speed line. Americans tuning into the Tokyo Summer Olympics saw bubble-nosed electric trains whooshing past Mount Fuji at the astounding speed of 130 miles per hour. These trains flew over welded rail fastened to concrete ties on a route free from the freight and commuter traffic that clogged US lines. The fast, sleek, and impeccably timely bullet train came as a revelation to Americans — a zero-altitude Sputnik moment that coincided with President Johnson's transit-based schemes for urban renewal.

Americans lusted for their own bullet train. But the Shinkansen was more than a shiny toy: its performance presumed immense infrastructure investment (partly supplied by a World Bank loan) and a radical reimagination of what railroading entailed.[19] "The Shinkansen is designed to move people," explained an American engineer after returning from a field trip to Japan. "It is not a cost savings device."[20] To catch on in the United States, high-speed trains required a sponsor who could sell politicians on an expensive technology—someone patient enough to play the planning long game and sufficiently domineering to quell opposition. Trains needed their own Robert Moses.

They instead got Rhode Island's junior senator. Claiborne de Borda Pell grew up among the marble cottages, tennis lawns, and noblesse oblige of Newport before earning a history degree at Princeton. The son of the US ambassador to Portugal and Hungary, Pell drove trucks of Christmas presents to British POWs during the war then briefly roughnecked on an Oklahoma oil rig. Pell believed in psychic powers and wore tattered suits. His wife judged him "the worst driver I ever knew."[21] John F. Kennedy called Pell the "least electable man in America."[22]

And yet Pell won six consecutive terms in the US Senate. He championed the National Endowment for the Arts, the National Endowment for the Humanities, and the federal tuition subsidies called Pell Grants. On his death in 2009 *Wonkette* columnist Sara K. Smith called Pell "a big fat liberal and a millionaire who was obsessed with UFOs and jogged around Newport in his old Princeton letter sweater and drove a Mustang with a roll-bar because he was such a bad driver. . . . It really is too bad that they don't make rich people like that anymore."[23] Among his eccentricities, Pell loved trains and fought for their revival. He would become the modern corridor's founding father and kooky uncle.

Pell knew the agony of train travel from his regular commutes between Providence and Washington aboard the Federal Express. He spent restless nights in drafty sleeping compartments.[24] He felt the clunk of spalled wheels over rough rail. On one trip, a brake shoe snapped off the baggage car and smashed Pell's window, sending glass splinters into his left eye. "There was considerable consternation when the chief Senatorial advocate of railroad passenger service was found on the floor with a bloody face," Pell recalled.[25] He emerged from the hospital with an eye patch and puzzled reporters by suggesting that the accident had "elements of sardonic humor, that the fellow who is very interested in the railroad gets beaned on it."[26]

From his personal experience and extensive reading, Pell knew that trains were failing the northeast. The senator subscribed to Jean Gottmann's gospel of regionalization, *Megalopolis*, published in 1961. He saw in the premerger New Haven and PRR "one long metropolitan industrial unit" struggling to coalesce.[27] "We need coordinated leadership to define the choices that must be made to best serve the public interest," Pell insisted in *Megalopolis Unbound*, a sequel he penned to Gottmann's monograph. "We can no longer rely on chance evolution of competitive systems."[28]

In 1921, William Murray coined the term *superpower* to advocate an interstate coordination of energy resources. Pell likewise found a catchphrase to convey his infrastructural vision: "Another term for the area used by transportation analysts is the 'Northeast Corridor,' for the axis of Megalopolis is indeed a passageway for gargantuan surges of movement along our Northeast seaboard."[29] The phrase "northeast corridor" previously described architecture. The ancient Greek Palace of Nestor had a northeast corridor, as do the Art Institute of Chicago and the United States Capitol Building. When applied to a deteriorating railroad, the phrase conveyed stability, grandeur, nearness—as if trains placed Trenton down the hall from Stamford, Boston around the bend from Baltimore.

In 1962 Pell pressed fellow New England Democrat President John F. Kennedy to create a multistate authority that would oversee northeastern railroads, highways, and airports. His proposed compact joined Massachusetts, Rhode Island, Connecticut, New York, New Jersey, Pennsylvania, Delaware, Maryland, and the District of Columbia "for the express purpose of owning, operating, and maintaining railroad passenger service within Megalopolis."[30] Kennedy acknowledged the "urgent need for the development of improved surface passenger transportation along the heavily-populated and heavily-traveled eastern seaboard megalopolitan area," but he found the federal government's role "not at all clear."[31]

The following May, Congress commissioned a corridor study.[32] The findings of the "Pell Committee" sprawled across reams of green graphing paper, megawatt consumption charts, hypothetical timetables, and track diagrams that resembled musical staffs, each note calling for a new signal, a welded joint, fresh ballast, replacement ties, tightened wire. The final report listed "track changes required to permit operation of high-speed passenger trains" while flagging several flaws beyond remedy.[33] The committee found, for example, no way to raise speed limits at Frankford Junction, the sharp bend in North Philadelphia where the corridor doglegs around Kensington.

Pell knew that importing Japanese-style trains to the northeast would require "financial and economic solutions" beyond physical engineering. The Shinkansen required an expert bureaucracy as much as it did good track. But Pell's colleagues had little interest in laying this institutional groundwork. They preferred to salivate over the bullet train alone while overlooking the administrative labor that maintained it.[34] President Johnson proceeded cautiously, advocating a demonstration project to gauge the public's appetite for fast trains. Consumer demand would tell government whether to proceed with high-speed rail.

The High-Speed Ground Transportation Act of 1965 authorized the Secretary of Commerce to research new "materials, aerodynamics, vehicle propulsion, vehicle control, communications, and guide-ways."[35] The signing ceremony took place in the East Room of the White House, where JFK had laid in state two years earlier. "Today, as we meet here in this historic room where Abigail Adams hung out her washing," Johnson began, "an astronaut can orbit the earth faster than a man on the ground can get from New York to Washington." The president pointed to Pell, thanking the senator who "harassed me week after week until he got me to take some action."[36]

Johnson explained that the Department of Commerce would work "in cooperation with private industry" soliciting train designs from contractors at "no cost to the Government."[37] This meant that high-speed rail would be the shared enterprise of elected officials like Pell, consulting engineers like those who staffed the Pell Commit-tee, train manufacturers, and railroad executives, most notably, PRR CEO Stuart Saunders, who saw the program as a way of greasing the skids for federal approval of the Penn Central merger.

State-incentivized capitalism could never match what Japan achieved by elevating public needs over profit motives. In 1964 Kenshiro Kunimatsu, a delegate from Japanese National Railways, toured the corridor and wrote, almost pityingly, "I am very glad to know that a plan of high-speed operation between New York and Washington is under way. I can well appreciate the effort to achieve a big economical success especially with reduced investment."[38] Kunimatsu knew that no true bullet train could fly over the corridor's choppy track bed or swivel through Elizabeth's S curve or overcome the fact that the 157 miles of track between New Haven and Boston remained unelectrified. But such facts would not stop his American counterparts from trying.

The High-Speed Ground Transportation Act boiled down to two machines: a gasoline train bound for the New Haven Shore Line and an electric train to race under the PRR's catenary. With the stroke of his Parker Eversharp felt pen, Johnson transformed the corridor into a laboratory. Rail car builders and aerospace firms submitted designs to the Department of Commerce. The PRR upgraded a section of track in Central New Jersey for testing and regeared an existing Pioneer III electric car to conduct high-speed experiments. "There are some things we don't know," said project manager J. Roland Smith. "We've never run a train at 150 miles an hour."[39]

The first prototype resembled a scruffy Shinkansen cousin. Engineered by the United Aircraft Company (UAC), the TurboTrain featured an aluminum fuselage, egg-shaped docking nose, and sloping dome cars. The seductive adjective *turbo* (from the Latin word for tornado) described the engine's cyclonic motion. A mixture of gasoline and compressed air entered each four-hundred-horsepower turbine. The fuel's combustion spun a rotor, which twirled a shaft, which turned the locomotive gears. The same Pratt and Whitney engines that lifted turboprop airplanes and Sikorsky helicopters drove TurboTrain down the tracks.

The Turbo was light and fast, combining what UAC called "the best in aerospace and railroad technology."[40] Its interior resembled a jetliner cabin, then the height of glamorous travel. Coaches featured carpeted floors, indirect lighting, cloth headrests, and fold-down tables. The windows had drapes. A brochure claimed the cars were "slightly pressurized to keep out dust and keep the noise level down."[41] The Turbo's pendulum suspension system let coaches bank into curves without flinging passengers from their seats.

On December 20, 1967, a test TurboTrain gusted through Princeton Junction at 170.8 miles per hour, setting a North American rail speed record that still stands in 2023.[42] But initial optimism evaporated when the TurboTrain entered service on the New Haven, where it bucked up and down Long Island Sound like a tight-leashed greyhound.[43] The winding Shore Line discouraged velocity. Only on the short stretch between Sharon, Massachusetts, and Boston's Boylston Street did the TurboTrain record triple-digit speeds. Elsewhere it puttered over worn angle bars and battered joints at an average pace of 63 miles per hour.[44]

Passengers liked the TurboTrain but found it strange to ride jet cabins through the Bronx, Bridgeport, and South Boston—the crumbling neighborhoods that Johnson's Great Society pledged to revive. Christopher Lydon titled his 1971 TurboTrain review, "A Study in Incongruities." He observed that the service "matches airline décor with railroad grime. It rides on jet-engine power, yet the engineer wears a steam engine smock that seems to capture the backward-looking spirit of an aging staff."[45] In Boston, passengers exited to the "cavernous gloom of the South Station onto the old outdoor platform, grimy and slippery after winter snow." Boarding riders tracked "fresh mud onto the train's already filthy green carpet."[46]

Turbo passengers could always draw the drapes, lean back in their headrests, and imagine cruising at 35,000 feet—until a hairpin turn or crossing chime recalled that they were stuck on a nineteenth-century railroad. The Turbo rolled on into the 1970s when it fell victim to politics. In 1971 Amtrak assigned yesterday's train of tomorrow to a tortuous route through the Alleghenies to appease West Virginia Representative Harley Staggers. New generations of turbos fanned out across the Midwest, the Hudson Valley, and upstate New York before spiking oil costs doomed the technology. By 1976 the original UAC trains that flew faster than anything in corridor history were rusting away on a spur beside the Providence River.[47]

The second high-speed prototype resembled a stainless steel pipe. Its self-powered carriages coupled together like subway cars. Each car pair sprouted a pantograph. Where the GG1 offered art deco elegance and the TurboTrain promised space-age ground flight, this locomotive-less column looked intentionally austere. The PRR hired marketing icon Al Paul Lefton to devise a suitably postmodern brand. Lefton tossed out some sedate monikers (Speedliner! Railblazer!) before settling on a portmanteau that welded the train to its region: Metroliner.[48]

Like its Turbo counterpart, the Metroliner impressed early observers. A Metroliner clocked 164 miles per hour outside New Brunswick

FIGURE 9.2 Penn Central advertisement displaying the blunt face of a Metroliner. Courtesy of David Reaves and Tom Diffenderfer.

in November 1967. Though a notch slower than the Turbo's top speed, this was no stunt. The Metroliner would carry real passengers over the same tracks. A bullet train seemed at least conceptually possible under the wires between New York and Washington. It became more feasible when the PRR (and then the Penn Central) upgraded the line. Track gangs replaced bolted rails with welded ones and copper catenary with cadmium bronze wire. They sealed off grade crossings and built new suburban park and ride stations at Iselin, New Jersey (Metropark), and Lanham, Maryland (Capital Beltway).

While Japan's Shinkansen required a dedicated right-of-way free from the burdens of history, American railroaders claimed their Metroliner could work on a rehabbed corridor. Neither Philadelphia's Frankford Curve nor Baltimore's twisting tunnels nor the presence of lumbering freights and skittering commuter trains would discourage them. Penn Central CEO Stuart Saunders went so far as to spin this patchwork approach as an accomplishment. He bragged that the Metroliner's thirty-two-month incubation period was "considerably shorter than the seven years of research, development, and testing which the Japanese required to initiate their Tokaido high-speed line."[49]

An industry consortium formed to create the Metroliner. Philadelphia's Budd Company manufactured the train's distinctive fluted car bodies. General Electric and Westinghouse supplied electrical components. This partnership soon frayed. Budd technicians could not make the Westinghouse parts work. Air compressor coils rattled. Coaches wobbled on turns. Metroliners drew so much current from the New Deal catenary system that they burned out corridor substations like an appliance overloading a circuit. The carriages rose and fell on the track bed like merry-go-round horses. Metroliners sometimes vacuumed up ballast stones and occasionally sucked windows from adjacent trains.[50]

As testing schedules lapsed, engineers and officials pointed fingers at one another. Their frustration poured out in crinkling mimeographs, telephone transcripts, committee memos, and marginal jottings—boxes upon boxes of frustration now stored at the Hagley Library in Wilmington, Delaware. One manila folder documents the time when a federal official held up the already delayed program to suggest that Metroliners include seatbelts, necessitating a "very brief study."[51] Another folder recounts a particularly star-crossed test run from 1969, when a Westinghouse-engineered Metroliner repeatedly lost power. The windshield wiper blades wouldn't even sit flush.[52]

By the time dignitaries christened the Great Society train at Union Station, the Great Society was over. Backlash to the Civil Rights Act of 1964 and the Voting Rights Act of 1965 cost Democrats forty-seven House seats. Lyndon Johnson dropped out of the 1968 Democratic primary. His figural war on poverty had been eclipsed by the literal war he escalated in Vietnam. The president did not attend the Metroliner's send-off. But the morning's keynote address, from incoming secretary of transportation, John Volpe, savored of Great Society optimism: "I want to say to the people of Washington and New York and all points in between: The Metroliner is your train. Use it. Tickets are ready."[53]

Claiborne Pell looked subdued. "This is the greatest evidence that the railroad is interested in passenger service," he told reporters.[54] To Pell the Metroliner was a hopeful sign at best, more probably a mirage, and certainly not the rebirth of megalopolis. With Richard Nixon entering the White House, the Rhode Islander had little hope of turning the Boston–Washington line into a world-class railroad anytime soon. Penn Central CEO Stuart Saunders felt no such ambivalence. The Metroliner had not carried one passenger—not moved one revenue-bearing inch—and yet he boasted that it already surpassed "any other cars in the world in speed, comfort, and luxury."[55]

The train, painfully shiny in bright winter sun, swayed through Union Station's yard tracks before ramping up to 110 miles per hour on welded rail. Maryland blurred by. Riders accustomed to the bumps and clanks of conventional coaches found the Metroliner surreally quiet. They examined the interior's brown carpets and mohair tomato seats. "Metro Misses" strolled the aisles in black blouses, orange skirts, and old-time engineer caps, explaining the tinted windows and vestibule telephones. These women were rank-and-file employees, secretaries and clerks whom the Penn Central pressed into hospitality for the occasion.

One reporter raved over the Metroliner's "excellent service" and claimed that "to be treated like a human being aboard an American train is, in itself, something of a miracle."[56] Metroliner staff received special training at the Human Development Institute of Georgia, where they took seminars in "basic psychology and sensitivity training."[57] The railroad recognized that onboard ambience was as critical as bottom-line speed. "People say 'I took a Metroliner,' not

'I took a train,'" observed Amtrak vice president Harold Graham years later.[58]

Creature comforts could not hide the fact that the Metroliner fell far short of Shinkansen standards. The train rarely broke 100 miles per hour, and when it did the coaches shook violently. Outgoing transportation secretary Allen Boyd joked, "these trains were not set up to be dance halls."[59] The Metroliners broke down so often that they needed onboard technicians to shoot down problems on the fly. Trains were sidelined for weeks at a time. In February 1970 a speeding Metroliner uncoupled near Baltimore, becoming two trains, both of which coasted along for miles before braking to a stop. A federal official later lamented, "if we had to do it over again, we would have gone much more carefully."[60]

Metroliners were too finicky for the corridor. Amtrak eventually banished them to Harrisburg service, where the train cut an absurd figure rolling past red barns and horse buggies in Amish Lancaster. Though propulsion problems sunk the Metroliner concept, passengers liked its columnar coach design. Some of the carriages survived in inanimate form, plucked of their pantographs and towed by conventional engines. Depowered Metroliners sometimes appeared behind GG1s, now soldiering into their fifth decade of service. Others carried riders to Hartford and Atlantic City. A few cars found their way across the continent where they rode out their days on Amtrak's San Diegan service, a northeastern artifact beside the Pacific surf.

Before it reached Elizabeth, RFK's 1968 funeral train passed Newark. Nowhere did the Great Society backfire more spectacularly than New Jersey's largest city. Here Mayor Hugh Addonizio used federal block grants to build a campus for the New Jersey College of Medicine and Dentistry in the largely African American Central Ward.[61] Neighbors protested the project, which threatened to displace twenty-two thousand residents.[62] Like the New Yorkers shoved into terrace projects

by Robert Moses's freeway binge, Newarkers of color resented officials uplifting them from their homes.

In July 1967 Newark cops beat a Black cab driver named John
Smith in front of the Reverend William P. Hayes Apartments. When
a false rumor claimed that Smith died in captivity, Newarkers rose
up. Twenty-six people died in the ensuing violence that engulfed the
same blocks Addonizio pledged to renew. Riot spread to Elizabeth
and Plainsboro. The long, hot summer of 1967 embarrassed the liberal
consensus around Johnson's antipoverty programs. Many Americans,
it turned out, wanted no part of his Great Society.

"The struggle for Black political power in Newark is not limited
to the ideas white people have about public political participation,"
claimed activist Amiri Baraka. "Newark, New Ark, the nationalist
sees as the creation of a base, an example, upon which one aspect
of the entire Black nation can be built."[63] The nephew of a "big tall
brawny Pullman porter on the Pennsylvania Railroad," Baraka envisioned Newark's rebirth as a Black-owned city-state in which "transportation and communications industries must be highly taxed and/
or 'nationalized.'"[64] Arrested during the Newark Riots, Baraka would
channel his radical worldmaking into a half century of dramatic art
and the state poet laureateship.

In 1970 Mayor Addonizio was indicted for accepting construction
kickbacks. He lost the Democratic primary to African American civil
engineer Kenneth Gibson, who became Newark's first Black mayor.
A builder of highways and housing projects, Gibson frustrated Newark revolutionaries by supporting commercial development, and
most controversially, a citadel of business towers connected to Newark Penn Station via skyways. Designed by Austrian American mall
pioneer Victor Gruen, Gateway Center gave commuters a climate-
controlled path from train to office. People now worked in Newark
without setting foot on its streets.

Like Gateway Center, the TurboTrain and Metroliner hurried
affluent northeasterners through poor communities. "By observing
where the train passes we can see where America hides her disgrace,"
said US Representative Bertram Podell after a Metroliner trip to

Washington. "On both sides of the tracks in every one of these communities we pass through block after block of rotten, dilapidated old
buildings, crammed to the rafters with people of the slums. Their
washing hangs in pitiful tatters from back porches of many of these
buildings."[65] Podell's dirge continued, "if ever our national urban
problems were presented in microcosm it is here. Look at it. Feel it.
Breathe it. Smell it. Know it."

The congressman closed his travelogue by absolving the Metroliner of the ills it exposed: "May I say that my remarks are not aimed
at the railroad. These problems are national difficulties, reflected in
the right-of-way." Podell rejected Claiborne Pell's equation of railroad
and region under the all-purpose term *corridor*. In Pell's vision, social
uplift required physical mobility. Podell, by contrast, believed state-
of-the-art trains had little to do with the communities they passed.
No vehicle could solve "national difficulties." No machine would raise
the people.

Hindsight condemns the Metroliner and TurboTrain projects
as costly boondoggles. People rode them anyway. Writing in 1999
journalist Don Phillips found it "totally beyond belief . . . that those
dogs were actually popular with the riding public."[66] Despite their
troubles, the demonstrations located a latent love of train travel that
survived decades of neglect, hostility, bad plans, and sloppy execution. It showed that people would take trains if the railroad tried to
make them worth riding. Trying, it seemed, was the whole point.

IV. RETURN

· 10 ·

IMPROVISING
AMTRAK

There is authorized to be created a National Railroad Passenger Corporation. The Corporation shall be a for profit corporation, the purpose
of which shall be to provide intercity rail passenger service, employing
innovative operating and marketing concepts so as to fully develop the
potential of modern rail service in meeting the Nation's intercity passenger
transportation requirements.

RAIL PASSENGER SERVICE ACT OF 1970[1]

The corridor's comeback began under the damp streets of Manhattan
in the final seconds of April 1971. As midnight approached, Madison
Square Garden's concrete cask sat dark. The Rangers were flying
home from Chicago. The Knicks had already bowed out of the play-
offs to Baltimore. The year 1971 would bring James Taylor, Jethro Tull,
the Temptations, the Jacksons, and the Concert for Bangladesh to the
Garden, but nothing graced its stage tonight. History was happening
downstairs, in the arena basement, where Penn Station endured in
cellar form.

Passengers perked their ears to boarding calls between gulps of
Budweiser. They slumped over benches and perched on luggage beneath the stale glow of panel lights. Under grimy linoleum, behind
terrarium shopfronts sweating with spring humidity, were relics of
Penn Station's former life. The glass floor bricks that caught sunshine.
The brass banisters beside the stairs. The mezzanine that now felt like
a forgotten utility closet. To veteran riders, the truncated hub felt

familiar but jumbled like the contents of a stress dream. Architectural form forgot its function in those fluorescent depths. Function grew formless.

Only on the platforms were things the same as ever: dark, warm, reeking of creosote mixed with wet night air. Catenary wires twitched with alternating current. Idle trains buzzed like spiteful refrigerators. When midnight tolled, the last train of the night became the morning's first departure. The 12:05 Clocker to Philadelphia featured a black GG1 and string of scratch and dent P70 coaches. The train bore Penn Central lettering. Its conductors wore Penn Central vests and punched Penn Central tickets. But by the time the last passenger boarded, the train was no longer Penn Central's. The engine nosed ahead, shaking out the slack between each carriage, and rumbled off under the Hudson River. April became May. The age of Amtrak had begun.

The subterranean launch of America's passenger rail system followed decades of scheming. By midcentury, few railroads wanted anything to do with riders. Carriers that once ran passenger trains as loss leaders to keep their freight business in the public eye began withdrawing from the market as car ownership and jet travel surged. The Penn Central lost $330 million moving humans between 1968 and 1970.[2] Its system, detailed in thick crepe-colored timetables, sprawled from Massachusetts to Missouri and included such curious routes as the Calumet (Chicago–Valparaiso), South Wind (Chicago–Louisville–Sarasota), and the Penn Texas (New York–St. Louis).

Chairman Stuart Saunders once offered to give a journalist the Penn Central's entire passenger system "lock, stock and barrel." He added, "It's a drag and a drain."[3] Saunders claimed he could put the Central back in the black on the strength of its freight network and speculative ventures if the Interstate Commerce Commission let him axe passenger service west of Buffalo and Harrisburg.[4] Exhausted by a broken-down railroad that resented their presence, riders formed a consumer interest group, the National Association of Railroad Passengers (NARP). Its members reasoned that if private companies like the Penn Central were unwilling to carry Americans, then someone had to relieve them.

Government seemed the obvious surrogate. Japan's Shinkansen showed what central planning and state money could achieve. The bullet train model had already inspired politicians in France, where La Société nationale des chemins de fers developed the Train à grande vitesse (TGV) to transport people rather than return profits. American trains, for their part, had been a public-private enterprise ever since John Stevens received his steam wagon charter from the New Jersey assembly. In the 1960s the pendulum swung toward state intervention with Lyndon Johnson's Great Society agenda, tax subsidies for commuter services in Boston and Philadelphia, and New York State's acquisition of the bankrupt Long Island Railroad.[5]

"A basic and difficult public policy decision must be made as to who shall pay for a service which appears to be essential but which nearly everyone agrees is basically unprofitable," wrote Claiborne Pell in 1965.[6] Many of Pell's colleagues still saw passenger trains as a money-making business. When in 1961 the Senate Committee on Commerce called for a federal corporation to operate the passenger trains that private carriers no longer wanted, the proposal went nowhere.[7] A later bill, cosponsored by Pell, would have made the Department of Transportation responsible for servicing passenger equipment. It failed as well. Americans, it seemed, were not ready to turn intercity trains into a public utility.

While these proposals languished, the Penn Central grew sicker. Drowning in debt, reviled by riders, plagued by scandal, scourged by infighting, and devoid of capital, the railroad begged for a federal bailout. Congress refused. On June 21, 1970, the Penn Central filed for Chapter 77 protection, precipitating the largest corporate bankruptcy in United States history (until Enron's 2001 collapse). As a century of American rail history plunged into the common grave of the Penn Central, a passenger solution grew urgent.

Enter Richard Nixon. As a child, the future president lay awake in Yorba Linda, California, listening to the whistles of Santa Fe steam engines. He dreamed of becoming an engineer.[8] Even in later years, when Nixon believed that passenger trains were as doomed as the alfalfa fields plowed under by the development of Orange County, he appreciated their grip on the American psyche. Nixon knew that presiding over the death of passenger trains would look bad at a time when other countries were pursuing high-speed projects, and the Metroliner sparked hope for a domestic rail revival.

The Penn Central bankruptcy presented two options. Nixon could save passenger trains through concerted intervention and risk aggravating Republicans who won office attacking Johnson entitlement programs. Or the president could abandon trains through laissez-faire indifference and risk blowback from an electorate-rich northeast where voters still rode the rails. Liking neither choice, Nixon ultimately settled on a compromise in the form of Congress's plan for a halfhearted industry buyout. The federal takeover gave the semblance of concern for riders without committing government to rehabilitating passenger trains. They could perish on someone else's watch.

The Rail Passenger Service Act of 1970 gave private railroads an ultimatum: they could either turn passenger trains over to a new National Railroad Passenger Corporation (NRPC) or promise to run them until at least 1975. Carriers who wanted to leave the business paid an exit fee equal to half their passenger losses in 1969.[9] These dues, plus forty million dollars in grants and one hundred million dollars in federal loan guarantees, formed the startup capital of the NRPC, a quasi-public company in the mold of such bureaucratic amphibians as the US Postal Service and the mortgage lender Fannie Mae. The NRPC would buy locomotives and cars from railroads exiting the passenger market and use them to operate a "basic system."

The law specified that the NRPC "shall be a for profit corporation."[10] The expectation that Uncle Sam's railroad make money, something no private carrier had accomplished in decades, may have seemed like harmless magical thinking or a sop to conservatives who wanted plausible deniability for their role in socializing trains. But the act made clear that Congress could force the NRPC to slash money-losing routes unless state or local government came forward to foot the bill. Since all passenger routes lost money, the entire system was under the gun before it began. In the words of industry journalist Rush Loving, Nixon had created a "cash-strapped passenger railroad destined to fail from starvation."[11]

Where Johnson celebrated the High-Speed Ground Transportation Act with photo op formality and rhetorical fanfare, Nixon did not even dignify the birth of America's passenger rail system with a signing statement. To this day no one knows what time Nixon signed the bill or in what room of his San Clemente house. His obscurity may have been deliberate, a tactic to keep people from looking too closely into the details of the country's new, self-canceling railroad. When the NRPC's maiden voyage trundled out of Penn Station on May 1, 1971, the American passenger train was born again and doomed to die.

The NRPC called itself Railpax, a neologism that took its suffix from the airline shorthand "pax" for passenger. Railpax promised the sophistication of flight with the old-time geniality of trains. Early promoters spoke of hiring jazz bands to play lounge cars. They imagined opening onboard barber shops and beauty salons. One abandoned venture called "Rent-an-Office-to-Boston" would have leased compartments, dictation machines, and stenography kits to business travelers.[12] These spitballed schemes suggested that a train could be viable transportation and a fun and productive place unto itself.

As launch date approached, the clunky Railpax moniker gave way to an even more cryptic acronym: American Travel by Track, or Amtrak.[13] The new brand came courtesy of Lippincott and Margulies, a New York ad firm cofounded in 1943 by GG1 progenitor Donald Dohner. Lippincott had already crafted pithy totems for Eastern Airlines, American Express, Chrysler, and Pizza Hut. An Amtrak press release touted the railroad's "short, powerful name, easy to pronounce and remember, with high visual impact."[14] Amtrak also received a horizontal chevron logo that supposedly depicted train cars rolling over track. Critics, who could not see the train cars, called this graphic the "pointless arrow."[15]

Amtrak inherited a hodgepodge railroad from its twenty-two predecessors. Before the NRPC could douse its hand-me-down trains in red, white, and blue paint, the rolling stock retained its original liveries. This meant that the Super Chief still rolled through Arizona in the Santa Fe's "warbonnet" red and silver. The Empire Builder blended patches of Burlington Northern cascade green with Milwaukee orange as it crawled across North Dakota. Most corridor trains wore the Penn Central's silver and black, sometimes mixed with the faded pigments of other fallen flags. Railfans savored this momentary "Rainbow Era," when the memory of extinct private trains lingered in multihued consists.

Early Amtrak's visual banquet reminded riders of what they had lost. The new network, sketched on a cocktail napkin by Federal Railroad Administration (FRA) official Jim McClellan, ran half as many trains as the systems it replaced.[16] *Texas Monthly* described the "eerie calm that descended on the member railroads' tracks" on the morning of May 1, when it sunk in that the Wabash Cannon Ball, Manhattan Limited, Panama Limited, Nancy Hanks, and Portland Rose now belonged to history.[17] The Associated Press reported that "more than 150 passenger trains doomed by Amtrak made their last runs, some in the glory of farewell celebrations, others in the ignominy of defeat. One train broke down during its final voyage, another collided with a truck."[18]

Amtrak's skeletal reality disillusioned early boosters. "Amtrak is operated by people who don't want it to succeed," snapped NARP cofounder Anthony Haswell, attacking the docile bureaucrats appointed to preside over the passenger train's burial.[19] The corporation's first president, former Pan American Airways executive Roger Lewis, showed little faith that Amtrak would survive. Lewis baffled legislators by declining additional congressional funds, leading Connecticut Senator Lowell Weicker to exclaim, "Either Mr. Lewis is a fool or he's fronting for someone in the administration or the private railroad industry."[20] Lewis at least had the common sense to commute by train from his Westchester home to Amtrak's L'Enfant Plaza headquarters in Washington, DC, though Rush Loving reports that the president often returned drunk in a private club car.[21]

Critics found Amtrak superficial—a patriotic drop cloth flung over rusted parts to counteract "public regard of American trains as dirty, slow, and undependable."[22] With its shoestring budget, impossible profit mandate, and compliant leadership, Amtrak obsessed over appearances. Coaches received eye-searing interiors complete with mauve carpets and amoeba pattern fabric seats. The psychedelic decors clashed with the exterior flag livery to create a postal burlesque effect.

Amtrak outfitted women working as sales ambassadors in polyester hotpants and white go-go boots. Designer Bill Atkinson justified the uniform, a throwback to the Penn Central's Metro Misses and nod to the sexualized marketing of airlines, by reasoning that "just because a guy is riding a train doesn't mean he's lost interest in girl watching."[23] In 2015, former Ambassador Tricia Saunders recalled that she and her colleagues "wanted to be hip and stylish, but we felt the hotpants were a little over the top."[24]

While pursuing what Lewis called the railroad's "creative new look," Amtrak displayed the lackluster maintenance habits of its predecessors.[25] Steam heating lines, air conditioners, and electrical systems failed on gussied-up legacy coaches. Toilets backed up. Aging locomotives broke down faster for lack of routine service. Amtrak fixated on visual effects partly because it lacked the necessary funds to make actual under-the-hood improvements to trains, tracks, and yards.

The railroad often papered over its problems with folksy commercials, jaunty buttons, and brazen appeals to the heterosexual male gaze. But Amtrak could also stare its problems in the face. One advertisement from the hard first year of 1971 shows a red-blazered Amtrak employee standing in the middle of tracks, cradling a model train car, a shock of sandy hair swooping across his forehead, his mouth twisted with worry. Amtrak "may not be the country's biggest headache. But it's close," reads the copy. "That's why when we took over we made only one simple promise. To make the trains worth traveling again. It's going to take time, and work. But we're going to do it. Just be patient. It's going to take time."[26]

It was no coincidence that Amtrak's inaugural train shoved off under the corridor wires. The railroad's architects regarded the electrified line from New York to Washington as their system's cornerstone. Federal Railroad Administration executive Jim McClellan recalled that "everyone, including the White House, understood that passenger trains made sense in the Northeast."[27] In 1973 Amtrak hired pop art illustrator David Klein to draw five posters promoting its nationwide service. Klein's "east" poster depicts a train rushing through a symbolic collage of the World Trade Center, Liberty Bell, and Capitol Building. By 1978 this region generated 56 percent of Amtrak's ridership and only 31 percent of its costs.[28] While the statutory profit mandate put long-distance routes under deferred death sentences or relegated them into land cruises, the corridor handled more passengers than it had under the Penn Central.

In 1973 the old line received a new opportunity to prove its worth. That October the Organization of the Petroleum Exporting Countries (OPEC) embargoed oil sales to the United States in retaliation for America's support of Israel in its war against Egypt and Syria over the Sinai Peninsula. Deprived of crude from Venezuela, Iraq, Saudi Arabi, Iran, Kuwait, and other member nations, Americans saw barrel prices quadruple, sending the country's fossil fuel economy into withdrawal. Filling stations ran dry. Cars cued in pump lines. The shortage hit hardest in the northeast, which lacked the Midwest's access to Alberta sands pipelines and the South's proximity to gulf rigs.

Ironically, the American petroleum industry began in the north-

FIGURE 10.1 1973 advertisement for Metroliner-esque Amtrak service between New York, Philadelphia, and Washington. National Railroad Passenger Corporation.

east in 1859, when Colonel Edwin Drake drilled the first profitable well near Titusville, Pennsylvania.[29] During the 1876 Philadelphia centennial celebrations, the Pennsylvania Railroad chartered a train of VIPs to tour the commonwealth's oil fields, "where petroleum is sucked from mysterious depths and forced through miles of small iron pipes to tanks at the railway stations, where it is loaded and sent to the markets of the world."[30] A century later, America found much of its oil abroad, and "gasoline fever" gripped northeastern drivers oblivious to the diplomatic wrangling that secured their fuel.

In February 1974 a line of cars at gas pumps in Bethel, Connecticut, stretched across tracks. Impatient drivers idled over the rails, then ran for their lives as a train flattened their cars.[31] The same thing happened again later that month in Neptune, New Jersey. In 1978 the Camp David Peace Accords instigated another OPEC embargo. This time, the ensuing fuel famine sparked riots in Levittown, Pennsylvania, at the Five Points Intersection where Quincy Hollow, Indian Creek, Red Cedar Hill, and Goldenridge converged. Residents of the "perfectly planned community" threw rocks at a Texaco station. They ignited a Ford Torino with stolen motor oil between chants of "more gas now!"[32]

As the northeast shuddered through energy crisis, electric trains powered by homegrown coal and domestic waterfalls appealed to budget-conscious travelers. "Save energy. Take our car," recommended one Amtrak billboard.[33] "Gas pains?" inquired another. "Take Amtrak for Relief!"[34] Like World War II, "gasoline fever" demonstrated the utility of trains to a rationing home front. In the 1970s one of the oldest forms of transportation proved the most economic—and ecological.

Embargo-era Amtrak also reminded passengers why so many of them had ditched trains in the first place. The cash-starved NRPC was in no shape to handle new riders, especially ones accustomed to the privacy of their own Datsuns and Oldsmobiles. Reluctant passengers crammed into coaches that were nauseatingly hot or icebox frigid depending on what equipment happened to be working. The railroad salvaged rolling stock from scrap spurs, pressing into service cars and locomotives it once judged too dilapidated for use.

"The trains are back," declared Amtrak's new slogan, inadvertently hinting at its habit of scavenging for old cars. The NRPC's desperate frugality agonized passengers but delighted federal officials. In 1973 Nixon signed the Amtrak Improvement Act, which increased subsidies, expanded routes, and authorized the railroad to acquire its own maintenance facilities. The once furtive president now publicly congratulated himself for "making the Federal Government a supporting partner with our Nation's passenger railroads," adding that the "energy efficiency of rail travel is an especially compelling argument for expansion of appropriate Federal assistance to Amtrak."[35]

In 1974 Nixon signed the Regional Rail Reorganization Act, paving the way for Amtrak to acquire most of the northeast corridor after the Penn Central's court-ordered liquidation. Where most Amtrak trains rode as guests on the tracks of freight companies—and do so to this day—the company now claimed most of the Boston–Washington line as home turf.[36] The corridor distinguished itself as the country's only intercity line where the conveyance of people took priority over the delivery of stuff.

Amtrak helped Nixon dodge the fallout of the Penn Central crisis and win reelection in a landslide, adding the corridor states of Connecticut, New York, and Pennsylvania to his 1968 electoral tally. When less successful sleights of hand forced Nixon's resignation during the Watergate scandal, his successor, Gerald Ford, allocated $1.75 billion to modernize the corridor.[37] Unlike the slap-dash preparations for the Metroliner and TurboTrain, the Northeast Corridor Improvement Program (NECIP) rebuilt the line from the ground up.

NECIP projects included new stations for the Connecticut edge city of Stamford and the Baltimore-Washington International Airport. Crews cleared "underbrush, abandoned automobiles, household appliances, and garbage" from the right-of-way.[38] Painters slapped fresh coats on rusting bridges over the Thames, Connecticut, and Hutchinson Rivers. Mechanics automated Maryland's Bush River drawbridge. Workers fenced off crossings, dug drainage ditches, and replaced catenary.[39] A bright orange work train nicknamed "the monster" spooled out miles of welded rail and replaced wooden ties with concrete ones.[40]

The NECIP contended with delays and overruns. Contractors accused one another of incompetence. The FBI investigated corrupt

procurement procedures.[41] An exasperated Brock Adams, secretary
of transportation, vowed that track work would proceed "even if
I have to go out myself with a pick and shovel."[42] Month by month,
the program nudged the corridor into decent working order. Having
abandoned their bullet train fantasies, officials set the more obtain-
able goal of running trains between New York and Washington in
under three hours.

This benchmark required new equipment to replace the GG1s
(long past their "useful economic life") and glitchy Metroliners
(which had never been economical at all).[43] Unfortunately for Amtrak, its acquisition followed the bankruptcy of the Penn Central
and an era of de-electrification during which freight carriers like
the Milwaukee Road and Great Northern snipped their wires and
bought diesel locomotives. Diesels generated their own electricity
from fuel, which meant they did not require catenary. But they also
lacked the speed and efficiency of electric engines tapping external
power sources. As diesels took over, manufacturers dropped their
electric motor lines, leaving Amtrak few options.

In 1974 the railroad bought a souped-up electric freight engine
from General Electric. The loaf-shaped E60 weighed roughly 30 percent more than the GG1 and lacked its graceful contours. In trials
the E60's wheels hunted (pitched from side to side) on acceleration,
inflicting lateral stress on the corridor's new welded rails. When an
E60 clonked off the tracks during acceptance testing, the Federal
Railroad Administration capped its speed at 85 miles per hour—too
slow to keep a Metroliner schedule. Amtrak decided to cut bait by
selling off the E60s to New Jersey Transit and New Mexico's Navajo
Mine Railroad, where the engines returned to the freight work for
which they were best suited.[44]

Amtrak's GG1 replacement arrived in 1978 not from Budd, Westinghouse, or General Electric, but from Sweden. The robotics manufacturer Allmänna Svenska Elektriska Aktiebolaget's stubby AEM-7
resembled nothing that had ever crossed corridor rails. The engine's
electrical components spilled out of its roof in a cascade of transformers, coils, hatches, and discharge outlets. Where American designers

hid function behind streamlined shrouds and stainless steel shells, the AEM-7 anticipated industrial chic décor by baring its machinery. The Swedish "toasters" paired perfectly with the corridor's improving but imperfect track. Though almost eighteen feet shorter than a GG1, the AEM-7 packed enough power to pull eight cars at 125 miles per hour. An Amtrak test driver said he had to "dog it" to avoid speeding.[45]

Some criticized Amtrak for importing "foreign trains" to the former "standard railroad of the world." Others noted that three-hour runtimes from New York to Washington were a far cry from Johnson-era promises of rocket trains and hovercraft. No AEM-7 would come close to touching the 171 mile per hour speed record set by the TurboTrain in 1967. But a new spirit of pragmatism reigned on the corridor. The AEM-7 did not need to compete with bullet trains, fulfill social mandates, or otherwise vindicate some belabored idea of Americanness. Like the era's other iconically sensible Swedish import, the Volvo, the AEM-7 could carry passengers quickly and reliably through the northeast, and that would be enough.

Amtrak retired its last GG1 in 1980. That same year, the locomotive's aesthetic consultant, eighty-seven-year-old Raymond Loewy, retired to Monaco. A few holdout GG1s continued to prowl New Jersey Transit's North Coast Line until 1983, when all surviving numbers were scrapped, parked in museums, or left rusting on spurs. Specimens of the engine survive in random settings: museums in Dallas, Green Bay, Baltimore, and St. Louis; the woods outside Cooperstown, New York; an exhibit in Elkhart, Indiana; a track beside the New York State Fairgrounds in Syracuse. Only one GG1, number 4859, the official state locomotive of Pennsylvania, rests beneath wires.

Over half a century after Nixon signed the NRPC into law, Amtrak still receives train passengers and federal subsidies. It remains the corridor's sole intercity carrier, its principal infrastructural steward, and a perennial target for conservative grievance. The NRPC is also just one of several public railroads born in the 1970s.

When, despite Amtrak's intervention, the Penn Central proved beyond saving, Congress created another company to contain the fallout. On April Fool's Day 1976, the Consolidated Rail Corporation (Conrail) took control of seventeen thousand miles of freight and commuter lines orphaned by the Penn Central, Boston & Maine, Lehigh Valley, Erie Lackawanna, Central of New Jersey, and Reading Railroads. With its arid bureaucratic name, fleet of ocean-blue engines, statutory profit expectation, and retinue of critics decrying "special interest socialism," Conrail became the Amtrak of freight.[46]

Conrail struggled through an era of stagflation that struck hardest in the railroad's Rust Belt heartland. But unlike the Penn Central, Conrail appealed to the legislators who created it. In 1980 the Staggers Rail Act let Conrail abandon two thousand miles of superfluous tracks without ICC approval. Conrail slashed its inherited workforce by sixty thousand employees, which exacerbated the recession but also transformed the corporation from "federal welfare project into a profit-maker."[47] Conrail received its last dollar of federal subsidy in 1981.[48]

Conrail initially operated freight and commuter trains. But when Congress realized that its carrier could make money as a cargo-only enterprise, it dumped riders on states and cities. Massachusetts was already underwriting New Haven Railroad commuter services. Philadelphia formed the Passenger Service Improvement Corporation to prop up trains run by the Pennsylvania and Reading Railroads. Conrail's exit from the passenger business catalyzed the creation of several new carriers. By 1983 the corridor that had briefly been the sole bailiwick of the Penn Central flew the colorful flags of the Massachusetts Bay Transportation Authority, Metro-North, New Jersey Transit, the Southeastern Pennsylvania Transportation Authority (SEPTA), and Maryland Area Regional Commuter (MARC).

These five agencies and Shore Line East, a Connecticut service founded in 1990, carry most corridor traffic today. For every Amtrak train that ran over the line in 2012, commuter authorities dispatched thirteen.[49] Many megapolitans have spent lives riding the tracks of the NRPC without setting foot inside an Amtrak train. A suitably hardy rider could hopscotch from one end of the corridor to the other on commuter trains provided they surmount one gap between Perryville, Maryland, and Newark, Delaware, and another between New London, Connecticut, and Wickford, Rhode Island.

By transforming passenger rail into public service, northeasterners returned the corridor to its local roots. Massachusetts again moves people between Boston and Providence over the tracks it chartered in 1831. Metro-North conveys commuters over the same Shore Line that P. T. Barnum once rode. New Jersey Transit clacks across the meadows that confounded antebellum swamp drainers. Pennsylvania pays for trains between Trenton, Philadelphia, and Wilmington. State and local funding have rejuvenated corridor service not just between big cities but throughout land that Adam Davidson calls an "empire of the in-between."[50]

BATTLE LINES

What we need is high-speed rail in the Northeast Corridor.
MICHAEL DUKAKIS[1]

All we needed were Metroliner tickets.
JAY-Z[2]

"Americans, who have always known that excessive bureaucracy is the enemy of excellence and compassion, want a change in life," Ronald Reagan told studio cameras on election eve 1980.[3] The Republican nominee's crinkled blue eyes and providential cheer blazed through monitors. "We shall be a city upon a hill," he proclaimed, quoting John Winthrop's seventeenth-century vision of a new Zion rising in Massachusetts. Just as Winthrop's "city upon a hill" answered its Puritan God, Reagan riffed, so must that benighted "city on the Potomac" face its people.

Reagan loved talking about Puritans despite living as far from them as possible in the telegenic warmth of Santa Barbara. The actor-turned-politician revered those hardy zealots who shivered through their first winter on Cape Cod. He also purportedly joked that "if the Pilgrims had landed in California instead of back East, nobody would have bothered to discover the rest of the country."[4] Reagan's putdown implicated weather while winking at his antipathy to the liberal institutions that defined eastern life: cities, unions, academia, and, above all else, government. The Californian ran for president on rhetorical sunshine and a budgetary battering ram aimed at whatever was left of the Great Society.

Reagan's victory threatened the corridor's existence. No sooner had citizens turned passenger trains into a public service then they elected a man who called Amtrak a "mobile federal money-burning machine," that lavished 7 percent of the Department of Transportation's budget on fewer than 1 percent of American travelers.[5] Reagan zeroed out the National Railroad Passenger Corporation (NRPC) in four consecutive budgets. In 1981 the White House cut $350 million from the Northeast Corridor Improvement Program, canceling plans to electrify the tracks from New Haven to Boston.[6] Reagan's budget director, David Stockman, seethed, "there are few programs I can think of that rank lower than Amtrak in terms of the good they do, the purpose they serve and the national need they respond to."[7]

Amtrak required federal subsidy to operate trains. Conrail, the government's freight salvage program, needed Amtrak to maintain the corridor right-of-way. State-run transit agencies also relied on Amtrak's tracks. Amtrak vice president Timothy Gardner wondered why a president who ran up a $200 billion deficit on defense spending would obsess over rail subsidies accounting for "less than one-tenth of 1 percent of the federal budget . . . it's bizarre that he is singling us out."[8] Fortunately for commuters, passenger rail advocates, and freight customers, Reaganite austerity ran headlong into a Democrat-controlled House of Representatives. Whenever the president scratched trains from his budgets, Congress restored at least some of their funding.

Stymied by Congress, Reagan tried to auction off the country's passenger rail network. Stockman went on *Meet the Press* to argue that Amtrak was actually "economically viable and would be reconstituted by private enterprise."[9] Stockman ignored the fact that private enterprise had left trains spectacularly unviable fifteen years earlier, when for-profit carriers dumped their passengers on the state. No one in their right mind, or with a shred of historical memory, would want to buy Amtrak. Passenger trains remained quasi-public under Reagan, even as privatization became a recurring conservative daydream. "Imagine what Donald Trump could do with passenger service," mused Heritage Foundation economist Stephen Moore in 1990.[10]

Reagan's attacks on Amtrak rallied northeastern Democrats around the cause of passenger rail. Representative James Florio (New Jersey) and Senators Frank Lautenberg (New Jersey), Daniel Patrick Moynihan (New York), and Joe Biden (Delaware) regularly sprung to Amtrak's defense. "The government made a commitment to a national rail passenger service that the private sector would not," Biden reminded his colleagues. "Since 1970, Amtrak has worked to clean up the problems caused by years of inattention by its previous owners."[11]

A lifelong northeasterner, Biden had seen the private sector fail Americans before. He grew up in Scranton, Pennsylvania, as a typhoon of Texas petroleum finished off the Pocono anthracite industry. His family moved to Claymont, Delaware, just blocks from the flagging Pennsylvania Railroad. As a senator, Biden would ride Metroliners over the PRR's former thoroughfare. He saw firsthand the run-down infrastructure that Amtrak inherited from the Penn Central and met the beleaguered employees scrambling to make trains "worth riding again."

Passenger trains gave Biden a parable for his "Delaware Way" economic philosophy, which considered private enterprise a constructive force that sometimes broke public trust. Government's job, he believed, was to "harness the power of regulated capitalism" while shielding consumers from its most harmful acts and rapacious practitioners.[12] By this logic Amtrak was a good investment. The NRPC gave American travelers more options and thereby made competing carriers more responsive to their customers. "For an administration that prides itself on understanding the economics of the free market, their study of Amtrak fails miserably," Biden fumed on the Senate floor. "I do not believe that you would see a continuation of a $19 flight between Washington, DC and New York without the competition Amtrak provides."[13] Rail subsidies, Biden believed, not only increased mobility but coaxed capitalism into becoming a better version of itself.

Reagan won forty-nine states in his reelection bid, sweeping the entire seaboard outside Washington. By his second term, Amtrak had become what Stockman called a "symbolic litmus test."[14] Rail subsidies represented another battlefront between free marketers, regulatory centrists, and progressives advocating the socialist planning that brought world-class systems to Japan and France. But Amtrak, the policy question and ideological trial, was still Amtrak the physical railroad, a transportation company that moved millions of human beings in metal containers. It soon reminded people of this fact.

Ricky Gates woke the first Sunday of 1987 feeling good despite downing six beers the night before.[15] The thirty-two-year-old Conrail engineer sloughed off his holiday weekend and drove to Baltimore's Bayview Yard. Gates clocked in, met his brakeman, Butch Cromwell, and climbed into a grimy blue General Electric B36-7 diesel locomotive. Someone had plucked out the cab's approach bulb, an indicator that copied trackside signal patterns.[16] Someone had wound duct tape around the alertor whistle, muffling the screech it emitted whenever a signal flashed anything other than "clear ahead." Neither issue kept Gates from pulling out of the yard.[17]

That same morning, Amtrak engineer Jerome Evans woke in his Baltimore home and drove to Washington. His train waited in the familiar labyrinth of tracks behind Union Station. The 12:30 Colonial carried passengers between Washington and New Haven, where it split into sections bound for Springfield and Boston. The "Colonial" moniker originally graced an 1892 express linking the "ancient colonies of Massachusetts and Virginia" (though the train never ran south of Washington).[18] Amtrak revived the label, along with several other bespoke historic titles. The Minute Man and Yankee Clipper had already departed Washington that morning.

Evans drove trains and loved them. "I ride my magic carpet / On ribbons made of steel / And my heart keeps pace / To the tapping of the wheel," he once rhymed in a trimeter poem.[19] Evans settled into the cab of his AEM-7 electric locomotive and surveyed the rows of selectors, indicators, gauges, and switches—a compact Swedish command control light years beyond Gates's tampered Conrail cab. That morning, the twelve-car Colonial would be drawn by two AEM-7s, with a combined output of fourteen thousand horsepower.

North of Baltimore, Gates and Cromwell were enjoying an easy run. Their train consisted of three engines bound for Enola Yard, Harrisburg. If the timing worked, the men could catch a bus back to Baltimore and hit the bars. Cromwell drank a bottle of soda, ate lunch, and lit a joint. He passed the joint to his engineer, who took three hits. Gates was known to smoke on the job—four packs of cigarettes daily and sometimes marijuana. The previous month he had been arrested for drunk driving.[20] Corridor engineer Susie Gaglia hated working with Gates. "I felt unsettled in my mind and in my gut the whole trip," she recalled. "I did not like the feeling, and it continued to tug at me. I just wanted to get the job done, get back, go home, and forget about it."[21]

Gates piloted his B36-7 up a sidetrack toward Gunpowder River, a scenic crossing where Charles Dickens feared that even "the smallest accident" would plunge his train into the river.[22] That same rickety bridge was set ablaze years later, first by Isaac Trimble's posse, then again by Confederate major Harry Gilmor's troops. The flammable pile trestle was replaced in 1913 by a concrete span designed by Austrian engineer Gustav Lindenthal shortly before he orchestrated his dramatic Hell Gate crossing.

The corridor right-of-way thins as it approaches the river: four tracks merge into three and then two. Gates rumbled toward the junction at sixty-three miles per hour, thirty-three over the speed limit. Had he unpeeled the tape from the alertor whistle, it would have squealed. Had Cromwell called the signals instead of getting high, there would have been time. "If the joint hadn't been there," Gates recalled wistfully.[23]

By the time he saw the home signal flash a bar of amber bulbs indicating "absolute stop," Gates could only throw the emergency brake and feel inertia drag his locked wheels onto the main line. The trio of B36-7 locomotives ground to a halt in the middle of the corridor. The last engine sat on the switch, its diesel-filled flank diagonal to the tracks. Behind the two men and three engines, through a tunnel of leafless trees, glimmered the white star of a headlamp.

Jerome Evans exited Baltimore at 128 miles per hour. This was too fast for any corridor train, let alone the Colonial, which carried a hand-me-down car from the Penn Central restricted to 105 miles per hour. Though Evans had received citations for speeding, colleagues described him as "very conscientious."[24] In the 1980s all Amtrak engineers felt pressure to meet the faster schedules that justified the multibillion-dollar Corridor Improvement Program. "If you run your train right up to the rules, you're going to be getting contact from dispatchers along the way wanting to know why you're losing time," explained an anonymous engineer.[25] Evans knew that he had exactly 201 minutes to reach New York.[26]

The Colonial's excess velocity meant nothing with 360 tons of bright-blue fuel cannister straight ahead. Evans entered the bend beyond Martin State Airport and saw the angled outline of a freight locomotive against the horizon. He pulled the emergency brake, saw the pneumatic control switch blink white, felt his wheels skate over polished rail, and waited through what he surely knew were the last fourteen seconds of his life.[27]

At 1:31 p.m. residents of Chase, Maryland, heard an explosion as the Colonial struck the rear Conrail engine at 105 miles per hour.[28] Evans died on impact as his AEM-7 crumpled and the B36-7 burst in a diesel comet. Behind him, stainless steel coaches tumbled over one another, tore apart, and blackened with smoke. The wreck ripped catenary wires from their bridges and welded rails from their bed. Passengers crawled from mangled cars. Enroute to New York, they found themselves in a forest. Neighbors emerged from the woods. They phoned ambulances, brought blankets, opened their homes, and cradled the dying. One man sprayed at the fire with his garden hose.[29]

"We just pushed the dead out of the way," recalled a paramedic.[30] "When you come into something of this magnitude you can't treat people."[31] Almost two hundred passengers sustained injuries. Fifteen died besides Evans.[32] The perished included a property appraiser, a lawyer, a state senate staffer, a retired special education teacher, a Polish tourist, a sixteen-year-old Princeton freshman, a Stanford junior, a widow, a second grader. A canvas tent served as the trackside morgue.[33] The right-of-way heaped high with Amtrak and Conrail debris. After years of politicians trading tired quips about budget wrecks and policy derailments, here was the literal collision of two federal programs.

Ricky Gates's locomotive remained intact, buffered by the two engines he was towing to Pennsylvania. Cromwell had leapt from the cab window right before the crash and limped away.[34] Gates stood at his control unhurt and terrified. He grabbed a fire extinguisher, dropped to the tracks, and tried to help, hoping that no one would die. But when investigators asked Gates how his train ended up in the Colonial's path, the engineer blamed a malfunctioning signal. Gates denied smoking pot in the cab and then for some reason elaborated, "what I do on my own time is my own business."[35]

Gates later confessed to using marijuana when tests found THC metabolites in his blood and urine. Cromwell turned state's evidence, testifying in exchange for criminal immunity. (Tests found traces of marijuana and PCP in his system.)[36] The ensuing trial shined a megawatt light on the obscure lives of modern railroaders. Train work could be tedious, lonely, boring, and dangerous. Assignments took engineers away their homes and families for days on end. Calls to come on duty rang at all hours of the night, leaving crews in a constant state of weary vigilance. Drugs and alcohol helped railroaders cope with the randomness and repetition of their professional lives.[37] Chemical release had soaked into the culture of trains.

Gates faced charges of vehicular manslaughter and lying to investigators. Like the case of John Wisker, the New York Central engineer who crashed in the smoky tunnels beneath Park Avenue, the railroad also stood trial. Gates personified a corridor that was fallibly human. He contemplated suicide. "Dressing up in my same clothes, and being ready for work, and coming here on the same day, and waiting for the same train," he trailed off in a television interview while gazing across the tracks at Chase.[38] Gates pled guilty and checked into a psychiatric hospital. He went to jail for four years and later became a drug counselor.

Though he never drove another train, Gates remained fond of railroading. In 2004 someone asked an online message board, "does anyone know what happened to Rickey Gates of Conrail who caused the big Wreck in Chase [*sic*]?" The thread received a few shrugs before going dormant. Six weeks later, a poster with the handle "Rick Gates" entered the conversation. His profile included the signature quote ("railroaders do it on steel") and a Tuscan GG1 avatar. "Rick Gates" appeared to know a lot about Conrail operations around Baltimore. He spoke to the events of January 4, 1987: "I'm alive and well. TY . . . I think. Excuse me for being a bit leery of this subject or opinions of it. I screwed up big time . . . I miss RR and still love trains."[39]

"It is, in short, a metaphor for today's Northeast: decaying and growing at the same time, staging a comeback even as it struggles with the problems of age, an evolving, haunting blend of past and present," wrote reporter William K. Stevens of 30th Street Station.[40] In 1985 Stevens visited Philadelphia to see the increasingly rare sight of "a real train station." The PRR's art deco palace had just turned fifty-two and showed its age. The waiting room surrendered its brilliance to scuffed windows and broken chandeliers. The limestone exterior bore verdigris stains. That year, Australian director Peter Weir opened his feature thriller, *Witness*, with a murder in 30th Street's men's room. The downtrodden station made a great crime scene.

But better times seemed near. As part of its corridor improvement program, Amtrak workers scoured 30th Street's facade and scrubbed its windows. Electricians relit the chandeliers. A modern food court anchored by McDonald's and Dunkin' Donuts replaced the Horn & Hardart commissary. There were plans to build skyscrapers over the station yards or even a new Phillies stadium. These schemes would complement rather than supplant the train hall; 30th Street Station could catalyze growth while retaining its dignity as a transportation hub where, as Stevens put it, "one feels connected to the rest of the Northeast in a solid, permanent way."[41]

Architect Marilyn Taylor noticed this new mindset while restoring Baltimore Penn Station's mosaic tile floors and Tiffany skylights. She watched officials who once regarded terminals as "processing places to move people" come to see them as a "visible and meaningful symbol of the community."[42] Corridor improvement was part technical enterprise, part art project. Carpenters, masons, and metalsmiths rehabbed old buildings while engineers consolidated dispatching operations, programmed an automatic train stop system, and eliminated the final road crossing between New York and Washington. Amtrak saw its corridor as an endlessly upgradable technology and a timeless cultural bequest.

This sense of history guided the line's splashiest improvement: a revived Union Station. Following its ill-thought conversion into a visitor center, Daniel Burnham's capital gateway followed familiar scripts of ruin pornography. Rain dripped through ceiling gaps onto filthy floors clumped with fungus.[43] Rats scuttled about. Metaphors of Roman ruin wrote themselves. Plywood ramps diverted passengers around the stewing chamber to a replacement station that one rider called "Hitler's bunker."[44] The rot grew too much even for Ronald Reagan, who in 1981 signed the Union Station Redevelopment Act. Reagan pledged to restore Union Station as a "commerce center with access to several modes of transportation."[45] His signing speech mentioned neither Amtrak nor trains.

Unlike New York and Boston, Washington took a mulligan on its neglected terminal. The visitor center debacle had the silver lining of tying up government, probably forestalling the same redevelopment

FIGURE 11.1 Workers repaint the ceiling of Washington's Union Station during the terminal's renovation. Library of Congress Prints and Photographs Division.

schemes that prevailed elsewhere during the 1960s and 1970s. Saved
by accident, Union Station required years of attention from crafts-
people before it could reopen. The ceilings were reglazed, repainted,
and regilded. The floor's red marble inlays were refreshed with stone
cut from the same Vermont quarry that Burnham sourced. A horol-
ogist refurbished the waiting hall clock. Technicians installed HVAC
ducts behind walls. At one point, crews uncovered the metal plate
that PRR workers flung over the 1953 wreck of the runaway Federal
Express.[46]

On September 9, 1988, Amtrak welcomed visitors to "the great
reunion."[47] Like 30th Street, the old and improved Union Station
came with new commerce. The developers had partnered with
several companies to convert the former train concourse into three
stories of shops and restaurants.[48] John Bortz, vice president of one
of the project subcontractors, characterized the barrel-vaulted room
as Washington's newest "social destination."[49] People would come

to Union Station not simply to board trains for elsewhere but to eat, drink, and shop in the presence of transit.

Critic Paul Goldberger described the subtle conversion of train hall into festival mall. Though he commended the painstaking work that restored Union Station's turn-of-the-century architecture and recognized the compromises needed to pull off such a job in an age of federal spending cuts and public-private partnerships, he sensed an underlying spiritual cost. The revamped terminal was "almost too clean, too fresh, too new—and a bit too suburban." Train stations were supposed to have a "slightly, shadowy, musty air; it should look like a grainy black-and-white photograph."[50] Union Station "now gleams," Goldberger conceded, echoing novelist Thomas Wolfe, "but it has lost the sound of time."

Amtrak emerged from the 1980s bloodied but alive. When Jimmy Carter left the White House in 1981, the NRPC received $1.24 billion in annual subsidy. By the time George H. W. Bush took office, federal support had shrunk to $603 million.[51] Funding cuts forced Amtrak to lay off staff even as ridership grew. Dining cars replaced cooked meals with microwaved platters.[52] The railroad let the telecom giant MCI lay fiber-optic cable beside the corridor tracks (a revenue venture that harked back to Samuel Morse stringing telegraph wires along the Baltimore & Ohio).[53] After years of fending off free marketeers, the NRPC was acting more like a business.

As the decade closed, Amtrak turned its attention to eastern New England, where the corridor tracks remained unelectrified. Plans to string catenary to Boston had languished for over half a century, rendering this 157-mile segment a sort of second-class annex. Boston-bound passengers felt this demotion at New Haven, where they waited twenty minutes for crews to replace electric engines with diesel locomotives. When the coach lights clicked back on, their trains lumbered off toward Massachusetts at an average pace of fifty-six miles per hour. The ride often took over three hours.[54]

"They're two different railroads," explained Amtrak's David Carol.[55] "South of New York, you have the rail lines with homes nearby, but you don't have grade crossings, and you don't have beautiful scenery and the shorelines that you have here. In southeastern Connecticut, we are literally in people's backyards."[56] The corridor's easternmost right of way bore little resemblance to the New Haven Railroad's commuter conveyor belt or the PRR's "traffic free steel boulevard." The line east of New Haven mostly had two tracks instead of four. Those tracks seemed to bend around every boulder and pebbled cove. Their slower, less frequent trains scarcely disturbed the seaside ambience.

But now with Ronald Reagan safely retired to his California ranch, Amtrak planned to unite the corridor's "different railroads" with one continuous band of alternating current. Officials saw a chance to sell the project to Reagan's former vice president and White House successor, George H. W. Bush. Five days before he lost reelection, the conservative but train-loving Connecticut native signed the Amtrak Authorization and Development Act, releasing $1.27 billion to establish "dependable passenger rail" between Boston and New York "in three hours or less."[57]

Opposition flared along the shoreline. The electrification project's environmental impact statement received 828 pages of public comments.[58] Trackside residents complained that catenary would spoil coastal vistas. Environmentalists pondered the harm posed to nesting osprey and shortnose sturgeon. A tennis club worried that increased train traffic would force members to "stop play more frequently." Some officials claimed the new trains would be too loud. Others asserted that the silence of electric engines imperiled pedestrians. A few revived the old panic that high-voltage wires emit "cancer-causing electromagnetic fields."[59] A group calling itself Citizens Against the Amtrak Electrification Project argued that the venture "doesn't help Southeast Connecticut. . . . New Yorkers and Bostonians benefit, not people along the southeastern coast."[60]

When Amtrak announced that it would add thirty-three trains a day to the electrified line, local anxiety centered around six movable bridges that carry the corridor tracks over coastal inlets. Upstream marinas needed these spans open so that sailboats and fishing charters could enter Long Island Sound. More trains presumably meant fewer openings. A Niantic boatyard owner urged the Department of Transportation, "our coastline is the most valuable asset Connecticut has. Please do not destroy this asset by eliminating access to the Long Island Sound and some of the best recreational and fishing waters in the world!"[61]

Amtrak, Connecticut, and the Coast Guard finally hammered out an agreement. By installing more sensitive signals, Amtrak could scale up train frequency while keeping the inlets open to boat traffic forty minutes per hour between 5 a.m. and midnight.[62] Amtrak received its final environmental permit. Construction began. The continent's busiest railroad would contain saltwater gaps for two-thirds of the waking day.

The electrification project broke ground in July 1996. Crews planted fifteen thousand catenary poles in New England's igneous coast.[63] In some places, the granite subsurface required jackhammers. Elsewhere vacuums sucked up marsh muck before concrete foundations could be poured. In Boston, workers wove their silver-copper wire through the rebar chaos of another megaproject, the Big Dig. Construction of the new I-93 tunnel made the corridor tracks sink.[64] Nothing came easy. But when the new millennium dawned over Massachusetts, the corridor's freshest catenary buzzed with current. On January 28, 2000, an Amtrak mail train pulled into Boston's South Station behind an AEM-7.

Passenger service began three days later with an "Electrification Celebration Special," which departed South Station, then abruptly tripped a breaker. The train slowed and the carriage lights dimmed. After a long moment, the lights blinked on and the engine regained speed.[65] The Special swept south across Massachusetts and slipped through the tunnels under Providence. It banked through Stonington, Mystic, Groton, Old Saybrook, and several other seaside towns that fought electrification. The Special paused in Penn Station before streaking across the toxic drownings of the Meadowlands, past the ceramic-dotted rowhomes of Newark's Ironbound, through the deer-filled woods north of Trenton, by the fractal reprise of Levittown, along the brown peaks of Delaware Bay, and across Gunpowder River.

The northeast that passengers saw through their windows was not a shining city atop some blessed hill but a blur of tooth-by-jowl variety. An ongoing argument. A string of tradeoffs. A begrudging compromise. Or, in the mixed metaphors of Amtrak president George Warrington, "a powerhouse of an engine that will help power the economy of a region."[66] Amtrak's largest investment in its greatest asset had drawn Boston back into the main line of northeastern life. Electrification also laid the groundwork for the corridor's third century, which opened with the age of Acela.

AFTER RUBBLE

Acela's fast, Acela's cool. Acela's modern. And Acela's stylish.
STAN BAGLEY, PRESIDENT OF NORTHEAST
CORRIDOR OPERATIONS[1]

Enter the Oak Room, a Back Bay drinking den tucked into the Copley Plaza Hotel. Crystal chandeliers blaze over copper counters. Piano chords patter through the din of laughter and scuffle of porcelain. Forks poke at oysters. Spoons ladle bisque. On a cold night in late 2000, a wood fire crackles. It looks like the ballroom from *Clue*, a plaster bastion where Brahmin life plays on in millennial Boston. A bartender rattles ice, vodka, and curaçao to a sapphire froth, plunks in three olives, then slides the shaker and a martini glass toward a leather-tufted barstool. The stainless steel concoction is called Acela-tini. It costs fifteen dollars and turns lips blue.[2]

One block from Copley Plaza, under Dartmouth Street, in a trench beside I-90, thrums an actual Acela. The gray train with blue accents has two engines—one leading, one trailing to form a reversible set. Its aerodynamic noses taper into canonical nubs. Its motors whirr through exhaust gills. The engines mesh with their power cars and carriages in a seamless cannular streak. Acela looks like a stylized torpedo. It looks sort of French. When the train hit 165 miles per hour on a test track in Pueblo, Colorado, it seemed to justify the Shore Line electrification, the corridor improvements, even Amtrak itself. Acela vindicated everyone who fought the American habit of eulogizing trains. It was the stuff drinks get named for.

The first Acela left Washington on November 16. Press gathered in Union Station for the 10 a.m. departure from track 20. National Public Radio's Jack Speer likened the christening to the "launch of an ocean liner."[3] Amtrak president George Warrington compared Acela's inaugural voyage to the "introduction of the jet engine and the building of the Interstate Highway System."[4] "The launch of Acela Express is one of those truly defining moments," Amtrak chairman and Wisconsin governor Tommy Thompson trailed off before cracking a champagne bottle across the train's beak, drenching Michael Dukakis.[5]

Acela entered regular service in the predawn murk of December 11. It ratcheted up to 135 miles per hour on the New Jersey straightaway where the TurboTrain once tested. After New York, Acela maneuvered through Metro-North traffic and bobbed along Connecticut's shore before opening up on the flats above Block Island Sound. Near Kingston, Rhode Island, Acela touched—and for a few hushed seconds held—150 miles per hour, the highest speed attained by a nontest train in American history. An hour later, Acela eased through Back Bay and entered South Station. Boston was now three and a half hours from Manhattan. Acela made the City on a Hill a true corridor terminus.

For one night, Acela was the toast of New England. The next morning brought hangover. The dazzling first run had damaged the lead engine's pantograph.[6] A backup Acela lacked hot water and a working freezer, so an AEM-7 substituted on the morning express, then stalled out in Bridgeport. In its first months, Acela delighted and disheartened riders. The sleek train impressed journalists and business travelers, but its pantograph tangled with catenary. Its undercarriage yaw dampeners cracked. Brush fires, landslides, and lightning strikes disrupted service.[7] By late summer, the corridor's bright future began to resemble its fraught past. Acela was, in the words of railroad writer Joseph Vranich, both "Amtrak's crown jewel" and a "remarkable fiasco."[8]

America's latest attempt at a bullet train began in 1992, when

Amtrak secured money to electrify the Shore Line. After its success with a Swedish import, the AEM-7, Amtrak decided to test-drive a pair of European trains: the Swedish-Swiss X2000 and the German ICE (Intercity Express). "I thought I'd stepped onto a cloud," mused one Amtrak rider stepping off the X2000, which banked into curves, reducing the G-forces felt aboard ordinary coaches.[9] The tilting train turned out to be too wispy. Scarred by the Gates wreck, the Federal Railroad Administration required passenger trains to have enough mass to sustain an impact generating eight hundred thousand pounds of horizontal force.[10] The Swedes and Germans refused to bulk up their designs and went home.[11]

With no off-the-shelf option, Amtrak asked Canada's Bombardier Corporation and the French firm Alstom to develop a compliant solution.[12] The resulting machine combined the TGV's propulsion system with the tilt mechanism that helped the X2000 navigate the twisting tracks between Stockholm, Gothenburg, and Oslo. Alstom-Bombardier's train offered speed and versatility on the corridor's rugged terrain. The consortium clinched the deal by financing Amtrak's purchase—the cash-strapped railroad essentially paid no money down.[13] Alstom-Bombardier even agreed to assemble the trains in two depressed American cities: the former granite hub of Barre, Vermont, and Plattsburgh, New York, devastated by the closure of a local air force base.[14]

Problems began with the train's regulatory heft. Acela looked like a TGV but weighed twice as much as one. French engineers called it *cochon* (pig). Former Amtrak president Tom Downs preferred "high-velocity bank vault."[15] The coaches somehow wound up four inches wider than intended, which meant that Acela could not fully tilt around turns without sideswiping adjacent trains. Acela languished in testing. Its launch drifted from early 1999 to late 2000.[16] Amtrak leased billboards along I-95 to showcase its new service to haggard motorists, but the signs, which featured a woman with blunt bangs, one eye shut, and a train popping out of her ear, mostly came down before Acela hit the rails. Relations between Amtrak and Alstom-

Bombardier chilled in a flurry of fines, suits, countersuits, and endless bickering over interior décor. Curtain design became an intractable sticking point.[17]

The train was initially called "American Flyer," after a model railroad kit sold by erector set inventor and New Haven catenary enthusiast Alfred Carlton Gilbert. In 1999 marketers debuted a new name that mushed together the words "acceleration" and "excellence." No one knew how to say "Acela" at first. The sibilant puree bedeviled newscasters, who mispronounced it every which way (Ak-sell-ah, A-ceel-ia, Ah-chel-a, Ace-la, Es-a-la).[18] Journalists snuck phonetic assistance (Ah-SELL-a) into their articles.[19] Were the word not baffling enough, Amtrak applied it to multiple corridor trains, including the new Alstom-Bombardier service (Acela Express) and conventional intercity runs (Acela Regional). For a time the railroad considered renaming its Clockers, which lumbered between New York and Philadelphia, "Acela Commuter."

Acela's postmodern marketing campaign invited riders to "depart from your inhibitions" and "return your mind to its upright position."[20] Posters stamped with the tagline "Life on Acela" appeared to sell something more conceptual than trains, like life insurance, or, one journalist suggested, antidepressants.[21] Amtrak accessorized the Acela lifestyle through a catalog of merchandise that included mousepads, CD cases, a plush bear named Ace, and gourmet chocolates confected by French chef Georges Perrier.[22] "Acela is more than just a name," George Warrington told his employees. "Acela is a brand representing a whole new way of doing business."[23]

Acela Express carried over a million riders in its first year. Amtrak's split of the air-rail travel market between New York and Boston jumped from 18 percent to 40 percent.[24] Acela-skeptics noted that the new train reached its vaunted top speed of 150 miles per hour on less than two dozen miles of track, and that it saved more time skipping stops than it did from dynamic tilting. Acela, critics claimed, was a timetable mirage that lagged far behind global benchmarks for high-speed rail. (A TGV topped 320 miles per hour in 1990.)[25] Passengers did not seem to care.

Nine months into service, Acela ridership spiked when the September 11th terrorist attacks sent traumatized flyers crowding onto trains. The corridor provided a logistical backstop during the two-day closure of American civilian airspace. Amtrak's passenger swell abated as airports reopened and the federal government orchestrated a five-billion-dollar airline bailout. Some northeasterners stuck with trains, however, thanks partly to the new Department of Homeland Security's laborious screening procedures, which made shuttle flights less efficient. A 2009 Acela advertisement enticed customers with the option of "taking off your shoes—only if you feel like it."[26] After decades of emulating airlines, Amtrak touted the pleasures of staying grounded.

Acela became a new symbol of northeasterness. The brisk blue-gray train distilled the pounding pace and supposed sophistication of corridor life. Pundits coined the phrase "Acela Primary" for the presidential nominating contests that occurred on one night in Rhode Island, Connecticut, Pennsylvania, Delaware, and Maryland.[27] Sportswriters christened the 2009 Phillies-Yankees Fall Classic an "Acela Series," just as journalists referred to the 1983 Phillies-Orioles championship as the "Metroliner Series."[28] The phrase "Acela Corridor" seeped into pop sociology as shorthand for elite and aloof seaboarders.

And yet few northeasterners actually lived "life on Acela." In 1961 Jean Gottmann's Megalopolis contained over fifty-two thousand square miles. Megapolitans lived in New York and Washington as well as Harrisburg, Scranton, Schenectady, and Manchester. Acelaland, by contrast, extended only to the corridor's largest stops and most affluent riders. Many northeasterners balked at Acela's premium fares. "For years we've been hearing about 33-minute trips between Boston and Providence, but they really won't be available to your average commuter," a Rhode Islander complained of the $28 one-way fare.[29] "We are not a commuter service," replied an Amtrak spokesperson, relegating the average rider to lesser trains.

Acela added a new rung to the corridor's socioeconomic ladder. The same tracks now carried spartan commuter cars with worn joints and jaundice lighting, Amfleet coaches with gun slat windows and the briny scent of microwaved hot dog, and Acela first-class, where passengers drained expense accounts on craft ales served seatside. Journalist Alexander Burns surmised that Acela was less famous for "moving passengers" than for "sorting them into a cultural set."[30] The corridor's expanding fleet of trains reflected the country's deepening class divisions.

Acela backlash ironically played into the hands of the Harvard-Yale-educated Connecticut scion who became America's forty-third president. Born one mile from New Haven's Union Station, George W. Bush fit the profile of an Acela rider. But America's first MBA-in-chief would revive Ronald Reagan's antipathy to trains. Bush the Texan rancher and failed oilman rose to power in a petroleum paradise of cars and jets. Bush the Sun Belt governor believed that private markets should provision citizen needs. Unlike Reagan, Bush enjoyed over two years of a Republican-controlled Congress poised to cut passenger rail.[31]

Bush tried to confiscate Amtrak's corridor through the Amtrak Reform Council, an oversight body created under Bill Clinton to enforce "operational self-sufficiency."[32] "Placing the ownership burden on Amtrak, which is the minority user, has not been effective," the council reported, "because Amtrak has never received the funding that is needed to fund the corridor's needs."[33] Instead of increasing Amtrak's subsidy, council members wanted to turn the line over to a joint federal-state operating company. Only by seizing the corridor, members argued, could government remedy a situation that was "bad for Amtrak's nationwide train operations and bad for NEC infrastructure."[34]

Rail advocates recognized that Bush was trying to strip Amtrak of its most valuable asset and dependable passenger base. "Selling the Northeast Corridor is the first step in President Bush's plan to destroy Amtrak and intercity rail service in America," warned New Jersey Senator Frank Lautenberg.[35] Amtrak's new president, the gruffly candid David Gunn, testified that "no national rail passenger system in the world is profitable."[36] A Bush appointee, Gunn claimed that the mere pursuit of profit incentivized short-term revenue grabs at the cost of "incremental but critical improvements to plant and equipment." When Gunn refused to help dismantle the National Railroad Passenger Corporation, Amtrak's board of directors fired him.

In 2004 Bush won reelection without earning a single northeastern electoral vote. He opened his second term by eliminating Amtrak's subsidy in a brazen attempt to bankrupt the railroad. Bush's budget enacted a Republican party platform, which acknowledged that "Amtrak provides a valuable service to passengers, especially in the Northeast corridor" while asserting that the "financial problems plaguing Amtrak cannot be solved simply by continued infusions of taxpayer dollars."[37]

Though Amtrak's $1.2 billion budget line constituted less than one tenth of 1 percent of the federal government's $2.2 trillion overall outlay, the mere existence of train subsidies rankled a president who drew support from rural voters, campaign donations from fossil fuel extractors, and guidance from the ineluctable laws of supply and demand.[38] If consumers could not support intercity passenger trains, the conservative logic went, then they did not need to run.

Like Reagan before him, Bush was ultimately foiled by legislators. The 108th United States Congress included several Republican friends of Amtrak from states far outside the northeast, including Kay Bailey Hutchison (Texas) and Conrad Burns (Montana).[39] "Preserving national passenger rail service shouldn't be based on partisan ideology or Amtrak's profit margins," argued Mississippi Republican senator Trent Lott in 2007, "[it is] about ensuring that America has a complete transportation system — one that includes planes, trains, and ports."[40]

Claiborne Pell died on New Year's Day 2009 at the age of ninety. His family, friends, and colleagues packed Newport's Trinity Church to the balcony pews. Attendants included former president Bill Clinton and Massachusetts senator Edward Kennedy, whose brother John had called Pell "the most unelectable man in America." In a moseying eulogy, vice president-elect Joe Biden recalled his fellow small-state senator's achievements and eccentricities. Stories concerned Providence stevedores and the Prince of Lichtenstein. Then, as ever, out of nowhere, Biden asked those gathered to "think about what happened when the Penn Central Railroad system shut down."[41]

Whether any of Biden's listeners could remember the ill-fated carrier's 1970 demise was unclear and immaterial. "He [Pell] went off and wrote a book," Biden explained, turning to Clinton, "remember you and I talked about this, Mr. President, *Megalopolis Unbound*," then turning to the full congregation, "he envisioned before anybody the vibrancy of the northeast corridor and rail." "Were it not for your husband," Biden shifted his gaze to Nuala Pell, "I would not have stayed in the Senate. . . . He had a vision. A vision of what he saw for the whole region."

Pell never rode Acela Express, the train that he foresaw forty years ahead of schedule, but he did get to watch one fly under the wires through Kingston.[42] For all its problems, Amtrak's premier train represented an enormous improvement on the "seedy and inadequate, always dirty, and often late" Federal Express that Pell took to Washington.[43] Beyond the tracks, Acela conveyed the same hope of regional economic integration that burned bright in Gottmann's keyword, *megalopolis*. The northeast corridor remained imperfect on the day of Pell's death, but as Biden recognized, it was again becoming a vital conduit "for the whole region."

Following the 2008 financial crash, a Democratic-controlled Congress passed the American Recovery and Reinvestment Act. President Obama's stimulus package funneled millions of tax dollars into trains. Amtrak used some of this money to rehabilitate its aging Amfleet coaches. In 2010 it contracted with Germany's Siemens Corporation to design a new corridor workhorse to replace the AEM-7. An electric traction pioneer since the days of Thomas Edison, Siemens delivered the first ACS-64 City Sprinter locomotive in 2013. By 2018 the once-ubiquitous Swedish toasters were gone.

Amtrak's corridor ridership increased by 38 percent between 2004 and 2019.[44] Trains doubled their share of northeastern air-rail traffic.[45] Even longtime Amtrak critics became riders of convenience, including New Jersey governor Chris Christie, who canceled state funds to build new corridor tunnels under the Hudson River, and former House speaker Newt Gingrich, who once described national passenger rail as a "case study of how bureaucracy, political pork, and unions fail the public."[46] Conservative columnist George Will denounced trains as a totalitarian plot to erode "Americans' individualism in order to make them more amenable to collectivism," then was spotted two months later deboarding one of Amtrak's wheeled communes at Union Station.[47]

Aughts-era Amtrak benefited from savvier marketing. When the NRPC debuted its first website in 1996, it included the proviso that the page was "best viewed in Netscape Navigator."[48] A decade later customers could book train tickets online or apply for an Amtrak Mastercard. In 2010 Amtrak adopted a perfunctorily snarky Twitter persona that cast shade on airline competitors and Quiet Car scofflaws. In 2014 Amtrak introduced a writer residency program that offered free train tickets to authors who blogged their travels (typically on long-distance routes more scenic than the corridor). The once clunky bureaucracy had become a slick supplier of wageless gig work.

Amtrak also capitalized on demographic shifts beyond its control. Train travel appealed to millennials, who were more apt to live in cities than their parents, more likely to forego car ownership, and more inclined to savor the efficiencies of working enroute.[49] Train time offered screen time to young professionals immersed in devices. Ideologically, those who came of age through the subprime mortgage crisis and its tax-funded bailout were less prone to regard Amtrak as what Reagan called a "federal money-burning machine."[50] The railroad delivered a solid and self-evident service to a generation disillusioned by the publicly backed promises of private banks. Millennials, it turned out, were the perfect Americans to rediscover passenger railroading. They were the megapolitans Pell had been waiting for.

In 2014 Berlin muralist Katharina Grosse blazed five miles of North Philadelphia's corridor with pink, lime, white, and orange paint. The spray-gunned pigment coated walls, windows, a ballast pile, a chain-link fence, and the splintery remnants of a trestle. Grosse made a vacant warehouse glow like a bottle of Fanta. An embankment of unintended saplings turned cotton candy. "My painting is a strange thing to happen to a city," she said.[51]

One journalist criticized the installation, called *psychylustro*, as an example of "hipster economics" meant to "block poverty from the public eye."[52] But the paint masked nothing. To the contrary, Grosse highlighted the innercity's detritus, drawing passenger eyes to what "often remains overlooked," in the words of painter Dushko Petrovich.[53] Or, as city mural arts director Jane Golden put it, "we wanted to illuminate the rubble."[54]

And what rubble it was. Here had stood American Machine, Global Dye, Albion Carpet, Asher Candy, Stetson Hats, Frankford Arsenal, Bromley Mills, Pearson Steam Packing, Cramp Shipyard, Tasty Baking, and Quaker Lace. In Philadelphia's former "workshop of the world," corridor trains pass near the Midvale Steel Works where Frederick Winslow Taylor turned labor management into science, setting off a time-motion "efficiency craze." Every day, Amtrak passengers thumbing out texts, knee-deep in email, run a corbelled brick gauntlet where the productivities of yesteryear persist as paintable debris.

Grosse's mural capitalized on the fact that the corridor has always felt part abandoned. Interlocking towers crumble. Spurs dissolve into weeds. Dead engines litter sidings. Riding a corridor train can feel metropolitan one moment and like trespassing through a junkyard the next. The right-of-way is strewn with dented shopping carts, worn tires, bags, bottles, and an empty Pennzoil jug. It sits at the center of everything while seeming dispossessed. It promises the future while looking lost to time.

Some of the line's most critical infrastructure remains ancient. In Secaucus, New Jersey, Acelas whip across the Hackensack River on a Bessemer steel span erected in 1910. Slated for replacement in 2027, the Portal Bridge periodically swings open on wedge blocks so that sewage barges can pass downriver. When the bridge shuts, its mitered rails sometimes misalign. A fouled closure derailed an Amtrak train in 1996. The engine caromed back and forth, ripping up tracks and sideswiping another train before vaulting into the riverbank.[55] Thirty-four people sustained injuries, but no one died thanks to the train's soft landing in sawgrass marsh.

Five miles up the line, the North River Tunnels have also entered their second century of service. The twin tubes had already reached capacity in 2012 when Hurricane Sandy sent a gray deluge across the Meadowlands, turning the tunnels into log flumes. When the brine receded, it left the lining and catenary caked with salt crystals. "We have to gut the tunnel," lamented Amtrak spokesman, Craig Schulz.[56] Sandy also inundated New Jersey Transit's Kearney repair shops, damaging locomotives and coaches.[57] In Trenton, Assunpink Creek overspilled its concrete trough, submerging a SEPTA train up to its headlights.

Sandy seemed like a harbinger of meteorologies to come, a disconcerting prospect for corridor passengers who ride over, under, and along seawater for much of their journeys. In 2014, Amtrak hired Booz Allen Hamilton consultants to assess the corridor's vulnerability to climate change. The report, made public by a Bloomberg Media records request, indicated that sections of track in Delaware, Connecticut, and New Jersey could face "continual inundation" over the next century.[58] The same rising seas and storm surges that menace coastal communities pose existential risks to the corridor's low-slung electric infrastructure, especially where it passes through South Wilmington's wetlands and North Jersey's marsh.

While steeling itself for climate disaster, Amtrak has competed with less encumbered carriers. In 1997 the charter motorcoach lines known colloquially as the Chinatown Bus began selling cheap tickets between New York, Boston, Philadelphia, and Washington. Initially marketed to Chinese Americans, the service soon drew budget-conscious travelers from all nationalities. Fung Wah was the first line to hone the Chinatown Bus method, which evaded terminal docking fees by collecting and depositing passengers on sidewalks. A parade of "curbside" carriers followed: Sunshine Travel, Eastern Shuttle, Dragon Coach, and Lucky Star—later joined by the "corporate curbside buses" Megabus and Bolt Bus.[59] In 2011 transportation analyst Joseph Schwieterman calculated that buses were the country's "fastest growing form of intercity travel."[60]

Politicians, meanwhile, have begun advocating various high-tech, postrail transit concepts, including magnetic levitation (maglev) systems, which float vehicles above electromagnets. In 2003, a Shanghai maglev reached 268 miles per hour. In April 2015, Japan's Lo Series maglev topped 375 miles per hour on its Mount Fuji test track. When the Federal Railroad Administration and Maryland Department of Transportation considered a demonstration maglev between Washington and Baltimore, Japanese prime minister Shinzo Abe offered to build the guideway free of charge.[61] Maglev impressed a trio of former northeastern governors, George Pataki, Ed Rendell, and Christine Todd Whitman, who advocated the technology as long as it be "complementary to Amtrak, not competitive."[62]

Three weeks after Japan's maglev broke its own world speed record outside Tokyo, the corridor's frailty came into tragic focus. On the rainless night of May 12, 2015, engineer Brandon Bostian climbed into the cab of a sparkling new City Sprinter locomotive. The thirty-two-year-old Tennessean had always dreamed of driving fast trains and that spring he got his chance on the corridor.[63] At 7:10 p.m., Bostian's train, Acela Regional 188, rolled out of Union Station. The Regional arrived ninety minutes later at Wilmington, where Delaware senator Tom Carper deboarded.[64] At 9:16, 188 arrived in Philadelphia, and at 9:19, it departed north through Katharina Grosse's neon canvass.[65]

Bostian listened to his cab radio. "Coming out of Mantua, right at, uh, almost at the Diamond Street under grade bridge. Something hit our windshield. I don't know if somebody threw something, or somebody—but our windshield is shattered," reported the engineer of SEPTA train 769. "I just got glass in my face. I saw a trespasser by the freight tracks. I blew the horn." He continued, "I've seen people throw rocks here before."[66] The SEPTA train stopped. Bostian's Regional passed it moments later. "I was really concerned for the SEPTA engineer," Bostian later told interviewers. "I had a coworker in Oakland that had glass impact his eye from hitting a tractor-trailer, and I know how terrible that is."[67]

Stonings terrify engineers. Bricks and ballast cobbles can crack windows and maim drivers. Such fears led the Penn Central to replace glass windows with lexan polycarbonate in 1971 and Amtrak to cover E60 windshields with cages. Projectiles also popped the cultural bubble separating professional-class corridor riders from their often impoverished surroundings. Amtrak Train 188 carried lawyers, bankers, startup CEOs, a college dean, an acclaimed chef, and a former congressman through a census tract where the median income hovered under twenty-one thousand dollars a year.[68] Most riders had little connection to the "often overlooked" world beyond their windows.

Bostian sped toward Frankford Junction, where the PRR's Congressional Limited derailed in 1943. The corridor bends wickedly here, an elliptical monument to the 1840 Kensington uprising. Frankford Curve is so sharp that engineers can take it at no more than fifty miles per hour. For reasons that remain unknown, Train 188 approached at 106 miles per hour. Blood-alcohol tests later confirmed Bostian's absolute sobriety. Mobile records showed no incoming or outgoing transmissions from his cell phone. Some speculate that a rock clunked against the Sprinter's windshield, knocking Bostian unconscious. Others guess that the engineer forgot where he was. Bostian himself cannot recall.

At 9:23 p.m. a white light popped from the Sprinter's pantograph as it lost contact with the catenary. The speeding engine tipped to its side and sledged off the right-of-way, dragging the train with it. Three

Amfleet coaches overturned. The business-class car was shredded beyond recognition. Eight people died in the ravaged train, now as crooked as its right-of-way. "Along the Northeast Corridor, Amtrak is a way of life for many," Barack Obama said in a statement that night. "From Washington, D.C. and Philadelphia to New York City and Boston, this is a tragedy that touches us all."[69]

Joe Biden mentioned the Penn Central at Claiborne Pell's funeral to honor his late colleague's support of passenger trains. But in 1970 the Central's bankrupt empire extended far beyond what Chairman Stuart Saunders called the "fucking railroad."[70] Nontrain assets included Ohio petroleum pipelines, Texas industrial parks, executive jets, a share of the New York Knicks, and land holdings nationwide. All of these properties hit the auction block as part of the corporation's court-ordered estate sale. The Penn Central's carcass would fertilize a new generation of northeastern enterprise.

Among those angling to snap up the Central's relics was thirty-two-year-old Queens developer Donald Trump. In 1975 Donald and his father finagled a package of loans and tax abatements from New York City to buy the Penn Central's Commodore Hotel, next door to Grand Central Station.[71] Trump gutted the building, named after the Hightstown rail wreck victim and robber baron Cornelius Vanderbilt, who never let his lack of naval commission get in the way of calling himself "commodore." Trump entombed the hotel's masonry facade with a skin of black reflective glass. In 1980 the Commodore reopened as the Grand Hyatt New York.

Trump then turned his attention to two Penn Central freight yards on Manhattan's West Side. He brokered a deal between the railroad and city that transformed the plot between 30th and 39th Streets into the Jacob Javits Convention Center. Trump intended the northern site, between 59th and 72nd Street, for something called "Television City," a concept that recalled an earlier generation's wildest Penn Station redevelopment fantasies.[72]

In 1988 Trump entered the transportation industry himself by purchasing and rebranding Eastern Airlines' network of commuter flights between New York, Boston, and Washington. The "Trump Shuttle" boasted plush chairs, chrome seatbelts, and lavatories decked in gold paint and granite. Despite its perks, the gaudy carrier could not overcome rising fuel costs and the resurgent AEM-7-hauled Metroliners, which Amtrak shrewdly dubbed the "smarter shuttle."

In 2016 presidential candidate Trump fashioned himself as a builder-in-chief who would deliver the "biggest and boldest infra-structure investment in American history."[73] He promised the "next generation of roads, bridges, railways, tunnels, seaports, and airports" with the confidence of a twenty-first-century Robert Moses.[74] That November, Trump the self-styled public works enthusiast convinced enough voters to crack the Democratic "blue wall" of midwestern states and flip the Commonwealth of Pennsylvania. For the first time in twenty-four years, corridor trains crossed a red state. Nowhere was the shock more visceral than at the official Clinton watch party in the Javits Center, whose 1986 construction over a Penn Central rail yard Trump himself arranged.[75]

Two months later, former vice president Joe Biden left Washing-ton by train. "Hey guys, back on Amtrak!" he shouted from Union Station's platform before boarding a chartered Acela Express.[76] Ex-actly eight years earlier, Biden had ridden a Pullman observation car on Obama's inaugural special. This ride held none of that euphoria. Biden watched familiar scenery streak past under grim winter skies. Rain splattered against his window. "You ride along here at night, and you look in the windows, and you see the lights on, and . . . I think, what's going on in that kitchen?" Biden looked around the train car. "This is my family," he said. "This is why I wanted to go home the way I came."

REBORN AGAIN

The historical signature of the railroad may be found in the fact that it represents the first means of transport—and, until the big ocean liners, no doubt also the last—to form masses.

WALTER BENJAMIN[1]

The corridor's next chapter opened on a gray winter morning in the Allegheny foothills. Hornell, New York, formed at the junction of four railroads, including the Erie Company's Hoboken-Chicago main line. The Erie built shops here beside the Canisteo River to tune up carriages and water locomotives. Train maintenance became Hornell's lifeblood. In 1882 a passing rider marveled at the "immense amount of side-tracks, ample engine-houses, repair-shops, and other railroad-structures" anchoring a community with "banks, newspapers, [and] a flourishing library association, which maintains a course of popular lectures."[2]

When the Erie dissolved into Conrail in 1976, Hornell's prospects dimmed. The shops shuttered in 1978. The town lost half its population. Hornell's industrial development director bought the Erie plant in the hope someone would reopen it.[3] A string of short-term tenants passed through until 2002, when the French train manufacturer Alstom made Hornell its American headquarters. The Erie shops returned to life, churning out locomotives for New Jersey Transit and double-decker commuter coaches bound for Boston and Chicago.

The New York MTA's first R160 subway car sparked to life in "Maple City."

On the morning of February 17, 2020, photographers staked positions beside Alstom's snow-crusted yard. Their cameras glimpsed a bizarre train. It had two Amtrak diesel engines and a baggage car up front, a sleeper at the rear, and sandwiched between them, Avelia. Avelia was itself a train, the newest and fastest train in North America. Onlookers gawked at the machine, so sleek and French as to seem photoshopped into Steuben County. The train's train grumbled forward through chain-link gates. It accelerated past the Save-A-Lot grocer, the ServU Credit Union, and the Hornell Bible Church into a valley of pine stands and frozen stubble.

Several hours later, Avelia swept through South Buffalo, where empty silos salute a cereal trade that moved elsewhere (except for the single General Mills plant that still emits a Cheerio scent). More railfans huddled with tripods and radio scanners to see the new train towed through the Old First Ward. The convoy crossed the Buffalo River and brushed past the solar panel factory that Tesla raised atop the ruins of Republic Steel. Avelia—its aluminum skin as smooth as its velveteen name—passed a nature preserve weeding over abandoned port slips. It pitched south along the interior ocean of Lake Erie and thundered out of view.

In 2014 Amtrak initiated the process of replacing its Acela fleet with lighter and faster trains. The railroad issued a joint request for proposals with the state of California, then planning electrified service between San Francisco and Los Angeles. Launched in 1996, California's high-speed rail initiative has shown how hard it is to build a corridor from scratch. Bogged down by land purchase battles and construction overruns, the state dropped out of the acquisition. Amtrak soldiered on, soliciting bids from any vendor that could produce equipment "capable of carrying up to 450 passengers at speeds of at least 160 miles per hour."[4] The corridor needed a tried-and-true solution this time, not another narcissistic experiment or bespoke compromise.

When it enters service in 2024, Avelia will send the original Acelas to the scrapyard. But the Acela brand will live on to grace Alstom's next-generation speedsters. Once maligned as pretentious jargon, the made-up mash-up of excellence and acceleration will outlive every other facet of the American Flyer project. "We don't want anyone asking, 'Why are you getting rid of Acela?'" said Caroline Decker, Amtrak's vice president for Northeast Corridor Operations.[5] Though Acela never quite lived up to its millennial hype, the name stuck in the minds of riders and pundits to the point that it represented the region. The northeast will retain its Acela Corridor after Acela retires.

Like the original Acela, Avelia will tap only a fraction of its potential power. Amtrak predicts that Alstom's train will top 160 miles per hour on the corridor. Straighter tracks and better signals could raise that limit to 186 miles per hour, approximately what Thomas Edison boasted his electromagnetic railway could achieve in 1881. But even this aspirational figure falls short of the 225 miles per hour that Avelia Horizon will clock on dedicated track in France. "You have a 21st-century train on 19th-century infrastructure," Decker acknowledged. "But we're going to get everything we can out of these new trainsets."[6]

By the time Avelia reached Colorado's High Speed Ground Test Center, COVID-19 had found its first American hosts. The contagion that spread at the speed of breath struck hard in places where people lived close together, most lethally in New York City. Just as yellow fever locked down the eighteenth-century seaboard, COVID-19 sowed fear along the corridor. Travel bans took hold. The politics of quarantine divided governors and federal officials. Commuters forsook mass transit and Amtrak ticket cancellations jumped by 300 percent.[7] Megalopolis stopped moving.

Before the pandemic, Amtrak forecast that its revenues would for the first time "break even on a net operating basis."[8] If not technically profitable, Amtrak at least approached a kind of self-sufficiency. When coronavirus trashed the dream of budget neutrality, the railroad instead became an essential service, operating for the public good despite mounting losses at a time when trains resembled what journalist Dan Berry called "ghost ships, their interior lights illuminating absence."[9]

The pandemic sidelined Acela. It also suspended the 2020 Acela primaries. When Connecticut counted its final ballot in August, Joe Biden had won forty-two states and the Democratic nomination. The man who lionized Claiborne Pell and amassed power through Delaware's third-way politics promised a return to normalcy. Biden wagered that the center would hold. Pandora could be reboxed. America could "build back better," a campaign slogan that stripped Trump's construction-speak of its vainglory. After the first debate, Biden rode a "Build Back Better Express" train junket from Cleveland to Johnstown, Pennsylvania, through a swing state heartland the Delawarean hoped to make blue again.

On election night, Americans toggled between vote tallies in Ohio, Michigan, Wisconsin, Florida, Arizona, Georgia, even Omaha—clueless when and which electors would assign victory. The race came home to Pennsylvania five days later as canvassers counted ballots inside Philadelphia's convention center—a facility built out of a former Reading Railroad terminal. On Saturday morning at 11:26 a.m., the Associated Press called Pennsylvania for Biden.[10] In reverting to a solid blue block, the corridor vaulted its most famous patron to the presidency.

As Biden's term approached, everyone expected another storybook send-off from Wilmington Station—until the January 6th insurrection canceled plans for a second inaugural express. Biden flew the seventy-eight miles to Andrews Air Force Base instead. But the president would return to trains on a warm afternoon that April, fifty years to the date that passengers boarded Amtrak's first Clocker. Biden stood before a fleet of engines parked outside Philadelphia's 30th Street Station. The president namechecked local dignitaries like cousins. He called out his old conductor, Gregg Weaver, and joked about sleeping through his stop: "I only did it about four times."[11]

Amtrak's fiftieth birthday gave Biden a chance to draw trains into the zeitgeist. "Imagine what we'd have to do—a single day without the

Northeast Corridor," he asked.[12] "You'd have to add seven new lanes of highway on I-95." The president then announced his American Jobs Plan, an infrastructure blueprint that would, among other things, "modernize the high traffic Northeast Corridor."[13] Surrounded by tracks laid by the Pennsylvania Railroad, beneath wires strung with New Deal subsidy, beside a station owned by Amtrak and served by state-owned transit agencies, Biden described how his $2.2 trillion spending package would launch a new era of public-private cooperation.

The Infrastructure Investment and Jobs Act that passed Congress in November 2021 gave fifty-eight billion dollars to Amtrak and Amtrak projects undertaken in partnership with states, other rail carriers, and the Department of Transportation. This money will address a backlog of corridor projects, including a new tunnel under the Hudson River, modern bridges along Connecticut's Shore Line, and two double-track spans over the Susquehanna River. Amtrak and the state of Maryland will spend four billion dollars to replace the Reconstruction-era shafts that carry corridor trains under Baltimore. Slated for completion in 2032, the Frederick Douglass Tunnel will modernize rail operations while honoring the line's emancipatory past.

These overdue renovations may herald more radical change. In 2021 the Northeast Corridor Commission, a body founded during the Bush presidency to coordinate maintenance costs, published a slick e-booklet titled *Connect 2035*. The PDF proposes building four "infill" stations in the Bronx, installing a climate-resilient power grid, and developing trackside "innovation districts" to incubate business and let riders "live, work, and play all in the same community, without requiring the use of a car."[14] Graphics depict carless and carefree sim people sauntering from trains to condos to cafes across leafy plazas—loving life in a Futurama of transit.

Connect 2035 follows an even more sweeping vision published by the Federal Railroad Administration. *NEC Future* (2015) ponders not just corridor upgrades but the creation of new high-speed spines between New York and Boston. These hypothetical corridors cut across northern Connecticut and under the Long Island Sound, accommodating six times as many trains as Amtrak's existing line.[15]

Nassau, Waterbury, Hartford, and the University of Connecticut receive high-speed service in one version, while the original corridor tracks through Stamford, Bridgeport, and New London become a secondary branch. *NEC Future* has faced heavy backlash. Detractors include businesses in existing corridor communities afraid that new lines will divert traffic and off-corridor residents who want to keep high-speed trains far from their homes.

When the commission sponsored a twenty-three-mile bypass around one of the corridor's knobbiest sections, between Old Saybrook, Connecticut, and Kenyon, Rhode Island, residents raised such an outcry that the detour became a "capacity study." Among those protesting were the Narragansetts, who said that new rails would violate their ancestral lands. The Mashpee Wampanoag called for an archeological survey of one site, the grounds of the Great Swamp Fight. They worried that Amtrak would further desecrate land where English colonists massacred hundreds of Indigenous people in a war that destroyed the Algonquian coalition.[16]

Federal Railroad Administration planners realized that modifying the corridor right-of-way meant digging deep into the region's past. They could not divert the tracks without moving the world around them or airing old wounds buried in the earth.

On the first morning of 2021, New Yorkers entered the mailroom. The Farley sorting office sat for so long behind brass-barred counter windows. Only postal workers knew its belts and ducts, its stamp-gum air, and the flutter of envelopes dropping through chutes. The mailroom now became something else. It transformed—transubstantiated— into a skylit hearth. The floor, eleven acres of Quaker Gray Tennessee marble, shone like a frozen puddle. Walnut benches gleamed in varnish. High-definition departure screens lent sans serif dignity to Ronkonkoma locals. A three-dimensional clock dangled down with the weight of a cast-iron radiator. Escalators treaded away to trains.

Four glass catenary vaults spanned everything. Their panes, thick

at the edges, ever more diaphanous toward their peaks, made in-
verse congruence with the trolley wires strung in the basement. The
glass hopscotched across three gray trusses stout enough to hold up
the Tenderloin sky. After decades under Styrofoam, passengers could
see clouds and the blue between them. On New Year's morning, some
people came by to watch the sun rise in quiet effulgence—welcome
peace after the loudest of years. Masks muffled what needed saying.
Rubber-soled sneakers cheep-chooped over the stone floor.

"Of course it's a nice day," Daniel Patrick Moynihan liked to say.
"It's the only one we've been given."[17] Born in Tulsa, raised in Manhattan, Moynihan polished shoes in the old Penn Station. He entered
City College of New York, then the Navy, then Tufts University, then
the London School of Economics, and, inevitably, politics. Moynihan's famously bipartisan career included stints in the Kennedy,
Johnson, Nixon, and Ford administrations. Senator Moynihan cast
progressive votes against Cold War defense spending, welfare cuts,
and the Defense of Marriage Act. He also railed against universal
healthcare and characterized African American families as a "tangle
of pathology."[18] In 1978 Moynihan sponsored a law to revive Washington's Union Station.[19] In 1991 he agitated for money to repaint the
Hell Gate Bridge.[20]

Late in life Moynihan mused to whomever would listen about
the outsized, underused James Farley Post Office on 8th Avenue.
McKim, Mead & White had designed the limestone sanctum to
complement their adjacent Pennsylvania Station. Farley perched on
pillars over the tracks in what one journalist called a "chunk of space
in the air."[21] The building facade bore the postal creed: "Neither snow
nor rain nor heat nor gloom of night stays these couriers from the
swift completion of their appointed rounds." Why, Moynihan asked,
could this handsome building not become a new Penn Station? It
took thirty years and four master designs before Moynihan Train
Hall welcomed passengers. The senator died seventeen years before
a surgical-masked Andrew Cuomo cut the ribbon.

The glossy hall packed with public art and an upscale food court
heads a reef of Midtown development. Moynihan sits across 9th Av-

enue from Manhattan West, a high-rise project that opened above
the corridor tracks in 2021, complete with skating rink, Whole Foods,
Peloton Shop, and a fiberglass lemon grove. West of Manhattan West
is Hudson Yards, another prefab habitat for the ultra-affluent spun
from the air over trains. Beside Hudson Yards runs the High Line,
a ribbon park fashioned from an abandoned freight railroad through
Chelsea.

Railroads are often the last place left to build in the urban northeast. In Queens, New York's Economic Development Corporation
plans to raise twelve thousand affordable homes on a 180-acre deck
over Sunnyside Yard.[22] In Washington, developers envision a "new
neighborhood" rising above the tracks that buried the old neighborhood, Swampoodle.[23] Named after Union Station's architect,
Burnham Place will "match the quality of the original, historic Union
Station and McMillan Commission urban plan."[24] Philadelphia and
Boston are also building up their corridor rights of way, intending es-
planades and skyscrapers over an increasingly subterranean railroad.

Moynihan Hall promised amends for Penn Station's mutilation
but could dispense only clemency. Most passengers still use the old
Penn Station, squalidly interred beneath Madison Square Garden,
including all New Jersey Transit patrons and the many Amtrak and
Long Island Railroad riders who exit trains in the direction of sub-
ways. Moynihan Hall has too little seating, and the bathrooms are
too far from the concourse. The tracks are buried so deep under the
marble floor that one can barely hear their engine bells over the din
of another Manhattan emporium. *Vice Magazine* journalist Aaron
Gordon called Moynihan an "office building that happens to have a
train hall in it."[25] No one wants to seem dumb for liking it.

And yet Moynihan—privatized, compromised, insufficient—
waved a signal flare of optimism in the gloom of pandemic winter,
extending a stone-wrought vow that people would again convene in
metropolitan palaces to travel between great cities. The Hall dignified
New York even as half its job was to remove people from Manhattan.
Architecture critic Michael Kimmelman wrote that "in the midst of

everything else, we need this. New York needs this."[26] The northeast does too.

Moynihan constituted a kickoff, a commencement, a down payment toward more work on the railroad. Like a switch, the sunny atrium routed past and potential on their respective courses through a region that blooms from the compost of history. Moments into service, Moynihan was already a classic. After two hundred years, the train line was making the northeast again. The corridor was still arriving.

ACKNOWLEDGMENTS

Many people helped me write this book. I could not have asked for a better advocate or editor than Monika Woods, who taught me how to find the plot of nonfiction. I am honored to be among the authors she represents at Triangle House. At the University of Chicago Press, I owe deep gratitude to Tim Mennel, who championed this project and read drafts with assiduous care and bullet train velocity. Tim's colleague, Susannah Engstrom, offered unfailing support through the daunting conversion of .docx into book. Thank you, Brian Chartier, for designing the gorgeous cover; Dennis McClendon, for capturing the corridor in map form; David Luljak, for compiling the index; and Fiona Young-Brown, for fact-checking with thoroughness and speed.

Comments from four anonymous readers improved this book immensely. I also benefited from wonderful nonanonymous readers, including Laura Marris, who shared her gift for summoning places with words, and Evan Kindley, who imparted his sharp sense of what makes narrative tick. My parents, Dave and Lorraine, read the whole manuscript, squaring my book's northeast with the one where they live. My parents-in-law, Henry and Nancy Rowan, supported me through the project's long development. I am delighted that Henry's stunning photograph of the Trenton Transportation Center appears here.

Eileen and Joe Morrell provided a sounding board for some of my earliest Corridor ideas. I so appreciate their enthusiasm, insights, and founding of the Train Lovers United text group. Photographs and recollections shared on the railroad.net message boards and the Amtrak Northeast Corridor Railfans Facebook group always reminded me what I was writing about.

Phil Maciak, Patricia Matthew, and Aaron Hanlon took time to show me how to write for readers beyond academia. I gratefully acknowledge editors who gave my unsolicited submissions a chance: Sarah Mesle at *Avidly*, Brian Rosenwald at the *Washington Post*, and Deborah Chasman at the *Boston Review*. My eighteenth-century writing group—rigorous scholars who are also talented public writers—offered good cheer, intellectual exchange, and searching questions about what and whom our discipline is for. Thank you, Jason Pearl, Stephanie DeGooyer, Rachael King, and Collin Jennings. Finally, thank you to my colleague in field at SUNY-Buffalo, Ruth Mack, for supporting this excursion into histories before and after the 1700s.

Images in *The Northeast Corridor* appear courtesy of the Hagley Library, the University of Connecticut Library, Temple University Libraries, DC History Center, MIT Press, and the Library of Congress. Amtrak allowed me to reproduce the 1970s-era "East" poster. Tom Diffenderfer gave me permission to use the Metroliner poster, and David P. Reaves III provided me with his high-definition image of it. Rosanna Warren let me use four lines from her poem "Northeast Corridor" (you can read the full work in *Raritan: A Quarterly Review* 31, no. 4 [2012]). A United University Professionals Individual Development Award underwrote a timely visit to Delaware's Hagley Library archives in 2022. Thank you to the Hagley librarians for helping me navigate the immense resources there.

I wrote most of this book in a warm and lively Buffalo carriage house. Lucy the locomoting mutt took me for walks when words wouldn't come. My daughter Mira taught herself which whistles go with freights and which belong to Amtrak. She brightens it all. I couldn't do much of anything without Katie, my editor, partner, best friend—my reader first and last. For this and everything else, thank you.

NOTES

INTRODUCTION

1. John McPhee, *The Pine Barrens* (New York: Farrar, Straus and Giroux, 1967), 4.

2. "Inaugural Train Passenger Boarding," C-Span, January 17, 2009, 1:38, https://www.c-span.org/video/?283449-1/inaugural-train-passenger-boarding.

3. Kenneth Bazinet, "Home Sweet Hotel: Obama Family Moves into Adams for Lead-Up to Inauguration," *New York Daily News*, January 1, 2009; Jeff Zeleny, "Obama Arrives in Washington after Train Trip," *New York Times*, January 17, 2009.

4. "Philadelphia Inaugural Train Rally," C-Span, January 17, 2009, 31:18, https://www.c-span.org/video/?283430-1/philadelphia-inaugural-train-rally.

5. Jeanne Meserve and Mike M. Ahlers, "President-Elect's Train Trip Poses Miles of Security Issues," *CNN*, January 9, 2009, http://www.cnn.com/2009/POLITICS/01/09/obama.train/.

6. *Northeast Corridor Annual Report: Operations and Infrastructure; Fiscal Year 2019*, March 2020, 16, http://nec-commission.com/app/uploads/2020/04/NEC-Annual-Report-FY19.pdf.

7. "The Impact of the Northeast Corridor and Amtrak on the Economy," Amtrak, https://blog.amtrak.com/2014/04/necimpact/.

8. *The Importance of the Northeast Corridor: Field Hearing before the Subcommittee on Railroads, Pipelines, and Hazardous Materials of the Committee on Transportation and Infrastructure House of Representatives*, 113th Cong. (2013), https://www.govinfo.gov/content/pkg/CHRG-113hhrg81370/pdf/CHRG-113hhrg81370.pdf.

9. "The Economic Landscape of the Northeast Corridor Region," *Real Transit*, http://realtransit.org/nec6.php.

10. Claiborne Pell, *Megalopolis Unbound: The Supercity and the Transportation of Tomorrow* (New York: Praeger, 1966), 21.

11. Jean Gottmann, *Megalopolis: The Urbanized Northeastern Seaboard of the United States* (Cambridge, MA: MIT Press, 1961), 9.

12. Gottmann, 25.

13. Gottmann, 632; Luca Muscarà, "The Long Road to Megalopolis," *Ekistics* 70, no. 418/419 (January/February–March/April 2003): 27.

14. Richard Florida, "Mega-Regions and High-Speed Rail," *Atlantic*, May 4, 2009,

https://www.theatlantic.com/national/archive/2009/05/mega-regions-and-high
-speed-rail/17006/.

15. In the thirty corridor counties, 13.8 percent of residents take public transit versus
2.5 percent nationally. US Census Bureau, 2021 American Community Survey, "Means of
Transportation to Work by Travel Time," table B08134, https://censusreporter.org/tables
/B08134/.

16. US Census Bureau, 2021 American Community Survey, "Income in the Past Twelve
Months (in 2021 Inflation-Adjusted Dollars)," table S1901, https://data.census.gov/table
/ACSST1Y2021.S1901?q=median+household+income+by+city+2021; "Educational At-
tainment," table S1501, https://data.census.gov/table?q=american+community+survey
+2021+Table+S1501.

17. "Presidential Election Results: Biden Wins," *New York Times*, https://www.nytimes
.com/interactive/2020/11/03/us/elections/results-president.html.

18. "The Sixties: The Years that Shaped a Generation," *PBS*, https://www.pbs.org/opb
/thesixties/topics/politics/legacy.html.

19. Alexander Burns, "Zippy Amtrak Train Gets Tangled in 'the Swamp,'" *New York
Times*, October 2, 2017.

20. F. H. Buckley, *The Way Back: Restoring the Promise of America* (New York: Encounter Books, 2016), 22.

21. J. D. Vance, *Hillbilly Elegy: A Memoir of a Family and Culture in Crisis* (New York:
Harper, 2016), 189.

22. Paul Krugman, "Acelaland versus Mayberry," *New York Times*, June 29, 2013, https://
krugman.blogs.nytimes.com/2013/06/29/acelaland-versus-mayberry/.

23. Joel Garreau, *The Nine Nations of North America* (Boston: Houghton Mifflin,
1981), xiv.

24. Colin Woodward, *American Nations: A History of the Eleven Rival Regional Cultures
of North America* (New York: Penguin, 2004), 4. Geographer Wilbur Zelinsky likewise
snuffed away northeasterness as an "image of territorial reality . . . hovering in the minds
of untutored." Wilbur Zelinsky, "North America's Vernacular Regions," *Annals of the Association of American Geographers* 70, no. 1 (March 1970): 1.

25. Wilmington Inaugural Train Rally. C-Span, January 17, 2009, 30:26, https://www
.c-span.org/video/?283431-1/wilmington-inaugural-train-rally.

26. Mark Leibovich, "Riding the Rails with Amtrak Joe," *New York Times*, September 16,
2008.

27. All speech is transcribed from "Wilmington Inaugural Train Rally."

28. Frederick N. Rasmussen, "Meet Carlyle Smith, the Engineer Who Drove the President's Train," *Baltimore Sun*, February 22, 2009, https://www.baltimoresun.com/news
/bs-xpm-2009-02-22-0902200088-story.html.

29. Joseph Vranich, *Super-Trains: Solutions to America's Transportation Gridlock* (New
York: St. Martin's Press, 1993), 248.

30. William D. Middleton, *When the Steam Railroads Electrified* (Bloomington: Indiana
University Press, 2001), 79.

31. *Importance of the Northeast Corridor*, 9.

32. Travis Humiston, "Dubois Bridge Piers," *Cecil Whig*, December 18, 2021.

33. Frederick Douglass, *The Life and Times of Frederick Douglass* (London: Christian
Age Office, 1882), 168.

14. Daniel Richter, *Facing East from Indian Country: A Native History of Early America* (Cambridge, MA: Harvard University Press, 2001), 6.

15. William Cronon, *Changes in the Land: Indians, Colonists, and the Ecology of New England* (New York: Hill and Wang, 1983), 38, 39.

16. Reginald Pelham Bolton, *Indian Paths in the Great Metropolis* (New York: Museum of the American Indian, 1922), 23.

17. "Journal of Madame Knight," Early Americas Digital Archive, 2003, http://eada .lib.umd.edu/text-entries/journal-of-madam-knight/; *The Journal of Madam Knight* (Boston: Small, Maynard, 1920), 11.

18. Wheaton J. Lane, *From Indian Trail to Iron Horse: Travel and Transportation in New Jersey 1620–1860* (Princeton, NJ: Princeton University Press, 1939), 26.

19. Quoted in Katherine Grandjean, *American Passage: The Communications Frontier in Early New England* (Cambridge, MA: Harvard University Press, 2015), 113.

20. Francis Lovelace, quoted in Eric Jaffe, *The King's Best Highway: The Lost History of the Boston Road, the Route That Made America* (New York: Scribner, 2010), 22.

21. Stephen Jenkins, *Post Road* (New York: G. P. Putnam's Sons, 1913), 13.

22. John F. Hart, "Takings and Compensation in Early America: The Colonial Highway Acts in Social Context," *American Journal of Legal History* 40, no. 3 (1996): 293.

23. Jaffe, *The King's Best Highway*, 14.

24. Benjamin Franklin, *The Autobiography of Benjamin Franklin*, ed. Peter J. Conn (Philadelphia: University of Pennsylvania Press, 2005), 21.

25. Franklin, 21.

26. Franklin, 22.

27. Franklin, 22.

28. Franklin, 22.

29. Letter to Henry Potts, April 23, 1761, Papers of Benjamin Franklin, https://franklin papers.org/framedVolumes.jsp?vol=9&page=302a.

30. Franklin, *Autobiography of Benjamin Franklin*, 23.

31. Franklin, 23.

32. Grandjean, *American Passage*, 5.

33. Letter to John and Sarah Van Brugh Livingston Jay, September 21, 1785. Papers of Benjamin Franklin, https://franklinpapers.org/framedVolumes.jsp?vol=43&page=434.

34. Seymour Dunbar, *A History of Travel in America* (New York: Bobbs-Merrill, 1915), 36.

CHAPTER 2

1. *The Federalist Papers: No. 14*, Avalon Project, Lillian Goldman Law Library, Yale Law School, https://avalon.law.yale.edu/18th_century/fed14.asp.

2. Martha Slotten, "Margaret Graeme Ferguson, a Poet in 'The Athens of North America,'" *Pennsylvania Magazine of History and Biography* 108, no. 3 (July 1984): 268.

3. Richard G. Miller, "The Federal City 1783–1800," in *Philadelphia: A 300-Year History*, ed. Russell F. Weigley (New York: W. W. Norton, 1982), 173.

4. "David Rittenhouse 1732–1796," University Archives and Records Center, Penn Libraries, University of Pennsylvania, https://archives.upenn.edu/exhibits/penn-people /biography/david-rittenhouse/.

5. "Philip Freneau 1752–1832," Poetry Foundation, https://www.poetryfoundation.org/poets/philip-freneau.

6. "Second Inaugural Address of George Washington," Avalon Project, Lillian Goldman Law Library, Yale Law School, https://avalon.law.yale.edu/18th_century/wash2.asp; Miller, "The Federal City," 179.

7. J. H. Powell, *Bring Out Your Dead: The Great Plague of Yellow Fever in Philadelphia in 1793* (Philadelphia: University of Pennsylvania Press, 2014), 1.

8. William Currie, *A Description of the Malignant, Infectious Fever Prevailing at Present in Philadelphia* (Philadelphia: T. Dobson, 1793), 4.

9. Currie, 4.

10. Powell, *Bring Out Your Dead*, 71.

11. Matthew Carey, *A Short Account of the Malignant Fever Lately Prevalent in Philadelphia* (Philadelphia: Matthew Carey, 1793), 37–38.

12. Carey, 47.

13. Powell, *Bring Out Your Dead*, 225.

14. Quoted in Katherine Grandjean, *American Passage: The Communications Frontier in Early New England* (Cambridge, MA: Harvard University Press, 2015), 113.

15. Van Wyck Brooks, *The World of Washington Irving* (New York: E. P. Dutton, 1944), 21.

16. Hugh Finlay, *Journal Kept by Hugh Finlay, Surveyor of the Post Roads on the Continent of North America during His Survey of the Post Offices between Falmouth and Casco Bay* (Brooklyn, NY: Frank H. Norton, 1867), 34.

17. Wheaton J. Lane, *From Indian Trail to Iron Horse: Travel and Transportation in New Jersey 1620–1860* (Princeton, NJ: Princeton University Press, 1939), 81.

18. Tench Coxe, *A View of the United States of America, in a Series of Papers* (Philadelphia: William Hall, 1794), 52.

19. Henry Adams, *History of the United States of America during the First Administration of Thomas Jefferson* (New York: Antiquarian Press, 1962), 1:11.

20. Thomas Jefferson, *Notes on the State of Virginia* (New York: Penguin, 1998), 9, 12.

21. Albert Gallatin, *Report of the Secretary of the Treasury on the Subject of Public Roads and Canals* (Washington, DC: United States Senate, 1808), 65.

22. Gallatin, 8.

23. Colin Woodard, *American Nations: A History of the Eleven Rival Regional Cultures of North America* (New York: Penguin, 2011), 160.

24. Eric Jaffe, *The King's Best Highway: The Lost History of the Boston Road, the Route That Made America* (New York: Scribner, 2010), 90.

25. "Report (1819)," in John C. Calhoun, *The Works of John C. Calhoun* (New York: D. Appleton and, 1855), 5:40.

26. Chet Raymo and Mureen E. Raymo, *Written in Stone: A Geological History of the Northeastern United States* (Chester, CT: Globe Pequot Press, 1989), 155, 217.

27. John Lauritz Larson described the Main Line as an "awkward amphibious network." John Lauritz Larson, *Internal Improvement: National Public Works and the Promise of Popular Government in the Early United States* (Chapel Hill: University of North Carolina Press, 2001), 85.

28. *Youth's Companion*, October 26, 1838.

29. Harriet Cheeney, "The Good Old Days: Traveling Westward in 1838 a Contrast to Luxury of Present Method," *Mutual Magazine*, February 1931, box 1, Robert B. Watson Collection, Hagley Library, Wilmington, Delaware.

30. Cheeney.

31. "The Erie Canal: Celebrating 200 Years of a National Landmark," pamphlet, Office of the New York State Comptroller, https://www.osc.state.ny.us/files/local-government /publications/pdf/erie-canal.pdf.

32. *Life and Works of Washington Irving*, ed. Richard Henry Stoddard (New York: Pollard and Moss, 1880), 833.

33. Stevens's resort entertained generations of northeasterners. In 1846, Hoboken's Elysian Fields hosted the world's first baseball game. "The First Baseball Game," NJ.gov, Official Site of the State of New Jersey, https://www.nj.gov/nj/about/baseball.html#: ~:text=On%20June%2019%2C%201846%2C%20at,23%2D1%20in%20four%20innings.

34. Roy Louis DuBois, "John Stevens: Transportation Pioneer," (PhD diss., New York University, 1974), 321.

35. DuBois, 318.

36. Quoted in M. J. T. Lewis, *Early Wooden Railways* (London: Routledge and Kegan Paul, 1970), 86.

37. Daniel Defoe, *The Complete English Tradesman, in Familiar Letters: Directing Him in All the Several Parts and Progressions of Trade* (London: Charles Rivington, 1726), 29.

38. Gallatin, *Report of the Secretary*, 106.

39. John Stevens, *Documents Tending to Prove the Superior Advantages of Rail-Ways and Steam Carriages over Canal Navigations* (New York: T. and J. Swords, 1812), 31.

40. Stevens, 37. Stevens conceded in a footnote that this "astonishing velocity is considered here as merely possible," though he believed that steam trains could soon reach "forty or fifty miles an hour" (133).

41. DuBois, "John Stevens: Transportation Pioneer," 304.

42. Jaffe, *The King's Best Highway*, 90.

43. Archibald Douglass Turnbull, *John Stevens: An American Record* (New York: Century, 1928), 379.

44. Turnbull, 380.

45. DuBois, "John Stevens: Transportation Pioneer," 322.

46. John G. Davidson, "Fourth of July—Foundation of the Railroad," *Niles' Weekly Register*, July 12, 1828, 316.

47. David Schley, *Steam City: Railroads, Urban Space, and Corporate Capitalism in Nineteenth-Century Baltimore* (Chicago: University of Chicago Press, 2020), 1.

48. James D. Dilts, *The Great Road: The Building of the Baltimore & Ohio, The Nation's First Railroad, 1828–1853* (Stanford, CA: Stanford University Press, 1993), 11.

49. Dilts, 80.

50. Franklin M. Reck, *The Romance of American Transportation* (New York: Thomas Y. Crowell, 1962), 78.

51. *Railroad Journal*, January 7, 1832.

52. George Wilson Pierson, *Tocqueville in America* (Baltimore: Johns Hopkins University Press, 1996), 591.

53. Alexis de Tocqueville, *Democracy in America*, trans. Henry Reeve, ed. Francis Bowen (Cambridge: Sever and Francis, 1863), 1:547.

CHAPTER 3

1. Quoted in John R. Stilgoe, *Metropolitan Corridor: Railroads and the American Scene* (New Haven, CT: Yale University Press, 1983), 250.

2. E. D. Galvin, "The Canton Viaduct," *Railroad History* 129 (Autumn 1973): 73.

3. D. A. Gasparini, K. Nizamiev, and C. Tardini, "G. W. Whistler and the Howe Bridges on the Nikolaev Railway, 1842–1851," *Journal of Performance of Constructed Facilities* 30, no. 3 (June 2016): 5.

4. Daniel T. V. Huntoon, *History of the Town of Canton, Norfolk County, Massachusetts* (Cambridge, MA: John Wilson and Son, 1893), 461.

5. Nathan Hale, *Remarks on the Practicability and Expediency of Establishing a Rail Road on One or More Routes from Boston to the Connecticut River* (Boston: Press of the Boston Daily Advertiser, 1827), 8.

6. Eric Jaffe, *The King's Best Highway: The Lost History of the Boston Road, the Route That Made America* (New York: Scribner, 2010), 112.

7. *Report of the Board of Directors of Internal Improvements of the State of Massachusetts, On the Practicability and Expediency of a Rail-Road from Boston to the Hudson River, and from Boston to Providence. Submitted to the General Court, January 16, 1829* (Boston: Press of the Boston Daily Advertiser, 1829), 75.

8. Hale, *Remarks*, 10, 57. Hale shared his name with his uncle, a Continental Army spy who was interrogated by Niagara incline pioneer John Montresor before his execution.

9. Hale, 4.

10. Hale, 7n.

11. Hale, 68.

12. *Plan of a Survey for the Proposed Boston and Providence Rail-Way by James Hayward, January 1828*, Barry Lawrence Ruderman Map Collection, Stanford University, https://exhibits.stanford.edu/ruderman/catalog/hp087ck4953.

13. Hale, *Remarks*, 74; Galvin, "The Canton Viaduct," 71.

14. Hale, 72.

15. *Providence Journal*, June 6, 1835.

16. Attleboro's Kirk Yard is now the Old Second Parish Church Cemetery.

17. *Railroad Journal*, February 4, 1832.

18. Patricia Tyson Stroud, *The Man Who Had Been King: The American Exile of Napoleon's Brother Joseph* (Philadelphia: University of Pennsylvania Press, 2005), 58.

19. Stroud, *Man Who Had Been King*, 78.

20. Bonaparte v. Camden & A. R., 3 F. Cas. 821 (US Cir. Ct. Dist. N. J., 1830).

21. Nicholas Wood, *A Practical Treatise on Rail-Roads: And Interior Communication in General* (Philadelphia: Carey and Lea, 1832), 445.

22. *Newark Advertiser*, March 8, 1832.

23. *Railroad Journal*, March 24, 1832.

24. George Washington Smith, "Appendix," in Wood, *Practical Treatise on Rail-Roads*, 529.

25. Wheaton J. Lane, *From Indian Trail to Iron Horse: Travel and Transportation in New Jersey 1620–1860* (Princeton, NJ: Princeton University Press, 1939), 288.

26. William Edgar Sackett, *Modern Battles of Trenton* (Trenton, NJ: John L. Murphy, 1895), 18.

27. Leslie E. Freeman Jr., "The New Jersey Railroad and Transportation Company," *Railway and Locomotive Historical Society Bulletin* 88 (May 1953): 110.

28. Quoted in Freeman, 115.

29. Alexander Mackay, *The Western World; or Travels in the United States 1846–47* (Philadelphia: Lea and Blanchard, 1849), 1:84.

30. Charles Lyell, *A Second Visit to the United States of North America*, Vol. 1 (New York: Harper and Brothers, 1849), 191.

31. Christopher T. Baer, *A General Chronology of the Pennsylvania Railroad Company: Its Predecessors and Successors and Its Historical Context, 1831*, Pennsylvania Railroad Technical and Historical Society, 1831, May 2015ed., http://www.prrths.com/newprr_files/Hagley/PRR1831.pdf.

32. "John Bull on Its Anniversary Run, 1981," Smithsonian, https://www.si.edu/object/john-bull-its-anniversary-run-1981%3Asiris_sic_5620.

33. "Gaslight on Cars and Boats," in *Scientific American* 13, no. 51 (August 1858): 405, https://www.scientificamerican.com/article/gaslight-on-cars-and-boats/.

34. Freeman, "The New Jersey Railroad," 127.

35. Freeman, 143.

36. Leo Marx, *The Machine in the Garden: Technology and the Pastoral Ideal in America* (Oxford: Oxford University Press, 2000), 22.

37. Mackay, *The Western World*, 106.

38. Tyrone Power, *Impressions of America* (London: Richard Bentley, 1836), 1:131. Power's great-grandson, Tyrone Edmund Power III, became a Hollywood film star in the 1930s and 1940s.

39. Power, 69.

40. Andrew Bell, *Men and Things in America: Being the Experience of a Year's Residence in the United States* (London: William Smith, 1838), 163.

41. Archibald Prentice, *A Tour in the United States* (London: Charles Gilpin, 1848), 24.

42. John Quincy Adams, *Memoirs of John Quincy Adams*, ed. Charles Francis Adams (Philadelphia: J. B. Lippincott, 1876), 30.

43. Power, *Impressions of America*, 1:131.

44. Power, 132.

45. Cassandra Schumacher, *Cornelius Vanderbilt: Railroad Tycoon* (New York: Cavendish Square, 2020), 41.

46. Adams, *Memoirs*, 31.

47. Power, *Impressions of America*, 1:133.

48. Daniel E. Slotnik, "Napoleon's Brother Lived in N.J.: Here's What Happened to the Estate," *New York Times*, January 31, 2021.

49. *An Act Authorising the Governor to Incorporate the Philadelphia and Trenton Rail Road Company* (Philadelphia, 1836), 21.

50. Joel Schwartz, "'To Every Man's Door': Railroads and Use of the Streets in Jacksonian Philadelphia," *Pennsylvania Magazine of History and Biography* 128, no. 1 (January 2004): 45.

51. Schwartz, 45.

52. Hale, *Remarks*, 57.

53. Charles Dickens, *The Works of Charles Dickens: Letters, Speeches, Plays and Poems*, ed. Frederic G. Kitton (New York: University Society, 1908), 27.

54. Isabella Bird, *The Englishwoman in America* (London: John Murray, 1856), 328.

55. Protest of Railroads, 1839, Getty Images, https://www.gettyimages.com/detail /news-photo/poster-against-the-development-of-railroads-in-philadelphia-news -photo/96823102.

56. Schwartz, "'To Every Man's Door,'" 57.

57. Geoff D. Zylstra, "Struggle over the Streets: Industrialization and the Fight over the Corporate Control of Street Space in Philadelphia, 1830–1860," *Journal of Urban Technology* 20, no. 3 (2013): 9.

58. "Riot on the Kensington Railroad," *Boston Investigator*, August 5, 1840.

59. "The Riot in Kensington," *New York Herald*, July 29, 1840.

60. Schwartz, "'To Every Man's Door,'" 60.

61. "Local Affairs," *North American*, June 22, 1842.

62. William Ferguson, *America by River and Rail; or, Notes by the Way on the New World and Its People* (London: James Nisbet, 1856), 94.

63. British troops built the pontoon during their eight-month occupation of Philadelphia, which began in September 1777. Its construction was overseen by omnipresent military engineer, John Montresor. Richard G. Miller, "The Federal City 1783–1800," in *Philadelphia: A 300-Year History*, ed. Russell F. Weigley (New York: W. W. Norton, 1982), 162.

64. John T. Faris, *Old Roads Out of Philadelphia* (Philadelphia: J. B. Lippincott, 1917), 30.

65. "John Brown: Passage of His Remains Eastward," *New York Times*, December 5, 1859.

66. Judith Giesberg, "The Most Northern of Southern Cities," *New York Times*, May 22, 2011.

67. Joshua Young, "The Funeral of John Brown," *New England Magazine* 30 (1904): 232.

68. James Silk Buckingham, *America, Historical, Statistic, and Descriptive* (London: Fisher, 1841), 1:269.

69. Joseph Sturge, *A Visit to the United States in 1841* (Boston: Dexter S. King, 1842), 95.

70. Mackay, *The Western World*, 101.

71. Mackay, 10. On the northern, pre–Civil War origins of the Jim Crow car, see Steve Luxenberg, "The Jim Crow Car, The North, the South and the Forgotten Origins of Racial Separation," *Washington Post*, February 20, 2019.

72. Frederick Douglass, *My Bondage, My Freedom*, ed. David W. Blight (New Haven, CT: Yale University Press, 2014), 257.

73. Leslie Ray Tucker, "Major General Isaac Ridgeway Trimble, CSA: The Individual and His Community" (PhD diss. Oklahoma State University, 2001), 140.

74. Charles P. Dare, *Philadelphia, Wilmington and Baltimore Rail Road Guide* (Philadelphia: Fitzgibbon and Van Ness, 1856), 59.

75. Scott L. Mingus and Robert L. Williams, *"This Trying Hour": The Philadelphia, Wilmington & Baltimore Railroad in the Civil War* (Scotts Valley, CA: Createspace Independent Publishing Platform, 2017), 29.

76. "Major Brown's Interview with President Lincoln," *New York Times*, April 24, 1861.

77. Dare, *Philadelphia, Wilmington and Baltimore Rail Road Guide*, 3.

78. Abraham Lincoln, "Message to Congress in Special Session," in *The Writings of Abraham Lincoln*, ed. Steven B. Smith (New Haven, CT: Yale University Press, 2012), 340.

79. Dare, *Philadelphia, Wilmington and Baltimore Rail Road Guide*, 43, 44.

80. Quoted in Steven Bernstein, *The Confederacy's Last Northern Offensive: Jubal Early, the Army of the Valley and the Raid on Washington* (Jefferson, NC: McFarland, 2010), 83.

81. Robert Ferguson, *America During and After the War* (London: Longmans, Green, Reader, and Dyer, 1866), 20.

82. Charles Sumner, *Charles Sumner: His Complete Works* (Boston: Lee and Shepard, 1900), 12:106.

83. Sumner, 129.

84. S. M. Felton, *Impolicy of Building another Railroad between Washington and New York* (Philadelphia, 1864).

85. Albert Churella, *The Pennsylvania Railroad*, vol. 1, *Building an Empire* (Philadelphia: University of Pennsylvania Press, 2012), 298.

86. Sumner, *Charles Sumner*, 107.

87. Tucker, "Major General Isaac Ridgeway Trimble," 295.

88. Tucker, 307.

89. Tucker, 310.

90. Tucker, 326, 327.

CHAPTER 4

1. Rosanna Warren, "Northeast Corridor," *Raritan: A Quarterly Review* 31, no. 4 (2012): 152.

2. "Bridgeport Housing Project to Close, a Victim of Crime," *New York Times*, July 9, 1994.

3. Andi Rierden, "The Last Farewell to Father Panik Village," *New York Times*, October 17, 1993.

4. Jack Cavanaugh, "Where Public Housing Meets the American Dream," *New York Times*, March 7, 1999.

5. Lynn Tuohy, "Father Panik Village, Where Dreams Turn to Dust," *Hartford Courant*, August 6, 1994.

6. Carolyn Ivanoff, "East Side Bridgeport: A Cityscape Made by the Great War," Bridgeport History Center, Bridgeport Library, https://bportlibrary.org/hc/business-and-commerce/bridgeport-a-cityscape-made-by-the-great-war/.

7. *Environment Impact Evaluation: Barnum Station Project* (Bridgeport: Connecticut Department of Transportation, 2017), 4–42.

8. P. T. Barnum, *Struggles and Triumphs; or, Forty Years' Recollections* (Buffalo, NY: Warren, Johnson, 1872), 261.

9. *Homes on the Sound for New York Business Men: A Description of the Region Contiguous to the Shore of Long Island Sound, between New York and New Haven* (New York: G. L. Catlin, 1875), 3, 4.

10. *Homes on the Sound for New York Business Men*, 47, 50.

11. *Homes on the Sound for New York Business Men*, 72.

12. Samuel Orcutt, *A History of the Old Town of Stratford and the City of Bridgeport Connecticut*, pt. 1 ([New Haven, CT]: Fairfield County Historical Society, 1886), 844; Barnum, *Struggles and Triumphs*, 357.

13. John L. Weller, *The New Haven Railroad: Its Rise and Fall* (New York: Hastings House, 1969), 35.

14. Robert B. Shaw, "The Great Schuyler Stock Fraud," *Railroad History* 141 (Autumn

1979): 10; Clarence Deming, "The Upbuilding of a Railroad System," *Railroad Gazette* 36, no. 17 (April 29, 1904): 317.

15. Frank Griggs, "Thames River Bridge," *Structure Magazine*, March 2019, https://www.structuremag.org/?p=14253.

16. John Stilgoe, *Metropolitan Corridor: Railroads and the American Scene* (New Haven CT: Yale University Press, 1983), 15.

17. Stilgoe, 13.

18. Barnum, *Struggles and Triumphs*, 653.

19. Barnum, 655.

20. Quoted in Weller, 16.

21. "The New Haven and New England," *Railway Age Gazette* 53, no. 25 (December 1912): 1172.

22. Weller, *The New Haven Railroad*, 41.

23. Vincent C. Carosso, *The Morgans: Private International Bankers, 1854–1913* (Cambridge, MA: Harvard University Press, 1987), 608.

24. Mark Aldrich, "Another Wreck on the New Haven: Accidents, Risk Perception, and the Stigmatization of the New York, New Haven & Hartford Railroad, 1911–1914," *Social Science History* 39, no. 4 (Winter 2015): 624.

25. Historian Mark Aldrich speculates that had "a Midwestern railroad attempted to monopolize Iowa interurbans or experienced a series of bad accidents, one imagines that its actions would have received less play in the eastern news media." Aldrich, "Another Wreck on the New Haven," 616.

26. Weller, *The New Haven Railroad*, 55.

27. 63rd Cong., 2d Sess., SD 543 (1914), 922.

28. "1911 St. Louis Cardinals Schedule," Baseball Reference, https://www.baseball-reference.com/teams/STL/1911-schedule-scores.shtml.

29. "12 Die in Wreck, 47 Injured, On Boston Flier," *New York Times*, July 12, 1911.

30. "12 Die in Wreck."

31. Chronicling America: Historic American Newspapers, National Endowment for·the Humanities, Library of Congress, https://chroniclingamerica.loc.gov/; Louis Brandeis, *Other People's Money and How the Bankers Use It* (New York: Frederick A. Stokes Company, 1913), 132.

32. Christopher Morley, *Christopher Morley's Philadelphia*, ed. Ken Kalfus (New York: Fordham University Press, 2007), 4.

33. Thomas Fitzpatrick, *A Transatlantic Holiday: or, Notes of a Visit to the Eastern States of America* (London: Sampson Low, Marston, 1891), 147.

34. Christopher T. Baer and Craig A. Orr, *A Guide to the Records of the Pennsylvania Railroad Company and the Penn Central Transportation Company* (Wilmington, DE: Hagley Library, 2009), 1:27.

35. The model railroad manufacturer Walthers markets one such PRR "fantasy scheme" on an HO-scale AEM-7 locomotive, an engine that entered service decades after the PRR ceased to exist. See https://www.walthers.com/aem-7-alp-44-electric-standard-dc-master-r-silver-pennsylvania-railroad-4939-fantasy-scheme-silver-red-single-stripe.

36. Ralph Keyes, *The Quote Verifier: Who Said What, Where, and When* (New York: St. Martin's Griffin, 2006), 175.

37. Albert Churella, *The Pennsylvania Railroad*, vol. 1, *Building an Empire, 1846–1917* (Philadelphia: University of Pennsylvania Press, 2012), xiv, 24.

38. Albert Churella, "Cassatt's Career: His Way of Running Pennsylvania Railroad," *American Citizen* (January 4, 1907).

39. "'The Pennsylvania Crowd': Now in the Public Eye," *New York Times*, June 10, 1906.

40. "Steel Rails on the Pennsylvania Railroad," *Iron Age: A Review of the Hardware, Iron and Metal Trades*, August 12, 1875.

41. "The Centennial Grounds Railroad and the Exhibition of Rolling Stock on It," *Railroad Gazette*, August 30, 1875; "Centennial Passenger Traffic of the Pennsylvania Railroad," *Journal of the Franklin Institute*, April 1, 1877.

42. *Official Catalogue of the International Exhibition of 1876*, pt. 1, *Main Building and Annexes* (Philadelphia: John R. Nagle, 1876), 122, 128, 133, 138, 140, 334.

43. A. C. Kalmbach, "The Era of Improvement," *Trains Magazine*, April 1946, 29.

44. "Railroad Hears Protests," *New York Times*, September 7, 1902.

45. "Topics of the Day among Residents of New Jersey," *New York Times*, August 30, 1903.

46. "President Cassatt, Head Officer of the Pennsylvania System, Was Trained from Early Manhood," *American Citizen*, July 21, 1899.

47. Churella, "Cassatt's Career."

48. Arthur E. McFarlane, "The Bottom Rounds of the Ladder," *System: The Magazine of Business* 10 (November 1906), 449.

49. Churella, "Cassatt's Career."

50. "The Pennsylvania Crowd."

51. Fitzpatrick, *A Transatlantic Holiday*, 148.

52. Barnum, *Struggles and Triumphs*, 388.

53. Samuel Orcutt, *A History of the City of Bridgeport, Connecticut* (New Haven: Fairfield County Historical Society, 1887), 392, 388.

54. Barnum, *Struggles and Triumphs*, 388.

55. George C. Waldo, ed., *History of Bridgeport and Vicinity* (New York: S. J. Clarke, 1917), 277.

56. *Republican Farmer*, November 21, 1854.

57. *Bridgeport 2020: A Vision for the Future: The City of Bridgeport, Connecticut, Master Plan of Conservation and Development* (New York: BFJ Planning, 2008), 144.

58. Crescent Crossings, "Apply Now," https://crescentcrossings.com/apply-now/.

59. Crescent Crossings, "Amenities," https://crescentcrossings.com/amenities/.

60. Jordan Grice, "Bridgeport's East Side Train Station Plans Halted," *Connecticut Post*, January 24, 2019.

61. Keila Torres Ocasio, "East Side Train Station, Development Projects Keep Chugging," *Connecticut Post*, December 18, 2016.

CHAPTER 5

1. Edith Wharton, *The Age of Innocence* (New York: Grosset and Dunlap, 1920), 287.

2. "Amtrak Ridership Statistics," Bureau of Transportation Statistics, US Department of Transportation, https://www.bts.dot.gov/browse-statistical-products-and-data/state-transportation-statistics/amtrak-ridership.

3. "Amtrak Offers *Acela Nonstop* Service between Washington, D.C. and New York

City," Amtrak Mediacenter, July 25, 2019, https://media.amtrak.com/2019/07/amtrak-offers-acela-nonstop-service-between-washington-d-c-and-new-york-city/.

4. "Opening of Boston's New South Station," *Boston Herald,* December 31, 1898.

5. David Brussat, *Lost Providence* (Charleston, SC: History Press, 2017), 152.

6. The U.S. Const., I.S8.C17.2.

7. Quoted in Kirk Savage, *Monument Wars; Washington D.C., The National and the Transformation of the Memorial Landscape* (Berkeley: University of California Press, 2011), 26.

8. Tyrone Power, *Impressions of America* (London: Richard Bentley, 1836), 1:129.

9. Charles Lyell, *Travels in North America with Geological Observations on The United States, Canada, and Nova Scotia* (London: John Murray, 1845), 1:128.

10. Henry Adams, *History of the United States of America During the First Administration of Thomas Jefferson* (New York: Antiquarian Press, 1962), 1:30.

11. Savage, *Monument Wars*, 35.

12. Solomon Northrup, *Twelve Years a Slave: Narrative of Solomon Northrup, A Citizen of New York* (London: Sampson Low, 1853), 42.

13. Gladys Baker, Wayne Rasmussen, Vivian Wiser, and Jane Porter, *Century of Service: The First 100 Years of the United States Department of Agriculture* (Washington, DC: US Department of Agriculture, 1963), 16.

14. Therese O'Malley, "'A Public Museum of Trees': Mid-Nineteenth Century Plans for the Mall," in *The Mall in Washington, 1791–1991*, ed. Richard Longstreth (Washington, DC: National Gallery of Art, 1991), 71.

15. Carol Highsmith and Ted Landphair, *Union Station: A History of Washington's Grand Terminal* (New York: Chelsea, 1998), 36.

16. *A Lecture on our National Capital by Frederick Douglass* (Washington, DC: Smithsonian Institution Press, 1978), https://tile.loc.gov/storage-services/service/gdc/lhbcb/02756/02756.pdf.

17. Olson Belanger, "The Railroad in the Park: Washington's Baltimore & Potomac Station, 1872–1907," *Washington History* 2 (Spring 1990): 10.

18. Charles Sumner, "Preservation of the Park at Washington, Remarks in the Senate, May 15, 1872," in *The Works of Charles Sumner* (Boston: Lee and Shepard, 1883), 20:74.

19. Sumner, 20:78.

20. Donald E. Press, "South of the Avenue: From Murder Bay to the Federal Triangle," *Records of the Columbia Historical Society, Washington, D.C.* 51 (1984): 54, 56.

21. "Union Depot," Cong. Globe, 42d Cong. 2d Sess. 1980 (1872).

22. "Ready for the Journey," *New York Times*, September 6, 1881.

23. "Taken from Washington," *New York Times*, September 7, 1881.

24. "The President's Special Train," *New York Times*, September 5, 1881.

25. "The Arrival at Elberon," *New York Times*, September 7, 1881.

26. American Institute of Architects, *Proceedings of the Thirty-Fourth Annual Convention of the American Institute of Architects*, ed. Glenn Brown (Washington, DC: Board of Directors AIA, 1900), 4.

27. American Institute of Architects, 31.

28. *The Improvement of the Park System of the District of Columbia*, ed. Charles Moore (Washington, DC: Government Printing Office, 1902), 12.

29. *Improvement of the Park System*, 12, 14.

30. *Improvement of the Park System*, 16.

31. "To Beautify Washington," *New York Times*, November 13, 1901.

32. "A Sanitary Pilgrimage!," *National Intelligencer*, November 11, 1865.

33. "A Visit to Washington," *Fayetteville Observer*, March 30, 1863.

34. Highsmith and Landphair, *Union Station*, 47.

35. Isabel Wilkerson, *The Warmth of Other Suns: The Epic Story of America's Great Migration* (New York: Vintage, 2010), 11.

36. *Children Playing on the Beach*, 1884; *Little Girl in a Blue Armchair*, 1878; *The Boating Party*, 1893/1894; *Woman with a Red Zinnia*, 1891.

37. "Pennsylvania Railroad: Fast Express Trains," box 1, 71.594.1, T-38, Allen H. Tweddle Collection of Railroadiana, Form 79, Hagley Library, Wilmington, Delaware.

38. "The Maryland Burned: Destruction of the Historic Old Transfer Steamer—No Lives Lost," *New York Times*, December 8, 1888.

39. "It Was a Narrow Escape," *New York Times*, December 9, 1888.

40. Fred Cicetti, "A Phantom Bridge Spans the Hudson at Hoboken," *New York Times*, June 1, 1980.

41. Archibald Douglass Turnbull, *John Stevens: An American Record* (New York: Century, 1928), 222.

42. "Pennsylvania's Tunnel under North River," *New York Times*, December 12, 1901.

43. "Photographs of Hudson River Tunnels," box 1, 71.594.1, T-38, Harry Hipler Collection for Pennsylvania Railroad, Hagley Library, Wilmington, Delaware.

44. "Completion of the Pennsylvania R.R. Extension at New York," *Scientific American*, May 14, 1910, 312.

45. "Completion of the Pennsylvania R.R. Extension at New York," 313.

46. "Bravest of Tunnel Men Dead under East River," *New York Times*, November 17, 1906.

47. "Truck Buried Near Waldorf," *New York Times*, December 15, 1906.

48. "The Pennsylvania Railroad's New York Improvement," *Bankers Magazine* 81 (1910): 698.

49. E. B. White, *Here Is New York* (New York: Little Bookroom, 1999), 28.

50. Linda Elsroad, "Tenderloin," in *Encyclopedia of New York*, ed. Kenneth Jackson (New Haven, CT: Yale University Press, 2010), 1289.

51. "Williams, 'ExCzar' of Tenderloin, Dies," *New York Times*, March 26, 1917.

52. "Race Riot on West Site," *New York Times*, August 16, 1900.

53. "A Disgrace to the Police," *New York Times*, August 17, 1900.

54. "Police in Control in Riotous District," *New York Times*, August 17, 1900.

55. "Deserted Village in Heart of New York," *New York Times*, August 3, 1902.

56. Hilary Ballon, "The First Pennsylvania Station," in *New York's Pennsylvania Stations* (New York: W. W. Norton, 2002), 137.

57. "Houses Set A-Tremble from a Heavy Blast," *New York Times*, November 19, 1904.

58. "Blast Endangers Lives," *New York Times*, December 5, 1905.

59. "Blast Endangers Lives."

60. *The New York Improvements and Extension of the Pennsylvania Railroad* (Philadelphia: [Pennsylvania Railroad], 1910), 19.

61. Langston Hughes, *The Collected Works of Langston Hughes*, vol. 1, *The Poems, 1921–1940*, ed. Arnold Rampersad (Columbia: University of Missouri Press, 2001), 223.

62. Ballon, "The First Pennsylvania Station," 34.

63. Albert J. Churella, *The Pennsylvania Railroad*, vol. 1, *Building an Empire, 1846–1917* (Philadelphia: University of Pennsylvania Press, 2012), 781.

64. *New York Improvements*, 14.

65. "Cover Memo by Joseph Richards," Joseph T. Richards Portfolio of Penn Station Project, Hagley Library, Wilmington, Delaware.

66. Christopher T. Baer, "1907," in *A General Chronology of the Pennsylvania Railroad Company: Its Predecessors and Successors and Its Historical Context, 1907*, Pennsylvania Railroad Technical and Historical Society, March 2005 ed., http://www.prrths.com/newprr _files/Hagley/PRR1907%20Mar%2005.pdf.

67. "Pennsylvania Linen Checkers Adopt a Natty Uniform," *Pullman News*, August 1922, 117.

68. "Pennsylvania Terminal," *Pullman News*, November 1922, 218.

69. Lewis Mumford, *Green Memories: The Story of Geddes Mumford* (New York: Harcourt, Brace, 2008), 13.

70. David D. Morrison, *Sunnyside Yard and Hell Gate Bridge* (Charleston, SC: Arcadia, 2016), 77.

71. Michael Nichols, *Hell Gate: A Nexus of New York City's East River* (Albany: State University of New York Press, 2018), 110.

72. "Blowing Up Flood Rock," *New York Times*, October 4, 1885; "Viewing the Explosion," *New York Times*, October 11, 1885.

73. Frank Griggs, "Thames River Bridge," *Structure Magazine*, https://www.structure mag.org/?p=14253.

74. Churella, *The Pennsylvania Railroad*, 795.

75. *Encyclopedia of the Haudenosaunee (Iroquois Confederacy)*, ed. Bruce Elliot Johansen and Barbara Alice Mann (Westport, CT: Greenwood Press, 2000), 210.

76. David Weitzman, *Skywalkers* (New York: Roaring Brook Press, 2010), 68.

77. Ken Johnstone, "The High-Flying Braves of Caughnawaga," *Macleans*, October 15, 1954.

78. Joseph Mitchell, *Up in the Old Hotel and Other Stories* (New York: Vintage Books, 2008), 279.

79. "Open All-Rail Line Boston to Capital," *New York Times*, April 2, 1917.

CHAPTER 6

1. *Review of Reviews* 2 (July–December 1890): 154.

2. "A Park-and-Ride Station Is Dedicated in Jersey," *New York Times*, November 12, 1971.

3. Joel Garreau, *Edge City: Life on the New Frontier* (New York: First Anchor Books, 1991), 3.

4. John F. Snyder, *Bulletin 67: The Story of New Jersey's Civil Boundaries, 1606–1968* (Trenton, NJ: Bureau of Geology and Topography, 1969), 8; Joseph Berger, "A Place Where Indians, Now New Jerseyans, Thrive," *New York Times*, April 27, 2008.

5. "Edison's Electric Railroad," *New York Herald*, June 11, 1880.

6. Carl W. Condit, "The Pioneer Stage of Railroad Electrification," *Transactions of the American Philosophical Society* 67, no. 7 (1977): 4–5.

7. "Edison's Electric Railway," *Frank Leslie's Illustrated Newspaper*, September 30, 1882.

Edison later scaled back this boast, conceding that at "130 miles an hour wheels of ordinary construction would fly apart by the operation of centrifugal force." "Edison's Electric Railway," *Galveston Daily News*, December 30, 1882.

8. "On Track: Siemens Presents the World's First Electric Railway," Siemens, https://new.siemens.com/global/en/company/about/history/stories/on-track.html.

9. "Memorial of Charles G. Page, Praying an Investigation of a Mode Discovered by Him of Applying Electro-Magnetic Power to Purposes of Navigation and Locomotion," H.R. and S. Doc. no. 30-2. (1849).

10. John J. Greenough, "The First Locomotive That Ever Made a Successful Trip with Galvanic Power," *American Polytechnic Journal* 4 (1854): 259.

11. Robert C. Post, "The Page Locomotive: Federal Sponsorship of Invention in Mid-19th-Century America," *Technology and Culture*, April 1972, 162.

12. T. A. Edison, Electric Locomotive, US Patent 475,491, filed June 30, 1880, and issued May 24, 1892.

13. "The Dead and Injured," *New York Times*, January 9, 1902.

14. "The Dead and Injured."

15. "The Dead and Injured."

16. "An Act to provide for further regulation of the terminals and approaches thereto of the New York and Harlem railroad at and north of Forty-second street in the city of New York," New York, Chapter 425, 1903.

17. Albert J. Churella, *The Pennsylvania Railroad*, vol. 1, *Building an Empire, 1846–1917* (Philadelphia: University of Pennsylvania Press, 2012), 786.

18. "Wm. Murray Dead; Noted Engineer, 68," *New York Times*, January 10, 1942.

19. William S. Murray, *Superpower: Its Genesis and Future* (New York: McGraw Hill, 1925), 1.

20. *National Register of Historic Continuation Sheet: Cos Cob Power Station* (Washington, DC: United States Department of Interior, 1990), sec. 8-2.

21. OED Online, s.v. "catenary, n. and adj.," https://www.oed.com.

22. Letter from Thomas Jefferson to Thomas Paine, December 23, 1788, Founders Online, National Archive, https://founders.archives.gov/documents/Jefferson/01-14-02-0156#TSJN-01-14-0181-fn-0002-ptr.

23. John Ruskin, *Modern Painters* (London: Smith, Elder, 1856), 4:277.

24. Allison Lee Palmer, *A Historical Dictionary of Architecture* (Lanham, MD: Rowman and Littlefield, 2016), 50.

25. "New Haven Electric Railroad," *Scientific American* 97, no. 5 (August 1907).

26. J. W. Swanberg, "Vanishing Triangles," *Railroad History* 182 (Spring 2000): 86.

27. Robert C. Stewart, "Electricity on the High Iron: Cos Cob Powers the New Haven Railroad," *Journal of the Society for Industrial Archeology* 23, no. 1 (1997): 58.

28. "Electrical Service Ready to Stamford," *New York Times*, October 5, 1907.

29. William D. Middleton, *When the Steam Railroads Electrified* (Bloomington: Indiana University Press, 2001), 79.

30. Middleton, 524.

31. Middleton, 79.

32. "Engineers at Odds on New Haven Work," *New York Times*, December 12, 1908.

33. Stewart, "Electricity on the High Iron," 50.

34. "Got 11,000 Volts and Lives," *New York Times*, May 5, 1907.

35. "Danger in New Haven Wires," *New York Times*, June 29, 1907.

36. "Lives after 12,000 Volts," *New York Times*, October 20, 1907.

37. "Engineers at Odds."

38. "Engineers at Odds."

39. Murray, *Superpower*, v.

40. Murray.

41. Murray, 223.

42. Murray, 5.

43. Murray, 41.

44. Murray, 13.

45. Murray, 41.

46. Murray, 44.

47. William J. Hausman and John L. Neufeld, "The Economics of Electricity Networks and the Evolution of the U.S. Electric Utility Industry, 1882–1935," *Business and Economic History On-Line* 2 (2004): 20, 22, https://thebhc.org/sites/default/files/Hausman Neufeld_0.pdf.

48. Michael Bezilla, "Steam Railroad Electrification in America, 1920–1950: The Unrealized Potential," *Public Historian* 4, no. 1 (Winter 1982): 46.

49. "Pennsylvania Railway Plans for Far Future," *New York Times*, November 18, 1928.

50. Michael Bezilla, "Railroad Electrification Strategy," *Business and Economic History* 9 (1980): 143.

51. "Pennsylvania Railway Plans for Far Future."

52. *New York Times*, November 1, 1928.

53. "Pennsylvania Railway Plans for Far Future," *New York Times*, November 18, 1928.

54. "Atterbury Predicts Big Business Year," *New York Times*, March 30, 1929.

55. "Railroads Give Free Wood," *New York Times*, December 17, 1930.

56. "The Pennsylvania Optimistic," *Railway Age* 87 (December 14, 1929): 1395.

57. Michael Bezilla, "The Development of Electric Traction on the Pennsylvania Railroad, 1895–1968," *Pennsylvania History: A Journal of Mid-Atlantic Studies* 46, no. 3 (July 1979): 206.

58. Bezilla.

59. United States Public Works Administration, *America Builds: The Record of the PWA* (Washington, DC: US Government Printing Office, 1939), 7.

60. United States Public Works Administration, 97.

61. United States Public Works Administration, 182, 189.

62. "P.R.R. Will Spend $77,000,000 at Once," *New York Times*, January 31, 1934.

63. "Needs Big Copper Tonnage," *New York Times*, November 5, 1928.

64. "100,000-Ton Order for Steel by P.R.R.," *New York Times*, April 1, 1931.

65. "P.R.R. Electrifying is 50% Completed," *New York Times*, August 19, 1934.

66. *The Pennsylvania Railroad Special Instructions for Employees in Electrified Territory* (1933), Allen H. Tweddle Collection of Railroadiana, box 1, Hagley Library, Wilmington, Delaware.

67. *Railway Age* 98, no. 2 (February 1935): 196.

68. Hampton C. Wayt, "Donald Dohner: The Man Who Designed 'Rivets,'" *Classic Toy Trains*, Summer 2009, 32.

69. Wayt, 31.

70. Wayt, 33.

71. Carroll Gantz, *Founders of American Industrial Design* (Jefferson, NC: McFarland, 2014), 69.

72. Raymond Loewy, *Never Leave Well Enough Alone* (New York: Simon and Schuster, 1951), 43.

73. Loewy, 4.

74. Raymond Loewy, *The Locomotive: Its Esthetics* (London: Studio, 1937).

75. Loewy, *Never Leave Well Enough Alone*, 139.

76. Loewy, 140.

77. Gantz, *Founders of American Industrial Design*, 70.

78. Gantz, 121.

79. Gantz, 69.

80. Michael Beschloss, "The Man Who Gave Air Force One Its Aura," *New York Times*, August 7, 2015.

81. Stewart, "Electricity on the High Iron," 43; "New Cos Cob Burners Ready," *New York Times*, August 5, 1979.

82. Stewart, 58.

CHAPTER 7

1. Albert Einstein, *Relativity: The Special and General Theory* (New York: Henry Holt and Company, 1920), 9.

2. Jim Holt, "Time Bandits: What Were Einstein and *Gödel talking* About?," *New Yorker*, February 20, 2005, https://www.newyorker.com/magazine/2005/02/28/time-bandits-2.

3. Albert Einstein, *The Ultimate Quotable Einstein*, ed. Alice Calaprice (Princeton, NJ: Princeton University Press, 2019), 73, 72.

4. Einstein, 71.

5. April C. Armstrong, "Princeton Junction and Back: Our Dinky," Seeley G. Mudd Manuscript Library blog, September 2, 2015, https://blogs.princeton.edu/mudd/2015/09/princeton-junction-back-our-dinky-archives/.

6. *Fitzgerald: My Lost City: Personal Essays, 1920–1940*, ed. James L. West (Cambridge: Cambridge University Press, 2005), 7.

7. David Walter, "Dinky or Bus?" *New York Times*, May 14, 2010.

8. J. D. Reed, "The Little Train that Can," *New York Times*, March 31, 2002.

9. Anne Margaret Daniel, "Riding the Dinky with John Nash," *Huffpost*, May 27, 2015, https://www.huffpost.com/entry/riding-the-dinky-with-john-nash_b_7440382.

10. *The Collected Papers of Albert Einstein*, vol. 10, *The Berlin Years: Correspondence, May–December 1920, and Supplementary Correspondence, 1909–1920 (English Translation Supplement)*, ed. Diana Kormos Buchwald, Tilman Sauer, Ze'ev Rosenkranz, József Illy, and Virginia Iris Holmes (Princeton, NJ: Princeton University Press, 2010), https://einsteinpapers.press.princeton.edu/vol10-trans/110?highlightText=electric.

11. Mike Frassinelli, "Proposal to Replace Princeton's Longtime 'Dinky' Train with Bus Line Saddens Sentimental Locals," *Star-Ledger*, July 18, 2010.

12. A. C. Kalmbach, "Epoch of Electrification," *Trains Magazine*, April 1946, 41.

13. "Pennsylvania Railroad: I," *Fortune Magazine*, May 1936.

14. "Elegy in a Railroad Station," *Saturday Review*, July 1954, 23.

15. "The New Haven's 'Comet,'" *Railway Age*, April 27, 1935, 633.

16. Peter Lynch, *New Haven Passenger Trains* (St. Paul, MN: MBI, 2005), 66.

17. "World's Fair: Enter the World of Tomorrow," *New York Public Library*, http://exhibitions.nypl.org/biblion/worldsfair/gallery/gallery-aquacade.

18. "1939–40 Railroads on Parade at the New York World's Fair," available at https://www.youtube.com/watch?v=WT8piY6kYNo.

19. John Martin "The Dance: Miscellany," *New York Times*, July 23, 1939.

20. Kurt Weill, "'Iron Horse Opera' Groomed for Fair," *New York Times*, April 16, 1939; Naomi Graber, *Kurt Weill's America* (Oxford: Oxford University Press, 2021), 101.

21. Eastern Railroad Presidents Conference, *Book of the Pageant. Railroads on Parade. New York World's Fair.* (New York: Select Printing, 1939).

22. E. B. White, *Essays of E.B. White* (New York: Harper and Row, 1977), 114.

23. "Marianne Moore, Letters to Hildegarde Watson (1933–1964)," ed. Cyrus Hoy, *University of Rochester Library Bulletin* 29, no. 2 (Summer 1976), https://rbscp.lib.rochester.edu/3572.

24. J. D. Salinger, *The Catcher in the Rye* (New York: Little, Brown, 1951), 60; William Faulkner, *Collected Stories of William Faulkner* (New York: Random House, 1950), 609; F. Scott Fitzgerald, *The Great Gatsby*, ed. Guy Reynolds (Hertfordshire: Wordsworth Limited Editions, 1993), 26.

25. Harry Warren and Mack Gordon, "Chattanooga Choo Choo," Sony/ATV Music Publishing, 1941.

26. Ron Cowen, "George Gershwin: He Got Rhythm," *Washington Post*, November 11, 1998.

27. "$35,000 Fund Asked for Czech Pavilion," *New York Times*, April 26, 1939.

28. Roosevelt first used this phrase in a 1943 address to Congress. "Arsenal of Democracy," *New York Times*, May 30, 1943.

29. Carl Landeck and Roger Thorne, "The Pennsylvania Railroad during World War II," *Tredyffrin Easttown Historical Society Historical Quarterly* 42, no. 2 (Spring 2005): 36.

30. Bradley Flamm, "Putting the Brakes on 'Non-Essential' Travel: 1940s Wartime Mobility, Prosperity, and the US Office of Defense," *Journal of Transportation History* 27, no. 1 (March 2006): 71.

31. Quoted in Thorne, "Pennsylvania Railroad," 41.

32. Thomas Guiler and Lee N. Penyak, "Braceros and Bureaucracy: Mexican Guest Workers on the Delaware, Lackawanna and Western Railroad during the 1940s," *Pennsylvania History: A Journal of Mid-Atlantic Studies* 76 (2009): 427, 429.

33. Guiler and Penyak, 429.

34. Theodore Kornweibel, *Railroads in the African American Experience: A Photographic Journey* (Baltimore: Johns Hopkins University Press, 2010), 55.

35. "P.R.R. Jobs for Negroes," *New York Times*, April 6, 1944.

36. "Women are Doing a Big Job on the Pennsylvania Railroad," *Life Magazine*, September 25, 1944.

37. Michael Nash, "Women and the Pennsylvania Railroad: The World War II Years." *Labor History* 30, no. 4 (February 1989): 614.

38. Ruth Hilger Hoffman, "The Molly Pitcher Poster, WW II Pennsylvania Railroad: The Real 'Molly Pitcher' Ruth Hilger Hoffman," available at https://www.youtube.com/watch?v=nYosnNaGalE.

39. Von Eike Frenzel, "Operation Pastorius: Hitler's Unfulfilled Dream of a New

York in Flames," *Der Spiegel*, September 16, 2010, https://www.spiegel.de/international /zeitgeist/operation-pastorius-hitler-s-unfulfilled-dream-of-a-new-york-in-flames-a -716753.html.

40. Richard Goldstein, "John Cullen, Coast Guardsman Who Detected Spies, Dies at 90," *New York Times*, September 2, 2011.

41. William Thiesen, "Jack Cullen, Nazi Spies and the Founding of the USCG Beach Patrol," *Maritime Executive*, September 16, 2019, https://maritime-executive.com/features /jack-cullen-nazi-spies-and-founding-of-the-uscg-beach-patrol-8.

42. Thiesen.

43. George John Dasch, *The Eight Spies Against America* (Chicago: Eumenes 2019).

44. *Transcript of Proceedings before the Military Commission to Try Persons Charged with Offenses against the Law of War and the Articles of War, Washington D.C., July 8 to July 31, 1942*, ed. Joel Samaha, Sam Root, and Paul Sexton (Minneapolis: University of Minnesota, 2004), http://www.soc.umn.edu/~samaha/nazi_saboteurs/nazi08.htm.

45. Andy Newman, "Terrorists among Us (1942): Detecting the Enemy Wasn't Easy Then, Either," *New York Times*, January 17, 2002.

46. *Transcript of Proceedings*; Newman, "Terrorists among Us."

47. Brian M. Harward, *Presidential Power: Documents Decoded* (Santa Barbara, CA: ABC-Clio, 2016), 133.

48. *Transcript of Proceedings*.

49. Von Eike Frenzel, "Operation Pastorius."

50. *New York Times*, June 17, 1942.

51. Von Eike Frenzel, "Operation Pastorius."

52. "Reviews Wars Pace," *New York Times*, September 8, 1943.

53. Frederick N. Rasmussen, "Labor Day Train Wreck among Worst," *Baltimore Sun*, September 1, 2001, https://www.baltimoresun.com/news/bs-xpm-2001-09-01-010901 0077-story.html.

54. "Survivors of Wreck Tell How Servicemen Helped," *New York Times*, September 7, 1943.

55. Rasmussen, "Labor Day Train Wreck."

56. Frank S. Adams, "More than 50 Are Killed in Wreck," *New York Times*, September 7, 1943.

57. Investigation no. 2726, "The Pennsylvania Railroad Company Report in Re Accident at Shore, PA, on September 6, 1943," Washington, DC.

58. "Pennsylvania Railroad Company Report," 8.

59. "Toll in 2 Wrecks Rises to 81 Dead," *New York Times*, September 8, 1943.

60. "Railroads and the National Defense," Association of American Railroads, available at https://www.youtube.com/watch?v=EbnCrTSSvbo.

61. Thornton Wilder, "The Happy Journey to Trenton and Camden," in *The Collected Short Plays of Thornton Wilder* (New York: Theater Communications Group, 1997), 1:97.

62. "The Bus Terminal Ready," *New York Times*, December 14, 1950.

63. "PRR's 232nd Dividend," *Pennsy Magazine*, January 1953.

64. "The Pennsylvania Railroad A.D. 205 Manual of Instructions Issued by the Accounting Department to Passenger Conductors, Ticket Collectors, and Train Baggagemen," Allen H. Tweddle Collection of Railroadiana, box 1, Hagley Library, Wilmington, Delaware.

65. "Pennsylvania Railroad A.D. 205 Manual of Instructions."

66. "Main Line Clear After Mishap," *New York Times*, January 15, 1953.

67. "Train Kills Musician," *New York Times*, January 15, 1953.

68. Carol Highsmith and Ted Landphair, *Union Station: A History of Washington's Grand Terminal* (New York: Chelsea, 1998), 84.

69. "Trains of Tomorrow Now," *Pennsy Magazine*, June 1952, 13.

70. *Union Station Train Accident: Hearing before the Committee on Interstate and Foreign Commerce*, United States Senate, 83rd Cong. 4 (1953).

71. Fred Rasmussen, "Runaway Train Crashed in D.C.," *Baltimore Sun*, January 26, 1997.

72. *Union Station Train Accident*, 19.

73. *Union Station Train Accident*; "Train Rams Station in D.C.: 18 from Baltimore Injured," *Evening Sun*, January 15, 1953.

74. "Station at Princeton Junction Burns, Victim of Hungry, Pyromaniacal Mice," *New York Times*, December 27, 1953.

75. "Station at Princeton Junction Burns."

76. "Station at Princeton Junction Burns."

77. "Station at Princeton Junction Burns."

78. "Station at Princeton Junction Burns."

CHAPTER 8

1. "The Bigger They Are . . . ," *New York Times*, November 19, 1972.

2. "Mercury Hits 65.7: Record for Date," *New York Times*, December 8, 1951.

3. Lawrence Lader, "Birth of a City," *Reader's Digest*, December 1951, 74.

4. "The Rancher," flyer, Levitt and Sons, 1952.

5. Dianne Harris, "'The House I Live In': Architecture, Modernism, and Identity in Levittown," in *Second Suburb: Levittown, Pennsylvania*, ed. Dianne Harris (Pittsburgh, PA: University of Pittsburgh Press, 2010), 155.

6. Lewis Mumford, *The City in History: Its Origins, Its Transformations, and Its Prospects* (New York: Harcourt, Brace and World, 1961), 494; Penn Kimball, "'Dream Town'—Large Economy Size: Pennsylvania's New Levittown Is Pre-planned Down to the Last Thousand Living Rooms," *New York Times*, December 14, 1952; Lewis Mumford quoted in Curtis Miner, "Pink Kitchens for Little Boxes: The Evolution of 1950s Kitchen Design in Levittown," in Harris, *Second Suburb*, 256.

7. Kimball, "'Dream Town.'"

8. Richard Longstreth, "The Levitts: Mass-Produced Houses and Community Planning in the Mid-Twentieth Century," in *Second Suburb: Levittown, Pennsylvania*, ed. Dianne Harris (Pittsburgh, PA: University of Pittsburgh Press, 2010), 155.

9. Kenneth Jackson, *Crabgrass Frontier: The Suburbanization of the United States* (New York: Oxford University Press, 1985), 4.

10. Lader, "Birth of a City," 75; Longstreth, "The Levitts," 134.

11. Jerry Jonas, "60 Years Later, the Levittown Shame that Still Lingers," *The Intelligencer*, August 12, 2017.

12. *The Saturday Evening Post*, vol. 227 (Evanston, IL: Northwestern University Press, 2011), 27.

13. "The March of Time," Getty Images, January 1, 1953, https://www.gettyimages.com

/detail/video/construction-sign-for-railroad-station-parking-for-1000-news-footage/5 12761465?adppopup=true.

14. Levittown Station History, sign, Levittown Station, Levittown, Pennsylvania.

15. "Levittown New Train Schedule Effective April 27," *Bristol Daily Courier*, April 15, 1953.

16. John Stilgoe, *Metropolitan Corridor: Railroads and the American Scene* (New Haven, CT: Yale University Press, 1983), 3.

17. "Levittown: Building the Suburban Dream," State Museum of Pennsylvania (2003), http://statemuseumpa.org/levittown/one/b.html.

18. "10 Hurt: P.R.R. Engine Breaks Down under Hudson," *New York Times*, October 3, 1952.

19. "Penn Station Bomb Blast Is Ignored by Commuters," *New York Times*, January 12, 1955; "None Hurt by Blast in a Station Locker," *New York Times*, March 9, 1955.

20. "2 Connecticut Workers Fined in Highway Blast," *New York Times*, October 6, 1956.

21. "Bomb Fells Man at Penn Station," *New York Times*, February 22, 1956; "Confession Pleases a Penn Station Porter Incapacitated for 11 Months by Explosion," *New York Times*, January 23, 1957.

22. "Iceberg Spotted off Jersey," *New York Times*, February 17, 1958.

23. Wayne Phillips, "Trains in Region Cut Back Sharply," *New York Times*, February 19, 1958.

24. Phillips, "Trains in Region."

25. Christopher Morley, *Christopher Morley's Philadelphia*, ed. Ken Kalfus (New York: Fordham University Press, 2007), 134.

26. "Pennsylvania Railroad Eastern Region, Philadelphia Terminal Division, Closing Broad Street Station, Information and Instructions for Employees, Incident to Abandonment of Broad Street Station," Robert B. Watson Collection, box I, Hagley Library, Wilmington, Delaware.

27. "Old Broad Street: Pennsylvania's Famous Station, in Last Days as in First, Figures in New Progress of Railroad," *The Pennsy*, June 1952, 4.

28. Quoted in Gregory L. Heller, *Ed Bacon: Planning, Politics, and the Building of Modern Philadelphia* (Philadelphia: University of Pennsylvania Press, 2013), 98.

29. Kevin Patrick, "Modernizing Center City: Philadelphia's Penn Center," *Pennsylvania Heritage*, Fall 2015.

30. "Last of Big Terminals," *New York Times*, February 16, 1912.

31. David W. Dunlap, "The Disappearance of Pennsylvania Station," *New Yorker*, June 7, 1958, 109.

32. Dunlap, 108.

33. William Taubman, *Khrushchev: The Man and His Era* (New York: W. W. Norton, 2003), 476.

34. "Zeckendorf Maps New Penn Station," *New York Times*, November 30, 1954; "Billy Rose Planning a 'Permanent Fair,'" *New York Times*, January 15, 1955.

35. Architects imagined 34th Street as the site of a World Trade Center and Freedom Tower decades before Minoru Yamasaki's twin towers ascended over the Battery. Paul Crowell, "'Palace' Plan Out: Bigger One Urged," *New York Times*, January 6, 1956.

36. Peter Kihss, "'Palace' Is Slated for Penn Station," *New York Times*, June 8, 1955.

37. "Racing of Every Kind: Madison-Square Garden Turned into a Hippodrome," *New York Times*, April 7, 1885.

38. Donal Henahan, "Hope Tops Card at Garden No. 4," *New York Times*, February 12, 1968; Mary Connelly and Alan Finder, "The Region; A Whiff of History," *New York Times*, December 1, 1985.

39. Foster Hailey, "Architects Fight Penn Station Plan," *New York Times*, August 3, 1962.

40. "Downtown Is for People," in *The Exploding Metropolis*, ed. William H. White (Berkeley: University of California Press, 1993), 165.

41. "Future of Penn Station," *New York Times*, May 17, 1962.

42. Foster Hailey, "Battle over Future of Penn Station Continues," *New York Times*, September 23, 1962.

43. "Redeveloping Penn Station," *New York Times*, August 23, 1962.

44. "End of a Landmark: The Demolition of Old Penn Station," *New York Daily News*, August 14, 2017.

45. Quoted in David W. Dunlap, "Longing for the Old Penn Station? In the End, It Wasn't So Great," *New York Times*, December 30, 2015.

46. *Hearing Held before National Transportation Policy Committee on Interstate and Foreign Commerce*, 86th Cong. 18 (1960).

47. *Hearing Held before National Transportation Policy Committee.*

48. "1962 Boston to New York New Haven Schedule," Allen H. Tweddle Collection of Railroadiana, box 9, Hagley Library, Wilmington, Delaware.

49. "South Station in Boston Sold," *New York Times*, August 13, 1965.

50. "Boston South Station Complex Is Getting More Attention," *New York Times*, May 1, 1966.

51. "Opening of Boston's New South Station," *Boston Herald*, December 31, 1898.

52. "Urban Plan Dooms Boston Rail Depot," *New York Times*, September 3, 1972.

53. Blaine Harden, "Union Station: Washington's Colossal Mess," *Washington Post*, November 16, 1980.

54. "Visitors' Center in Capital Urged," *New York Times*, September 17, 1967.

55. Steven Rattner, "Now Washington Wants Its Station Back," *New York Times*, May 8, 1978.

56. Harden, "Union Station."

57. Harden.

58. Campbell Gibson, "Population of the 100 Largest Cities and Other Urban Places in the United States: 1790 to 1990" (June 1998), https://www.census.gov/library/working-papers/1998/demo/POP-twps0027.html. The actual population table is available at https://www2.census.gov/library/working-papers/1998/demographics/pop-twps0027/tab14.txt.

59. "Poor Railroads, Poor Passengers," *New Republic*, June 1961.

60. David Bevan, "Financing Our Progress," *The Pennsy*, April 1953, n.p.

61. "Supreme Court Says Yes: Merger!," *The Pennsy*, February 1, 1968, 1.

62. Joseph R. Daughen and Peter Binzen, *The Wreck of the Penn Central* (Washington, DC: Beard Books, 1971), 206.

63. Rush Loving, *The Men Who Loved Trains: The Story of Men Who Battled Greed to Save an Ailing Industry* (Bloomington: Indiana University Press, 2006), 55.

64. "Supreme Court Says Yes: Merger!," 1.

65. "Supreme Court Says Yes: Merger!," 1.

66. John F. Stover, *American Railroads* (Chicago: University of Chicago Press, 1997), 234.

67. George Drury, *The Historical Guide to North American Railroads: Histories, Figures, and Features of More Than 160 Railroads Abandoned or Merged since 1930* (Waukesha, WI: Kalmbach, 1994), 215.

68. Richard Saunders, *Main Lines: Rebirth of the North American Railroads, 1970–2002* (Dekalb: Northern Illinois University Press, 2003), 6.

69. Christopher T. Baer, *A General Chronology of the Pennsylvania Railroad Company: Its Predecessors and Successors and Its Historical Context, 1968*, Pennsylvania Railroad Technical and Historical Society, April 2015 ed., http://www.prrths.com/newprr_files/Hagley/PRR1968.pdf.

70. Christian Wolmar, *The Great Railroad Revolution: The History of Trains in America* (New York: Hachette, 2012), 337.

71. Wolmar.

72. "Atterbury Says: Give Public What It Wants," *Railway Age* 86, no. 26 (May 25, 1929).

73. Saunders, *Main Lines*, 12.

74. "Call Us Penn Central," promotional film (1968), available at https://www.youtube.com/watch?v=EKcJIPpjhog.

75. "Bob Hope Show Opening of the Garden (2/12/68)," available at https://www.youtube.com/watch?v=BgRsTd2cpoc&t=385s.

76. Henahan, "Hope Tops Card at Garden No. 4."

77. "Penn Station Columns Dumped in Jersey," *New York Times*, October 9, 1964.

78. "Penn Station Columns Dumped in Jersey."

CHAPTER 9

1. "Pell's Statement on Northeast Rail Agency," *New York Times*, May 21, 1962.

2. Ernest Meyer, *Map of Elizabeth Town, N.J. at the Time of the Revolutionary War, 1775–1783* (New York: J. Schedler, 1879), Library of Congress, https://www.loc.gov/resource/g3814e.la002339/?r=0.323,0.145,0.763,0.341,0.

3. Andrew C. Zeek, "Tullytown, Pennsylvania, June 8, 1960," Super 8 film, San Francisco Museum of Modern Art, https://www.sfmoma.org/watch/andrew-c-zeek-tullytown-pennsylvania/.

4. Russell Baker, "They Line the Tracks to Say Goodbye," *New York Times*, June 9, 1968.

5. Alan Taylor, "A Portrait of America: Watching Robert F. Kennedy's Funeral Train Pass By," *Atlantic*, June 7, 2018, https://www.theatlantic.com/photo/2018/06/rfks-funeral-train-in-photos/562238/.

6. "Robert Kennedy, Shot and Killed in Los Angeles," *Newsweek*, June 16, 1968, https://www.newsweek.com/robert-kennedy-shot-killed-los-angeles-207078.

7. Edward C. Burks, "City-Bound Train Kills 2 Mourners," *New York Times*, June 9, 1968.

8. "2 Railroads Try Plastic Windows," *New York Times*, February 14, 1971.

9. Miloš Perović, "An Interview with Jean Gottmann on Urban Geography," *Ekistics* 420/421 (May/June–July/August 2003): 143.

10. Nick Kirkpatrick and Katie Mettler, "Reflecting on RFK's 200-mile Funeral Train," *Washington Post*, June 1, 2018.

11. Lyndon B. Johnson, "Remarks at the University of Michigan" transcript of speech delivered at the University of Michigan, May 22, 1964, American Presidency Project, University of California, Santa Barbara, https://www.presidency.ucsb.edu/documents/remarks-the-university-michigan.

12. Lyndon B. Johnson, "Remarks in Athens at Ohio University," transcript of speech delivered at the Ohio University, May 7, 1964, American Presidency Project, University of California, Santa Barbara, https://www.presidency.ucsb.edu/documents/remarks-athens-ohio-university.

13. Lyndon B. Johnson, "Remarks upon Signing the Urban Mass Transportation Act," transcript of speech delivered at the White House, July 9, 1964, American Presidency Project, University of California, Santa Barbara, https://www.presidency.ucsb.edu/documents/remarks-upon-signing-the-urban-mass-transportation-act.

14. Johnson, "Remarks upon Signing the Urban Mass Transportation Act."

15. Lyndon B. Johnson, "Remarks at the Signing of the High-Speed Ground Transportation Act," transcript of speech delivered at the White House, September 30, 1965, American Presidency Project, University of California, Santa Barbara, https://www.presidency.ucsb.edu/documents/remarks-the-signing-the-high-speed-ground-transportation-act.

16. "While at the Fair, see the Long Island Exhibit by the Long Island Railroad," brochure, http://www.trainsarefun.com/lirr/lirrworldfair/Worlds-Fair_LIRR-exhibit-map_BradPhillips.jpg.

17. Robert Caro, *The Power Broker: Robert Moses and the Fall of New York* (New York: Alfred A. Knopf, 2012), 903.

18. Caro, 899.

19. See *The Bank and Japan's Bullet Trains*, World Bank Group Archives Exhibit Series no. 009, World Bank Group, 2016, https://documents1.worldbank.org/curated/en/120191468195565266/pdf/104633-WP-PUBLIC-2003-02-The-Bank-and-Japans-Bullet-Trains.pdf.

20. J. A. Early, "2731—Amtrak—Reports on Observations of Japanese Nat'l RR (4/5/78)," Amtrak Corridor Improvement Project Records, box 4, Hagley Library, Wilmington, Delaware.

21. Wayne Miller, *An Uncommon Man: The Life and Times of Senator Claiborne Pell* (Hanover, NH: University Press of New England, 2011), 195.

22. Miller, 5.

23. Sara K. Smith, "None," *Wonkette*, January 1, 2009, https://www.wonkette.com/405223.

24. "Who Will Save the New Haven?," *Nation*, February 22, 1965.

25. Claiborne Pell, *Megalopolis Unbound: The Supercity and the Transportation of Tomorrow* (New York: Praeger, 1966), 10.

26. Miller, *An Uncommon Man*, 133.

27. "Pell's Statement on Northeast Rail Agency," *New York Times*, May 21, 1962.

28. Pell, *Megalopolis Unbound*, 16.

29. Pell, 33.

30. Pell, 164.

31. John F. Kennedy, "Letter to Senator Pell Concerning Interurban Transportation between Eastern Seaboard Cities," October 15, 1962, American Presidency Project, University of California, Santa Barbara, https://www.presidency.ucsb.edu/documents/letter-senator-pell-concerning-interurban-transportation-between-eastern-seaboard-cities.

32. Pell, *Megalopolis Unbound*, 185.

33. "891-Pell Committees Study-New York to Washington Improvements," 1964, Klauder: Metroliner and Turboliner, box 1, Hagley Library, Wilmington, Delaware.

34. Colin Leach argues that officials were less inclined to sponsor a "comprehensive rebuilding of underlying infrastructure" than to pursue "technologically advanced trains as a panacea for the Northeast's problems." Colin Leach, "Waiting for Supertrain: Trains, Technocracy, and the Great Society" (MA thesis, University of Maryland, 2014), 74.

35. Johnson, "Remarks at the Signing of the High-Speed Ground Transportation Act."

36. Johnson.

37. Johnson.

38. Letter from K. Kunimatsu, Japanese National Railways 1-1 Marunouchi Tokyo, Japan on April 22, 1964, to Louis T. Klauder, Klauder: Metroliner and Turboliner, box 1, Hagley Library, Wilmington, Delaware.

39. Philip H. Dougherty, "Pennsy Prepares for Speed Trains," *New York Times*, August 11, 1966.

40. *The Jet Train Is Here*, National Educational Television and Radio Center, December 17, 1967, https://americanarchive.org/catalog/cpb-aacip_512-gm81j98705.

41. "Sikorsky Turbo Train," Sikorsky Product History, Igor I. Sikorsky Historical Archives, https://sikorskyarchives.com/home/sikorsky-product-history/surface-vehicles/sikorsky-turbo-train/.

42. In 1966 a railcar strapped to rocket boosters reached 183 miles per hour on a stretch of New York Central track in Ohio. The experiment, widely seen as a publicity stunt, was never intended to develop operational service, https://www.hsrail.org/blog/worlds-fastest-trains/.

43. "Turbo Train's First Birthday," *Penn Central Post*, May 1970, 9.

44. Letter from Klauder to Mr. Clifford Gannet, November 27, 1968, Klauder: Metroliner and Turboliner, box 1, Hagley Library, Wilmington, Delaware.

45. Christopher Lydon, "The Turbotrain: A Study in Incongruities," *New York Times*, January 31, 1971.

46. Lydon.

47. Amtrak would toy with turbine power for decades. The National Railroad Passenger Corporation purchased new turbos from the French company, ANF, and then another batch from Rohr Industries, for use on its Hudson Valley line before abandoning the technology entirely in 2005.

48. Christopher T. Baer, *A General Chronology of the Pennsylvania Railroad Company: Its Predecessors and Successors and Its Historical Context: 1967*, Pennsylvania Railroad Technical and Historical Society, April 2015 ed., http://www.prrths.com/newprr_files/Hagley/PRR1967.pdf.

49. "America Greets the Metroliner," *Penn Central Post*, March 1969, 2.

50. "Suction of New Train Pulls Out 7 Windows," *New York Times*, January 23, 1969.

51. "Notes for and Record of Phone Conversation from Bob Smith," Klauder: Metroliner and Turboliner, box 1, Hagley Library, Wilmington, Delaware.

52. "Test-Run Westinghouse Cars 801 (South) and 807 (North), July 7, 1969," Klauder: Metroliner and Turboliner, box 1, Hagley Library, Wilmington, Delaware.

53. "America Greets the Metroliner," 1.

54. "America Greets the Metroliner," 1.

55. "America Greets the Metroliner," 1.

56. "In the Nation: Too Late the Metroliner," *New York Times*, February 6, 1969.

57. "Penn Central Railroad Employees Go to School," *Training and Development School*, August 1969, 59.

58. "Amtrak's Metroliner Service," *Amtrak News*, September 1, 1974, 8.

59. Richard Witkin, "High-Speed Train Starts Run Today," *New York Times*, January 16, 1969.

60. Robert Lindsey, "Mechanical Bugs Still Plague Metroliners after Year in Service," *New York Times*, January 16, 1970.

61. Edad Mercier, "'No Med School!' Black Resistance to the New Jersey College of Medicine and Dentistry (NJCMD) Urban Renewal Proposal, between 1960 and 1970," *Journal of Ethnic and Cultural Studies* 7, no. 3 (December 2020): 51.

62. Mercier, "'No Med School!'"

63. Amiri Baraka, "The Practice of New Nationalism" (typescript), 39–40, https://www.freedomarchives.org/Documents/Finder/Black%20Liberation%20Disk/Black%20Power!/SugahData/Essays/Baraka3.S.pdf.

64. Amiri Baraka, *The Autobiography of Leroi Jones* (Chicago: Lawrence Hill Books, 1997), 18.

65. Cong. Rec., H10246 (daily ed. April 24, 1969) (statement of Mr. Podell), https://www.govinfo.gov/content/pkg/GPO-CRECB-1969-pt8/pdf/GPO-CRECB-1969-pt8-3.pdf.

66. Don Phillips, "Amtrak's New Train: So Far, So Good," *Trains Magazine* 59, no. 1 (November 1999).

CHAPTER 10

1. "Rail Passenger Service Act of 1970," Amtrak: A History of America's Railroad, https://history.amtrak.com/archives/rail-passenger-service-act-of-1970.

2. Joseph R. Daughen and Peter Binzen, *The Wreck of the Penn Central* (Washington, DC: Beard Books, 1971), 131–32. In 1967 the US Postal Service began shipping priority mail by jet, depriving railroads of revenues that sometimes allowed passenger trains with mail cars to break even. Richard Saunders, *Main Lines: Rebirth of the North American Railroads, 1970–2002* (Dekalb: Northern Illinois University Press, 2003), 54.

3. Daughen and Binzen, *Wreck of the Penn Central*, 131.

4. Robert Bedingfield, "Penn Central Seeks to Abandon N.Y.–Chicago Passengers Runs," *New York Times*, March 5, 1970.

5. Geoffrey H. Doughty, Jeffrey T. Darbee, and Eugene E. Harmon, *Amtrak: America's Railroad; Transportation's Orphan and Its Struggle for Survival* (Bloomington: Indiana University Press, 2021), 36.

6. Claiborne Pell, "Who Will Save the New Haven?," *The Nation* (February 22, 1965), 186.

7. S. Comm. on Commerce, *National Transportation Policy: Report of the Committee on Commerce*, S. Rep. No. 87-445, 31 (1961).

8. Richard Nixon, *RN: The Memoirs of Richard Nixon* (New York: Simon and Schuster, 2013), 1913.

9. National Rail Transportation Act 1970, Pub L. No 91-518.

10. National Rail Transportation Act 1970, 1329. NARP president Anthony Haswell initially commended the law as a crucial step toward "rescuing the passenger train." Christopher Lydon, "Senate Unit Backs Subsidy for Rails," *New York Times*, March 13, 1970.

11. Rush Loving, "Amtrak's Creation Story: A Nitty-Gritty Narrative about the Origins of the National Passenger Railroad Corp," *Trains Magazine* (April 30, 2021).

12. Robert Lindsey, "Railpax Plans Innovations to Win Back Passengers," *New York Times*, April 11, 1971.

13. Steven A. Morrison, "The Value of Amtrak," *Journal of Law and Economics* 33, no. 2 (October 1990): 362n2.

14. "New Name for National Railroad Passenger Corporation," Amtrak press release, April 19, 1971, National Railroad Passenger Corporation, https://history.amtrak.com /archives/press-release-introducing-the-amtrak-name-1971/@@download/item/Press %20Release_New%20Amtrak%20Name.pdf.

15. *Amtrak: America's Railroad*, 69.

16. *Amtrak: America's Railroad*, 173.

17. Griffin Smith Jr., "Waiting for the Train: Why Amtrak Can't Get Us There from Here," *Texas Monthly*, August 1974.

18. "Amtrak Closes Book on Doomed Trains," Associated Press, May 1, 1971.

19. "2 Courts Uphold Amtrak System," *New York Times*, May 1, 1971.

20. William E. Thomas, "Amtrak Revisited: The 1972 Amendments to the Rail Passenger Service Act," *Transportation Law Journal* 5 (1973): 142.

21. Rush Loving, "Trains' Formula for Fixing Amtrak," *Trains Magazine*, March 2009.

22. Robert Lindsey, "Railpax Plans Innovations to Win Back Passengers," *New York Times*, April 11, 1970.

23. "Amtrak Designing Job Appealing," *Beaver County Times*, December 17, 1971.

24. "Amtrak Voices: Tricia 'Patty' Saunders, Part 2," History Blog, Amtrak, October 23, 2015, https://history.amtrak.com/blogs/blog/amtrak-voices-tricia-patty-saunders -part-ii.

25. "Amtrak Presents a New Look," *Penn Central Post*, February 1972.

26. "Amtrak Advertising through the Years," Amtrak's 50th Anniversary, Amtrak, https://www.amtrak.com/about-amtrak/50th-anniversary/advertising.html.

27. Jeff Davis, "Amtrak at 50: The Rail Passenger Service Act of 1970," Eno Center for Transportation, October 30, 2020, https://www.enotrans.org/article/amtrak-at-50-the -rail-passenger-service-act-of-1970/.

28. John W. Fisher and Teresa Ellis Brown, *The Northeast Corridor Improvement Project: An Overview* (Washington, DC: Congressional Research Service, 1979), 1.

29. Urja Davé, "Edwin Drake and the Oil Well Drill Pipe," Pennsylvania Center for the Book, https://pabook.libraries.psu.edu/literary-cultural-heritage-map-pa/feature -articles/edwin-drake-and-oil-well-drill-pipe.

30. "Centennial Excursion of the Pennsylvania Railroad," *Engineering and Mining Journal*, July 29, 1876.

31. "Shortages: Gas Fever; Happiness Is a Full Tank," *Time Magazine*, February 18, 1974.

32. J. D. Mullane, "Coronavirus Malaise and the Levittown Gas Riots of 1979," *Bucks County Courier Times*, April 25, 2020; David M. Anderson, "Levittown is Burning! The 1979 Levittown, Pennsylvania, Gas Line Riot and the Decline of the Blue-Collar American

Dream," in *Second Suburb: Levittown, Pennsylvania*, ed. Dianne Harris (Pittsburgh, PA: University of Pittsburgh Press, 2010), 48.

33. "Take Our Car," poster ad, Amtrak Archives, https://history.amtrak.com/archives /take-our-car.

34. "1970's Amtrak Oil Crisis Advertisements Gallery," Energy History, Yale University, 2018, https://energyhistory.yale.edu/library-item/1970s-amtrak-oil-crisis -advertisements-gallery.

35. Richard Nixon, "Statement on the Signing of the Amtrak Improvement Act of 1973," transcript of speech delivered at Key Biscayne, Florida, November 3, 1973, American Presidency Project, University of California, Santa Barbara, https://www.presidency.ucsb.edu /documents/statement-signing-the-amtrak-improvement-act-1973.

36. Amtrak also owns the ninety-seven miles of track between Porter, Indiana, and Kalamazoo, Michigan. Although Amtrak possesses the majority of corridor trackage, the Massachusetts Bay Transportation Authority, Connecticut Department of Transportation, and New York Metropolitan Transportation Authority own small sections of the line as well.

37. Christopher T. Baer, *A General Chronology of the Pennsylvania Railroad Company: Its Predecessors and Successors and Its Historical Context: 1976*, Pennsylvania Railroad Technical and Historical Society, April 2015 ed., http://www.prrths.com/newprr_files/Hagley /PRR1976.pdf.

38. *Northeast Corridor Improvement Project, Annual Report for Fiscal Year 1977*, 22, Amtrak Corridor Improvement Project Records, box 1, Hagley Library, Wilmington, Delaware.

39. Northeast Corridor Improvement Program, 49 U.S.C. chap. 249, http://uscode .house.gov/view.xhtml?path=/prelim@title49/subtitle5/partC/chapter249&edition =prelim.

40. Edward C. Burks, "Letter from Washington," *New York Times*, August 6, 1978.

41. Mick Rood, "Amtrak Northeast Plan Becomes a Nightmare," *Allentown Morning Call*, September 28, 1978.

42. Ernest Holsendolph, "Adams, Unhappy at Pace of Work on Rail Corridor, Acts to Speed It," *New York Times*, March 7, 1977.

43. Fisher and Brown, *Northeast Corridor Improvement Project*, 9.

44. Amtrak retained several E60s to haul its longest, heaviest corridor trains until 2003.

45. Edward C. Burks, "Swedish Technology to Join Northeast Rail Corridor," *New York Times*, October 6, 1976.

46. Joseph Albright, "Penn Central," *New York Times*, November 3, 1974.

47. Douglas B. Feaver, "Revitalized Conrail to Be 'Profitable Carrier,'" *Washington Post*, May 31, 1983.

48. Conrail rehabilitated Penn Central freight assets to the point that the company attracted private investment. In 1987 Conrail stock went public in a $1.6 billion initial offering. In 1997 CSX Transportation and Norfolk Southern Railway bought Conrail and divided its system between them. James Sterngold, "85% U.S. Stake in Conrail Sold for $1.6 Billion," *New York Times*, March 27, 1987.

49. *The Importance of the Northeast Corridor: Field Hearing before the Subcommittee on Railroads, Pipelines, and Hazardous Materials of the Committee on Transportation and Infrastructure, House of Representatives*, 113th Cong., 1st Sess. iv (2013), https://www.govinfo .gov/content/pkg/CHRG-113hhrg81370/pdf/CHRG-113hhrg81370.pdf.

50. Adam Davidson, "Empire of the In-Between," *New York Times*, November 2, 2012.

CHAPTER 11

1. *Work and Welfare: Hearings before the Committee on Labor and Human Resources, United States Senate*, 100th Cong. 181 (1987), https://www.google.com/books/edition /Work_and_Welfare/AcUlETWKB18C?hl=en&gbpv=1&dq=dukakis++%22northeast +corridor%22&pg=PA181&printsec=frontcover.

2. Jay-Z, *Decoded* (New York: Spiegel and Grau, 2010), 15.

3. "Ronald Reagan's Election Eve Address: 'A Vision for America' on November 3, 1980," Reagan Library, available at https://www.youtube.com/watch?v=fMx3KsU-Rcg.

4. Peter Robinson, "Notes from a Once Golden State," *National Review*, April 1, 2021, https://www.nationalreview.com/magazine/2021/04/19/notes-from-a-once-golden-state/.

5. Timothy Aeppel, "Amtrak: White House Wants to Privatize, Congress Subsidize," *Christian Science Monitor*, February 18, 1987; Drew Lewis, memorandum for the cabinet, "Administration's Proposal for Amtrak," Presidential Briefing Papers: Records, 1981–1989, 49–53, Ronald Reagan Presidential Library, https://www.reaganlibrary.gov/public /digitallibrary/smof/president/presidentialbriefingpapers/box-003/40-439-5730647 -003-033-2016.pdf.

6. Edward C. Burks, "Reagan Cuts Said to Imperil Northeast Rail Project Gains," *New York Times*, March 16, 1981.

7. Alfred Borcover, "Reagan Administration's Death Threat to Amtrak Makes No Fiscal Sense," *Chicago Tribune*, May 12, 1985.

8. Borcover.

9. *Reauthorization of Funds for Amtrak: Hearing before the Subcommittee on Surface Transportation of the Committee on Commerce, Science, and Transportation, United States Senate*, 99th Cong., 1st Sess. 36, 109 (1985), https://www.google.com/books/edition /Amtrak_Reauthorization/mQ4SAAAAIAAJ?hl=en&gbpv=1&dq=%22northeast +corridor%22+%22David+stockman%22&pg=PA109&printsec=frontcover.

10. William E. Schmidt, "The Nation: Finally, Amtrak Looks Like a Way to Run a Business," *New York Times*, January 14, 1990.

11. "Keep Amtrak Rolling," 131 Cong. Rec. S2210 (February 27, 1985).

12. Jeff Weiss, "The Elephant in the Room: Rick Perlstein on the Evolution of the American Conservative Movement," *Sun*, December 2021, https://thesunmagazine.org /issues/552/the-elephant-in-the-room.

13. "Keep Amtrak Rolling."

14. *Reauthorization of Funds for Amtrak*, 36.

15. Frank D. Roylance, "Ricky Gates: 6 Years Sober Yes, He Declares, Marijuana Caused 1987 Rail Tragedy," *Baltimore Sun*, June 16, 1993.

16. Ramsey Flynn and Steve D. Kaye, "On the Wrong Track," *Baltimore Magazine*, November 1987, https://www.baltimoremagazine.com/section/community/special-report -on-the-crash-of-amtrak-colonial-94/.

17. Roylance, "Ricky Gates: 6 Years Sober."

18. "The Colonial Express," *Day*, January 14, 1892. Amtrak kept the "colonial" designation even after lopping off the route's Virginia segment to Newport News.

19. Flynn and Kaye, "On the Wrong Track."

20. "Conrail Engineer Had History of Auto Violations with PM-Amtrak Investigation," Associated Press, January 14, 1987.

21. Susie Gaglia, *An American Railroad Dream* (Athol, MA: Haley's, 2018), 101.

22. *The Works of Charles Dickens* (New York: P. F. Collier and Son, 1911), 2:113.

23. Roylance, "Ricky Gates: 6 Years Sober."

24. "Thumbnail Sketches of Amtrak Crash Victims," UPI Archives, January 7, 1987, https://www.upi.com/Archives/1987/01/07/Thumbnail-sketches-of-Amtrak-crash-victims/5129536994000/.

25. William K. Stevens, "Metroliner Not Yet as Fast as a Speeding Bullet Train, but It's Getting There," *New York Times*, November 3, 1985.

26. National Railroad Passenger Corporation (Amtrak) timetable, October 26, 1986, through April 4, 1987, http://www.timetables.org/full.php?group=19861026&item=0020.

27. Flynn and Kaye, "On the Wrong Track."

28. Reginald Stuart, "2 Trains Were Speeding before Crash, Board Says," *New York Times*, January 14, 1987.

29. Robert D. Hershey Jr., "Floodlights Shine on Scene of Horror at Site of Collision," *New York Times*, January 5, 1987; Flynn and Kaye, "On the Wrong Track."

30. Reginald Stuart, "Amtrak Wreck Kills 12: Scores Injured," *New York Times*, January 5, 1987.

31. Hershey, "Floodlights Shine on Scene of Horror."

32. Reginald Stuart, "Rail Agency Picks Up Pieces after Amtrak's Worst Crash," *New York Times*, January 11, 1987.

33. Hershey, "Floodlights Shine on Scene of Horror."

34. William K. Stevens, "Conflict over Signal in Train Inquiry," *New York Times*, January 8, 1987.

35. "Engineer Denies Use of Drug in Collision That Took 16 Lives," *New York Times*, January 29, 1987.

36. Flynn and Kaye, "On the Wrong Track."

37. Reginald Stuart, "Alcohol and Drug Abuse Seen as a Key Issue in Railroad Safety," *New York Times*, January 19, 1987.

38. "VHS Newsreel—Chase Maryland Amtrak/Conrail Crash 1987," ABC 20/20, 1988, available at https://www.youtube.com/watch?v=6Cc4NVhhicY.

39. "Does Anyone Know What Happened to Rickey Gates of Conrail Who Caused the Big Wreck in Chase, Maryland," *Trains Magazine* Forum, January 1, 2004, http://cs.trains.com/trn/f/111/t/10404.aspx?page=1.

40. William K. Stevens, "About Philadelphia: A Comeback for a Real Train Station," *New York Times*, July 19, 1985.

41. Stevens.

42. David W. Dunlap, "Ideas and Trends: Other Stations on the Line Are Elegant Once Again," *New York Times*, April 3, 1988.

43. Blaine Harden, "Union Station: Washington's Colossal Mess," *Washington Post*, November 16, 1980.

44. Ben A. Franklin, "U.S. Hopes to End Union Station's Period as a Mess," *New York Times*, June 1, 1982.

45. "Statement on Signing the Union Station Redevelopment Act of 1981," transcript of speech, December 29, 1981, Archives, Ronald Reagan Presidential Library and Museum, https://www.reaganlibrary.gov/archives/speech/statement-signing-union-station-redevelopment-act-1981.

46. Carol Highsmith and Ted Landphair, *Union Station: A History of Washington's Grand Terminal* (New York: Chelsea, 1998), 112.

47. "1988 Redevelopment," DDOT Historic Collections, https://ddotlibrary.omeka .net/exhibits/show/union-station/1988redev.

48. Highsmith and Landphair, *Union Station*, 109.

49. "Washington, D.C. Union Station (1988)," available at https://www.youtube.com /watch?v=tEwEs9w7v5Q.

50. Paul Goldberger, "A Tale of Bloopers Ending in Success," *New York Times*, September 29, 1988.

51. "Federal Grants to Amtrak," Federal Railroad Administration, US Department of Transportation, https://railroads.dot.gov/grants-loans/directed-grant-programs /federal-grants-amtrak.

52. John F. Stover, *American Railroads* (Chicago: University of Chicago Press, 1997), 256.

53. Reginald Stuart, "Amtrak Rolls Past Shuttles in Number of Riders," *New York Times*, November 23, 1986.

54. National Railroad Passenger Corporation (Amtrak), timetables, effective September 26, 1989, through January 14, 1989, Museum of Railway Timetables, http://www.time tables.org/full.php?group=19880918&item=0010.

55. Robert A. Hamilton, "Connecticut Q&A: David J. Carol; Adding More (and Faster) Rail Service," *New York Times*, November 6, 1994.

56. Hamilton.

57. William C. Vantuono, "Gil Carmichael, 1927–2016," *Railway Age*, February 2, 2016.

58. *Northeast Corridor Improvement Project Electrification: New Haven, CT to Boston, MA*, vol. 4, *Comment Letters and Public Hearing Transcripts* (Cambridge, MA: National Transportation Systems Center, 1994).

59. Sam Libby, "Rough Ride for Amtrak Boston Plan," *New York Times*, June 21, 1992.

60. *Northeast Corridor Improvement Project Electrification*.

61. *Northeast Corridor Improvement Project Electrification*.

62. Sam Libby, "5 Bridges at Issue in Amtrak Project," *New York Times*, December 17, 1995.

63. "Building the Infrastructure for Acela Express," Amtrak: A History of America's Railroad, February 25, 2016, https://history.amtrak.com/blogs/blog/building-the -infrastructure-for-acela-express; Bob Johnston, "Wiring the NEC Is Not So Easy," *Trains Magazine* 58, no. 1 (January 1998).

64. *Office of Inspector General Audit Report: Amtrak's High-Speed Rail Electrification Project*, Report Number RT-200-020, December 14, 1999, https://www.oig.dot.gov/sites /default/files/rt2000020.pdf.

65. "Amtrak Begins Acela Service to Boston," *Train Rider: The Newsletter of Trains Riders/Northeast* 10, no. 1 (Spring 2000): 1, https://www.trainridersne.org/images /newsletters/Volume10-1.pdf.

66. Jayson Blair, "With Fanfare and a Delay, Amtrak Unveils a Faster Train," *New York Times*, February 1, 2000.

CHAPTER 12

1. "It's Official," Amtrak *Ink*, March 1999.

2. Betsy Wade, "Practical Traveler: The New Acela; An Assessment," *New York Times*, January 21, 2001.

3. "Acela Train," NPR, November 16, 2000, https://www.npr.org/2000/11/16/1114103/acela-train.

4. Robert Siegel, "Profile: Amtrak's New Acela Express High-Speed Train," *All Things Considered*, NPR, November 16, 2000.

5. "U.S.'s First Bullet Train Hits the Tracks," Associated Press, November 16, 2000.

6. "Acela Trains Sidelined on Second Day of Operation," Associated Press, December 13, 2000.

7. Raphael Lewis, "Amtrak Bullet Train Suffers On-Time Service Woes," *Boston Globe*, July 8, 2001; Laurence Arnold, "Fast Trains Slow Amtrak's Acela Not Meeting Ridership, Revenue Goals," Associated Press, August 21, 2001.

8. Joseph Vranich, *End of the Line: The Failure of Amtrak Reform and the Future of America's Passenger Trains* (Washington, DC: AEI Press, 2004), 71.

9. Martin Tolchin, "Fast and Posh, X-2000 Train Picks Up Fans," *New York Times*, February 2, 1993.

10. Bob Johnston, "New Acela Rising: Alstom and Amtrak Give TRAINS First Look at Acela 21, Set to Debut in 2021," *Trains Magazine*, September 2019.

11. James Dao, Matthew L. Wald, and Don Phillips, "Acela, Built to Be Rail's Savior, Bedevils Amtrak at Every Turn," *New York Times*, April 24, 2005.

12. The company spelled its name "Alsthom" until 1999, when it dropped the 'h' to become "Alstom."

13. Dao, Wald, and Phillips, "Acela, Built to be Rail's Savior."

14. "Former Plattsburgh Air Force Base, N.Y." Air Force Civil Engineer Center, https://www.afcec.af.mil/About-Us/Fact-Sheets/Display/Article/466131/former-plattsburgh-air-force-base-ny/#:~:text=Plattsburgh%20AFB%20was%20recommended%20for,30%2C%201995.

15. Dao, Wald, and Phillips, "Acela, Built to be Rail's Savior."

16. Don Phillips, "Amtrak's New Train: So Far, So Good," *Trains Magazine*, November 1999.

17. "Getting to Today's Northeast Corridor and the *Acela Express*," Real Transit, http://www.realtransit.org/nec4.php.

18. "Local News Anchors Pronouncing 'Acela Primary,'" Bloomberg Television, available at https://www.youtube.com/watch?v=WCLzdp4geZo.

19. Jayson Blair, "With Fanfare and a Delay, Amtrak Unveils a Faster Train," *New York Times*, February 1, 2000.

20. Jeroen Reuven Bours, "Amtrak-Acela," Darling advertising agency campaign, http://www.jeroen.nyc/amtrak/.

21. Phil Patton, "The High-Speed Train That Thought It Could, but Can't," *New York Times*, February 3, 2000.

22. Acela Source, Allen H. Tweddle Collection of Railroadiana, box 4, Hagley Library, Wilmington, Delaware.

23. Amtrak Acela (2001), Allen H. Tweddle Collection of Railroadiana, box 4, Hagley Library, Wilmington, Delaware.

24. Clifford Black, "The Acela Express," *Japan Railway and Transport Review* 40 (March 2005): 18.

25. "French Train Record," *Los Angeles Times*, May 10, 1999.

26. Stuart Elliott, "Acela Looks to Lure from the Skies and the Roads," *New York Times*, February 2, 2009.

27. "'Acela Primary': Voters Hit the Polls in 5 Northeastern States," NPR, April 26, 2016, https://www.npr.org/2016/04/26/475773268/acela-primary-voters-hit-the-polls-in-5-northeastern-states.

28. "Training for a Title: Cubs Fans Take Amtrak through the Night," *AP News*, October 27, 2016; Larry Eldridge, "The 1983 World Series," *Christian Science Monitor*, October 14, 1983. As of Spring 2023, the Phillies are 0–2 in train-themed World Series.

29. Kathleen Yanity, "Faster Train Service Comes at Higher Price for Providence, R.I.–Area Riders," *Providence Journal*, December 12, 2000.

30. Alexander Burns, "Zippy Amtrak Train Gets Tangled in 'The Swamp,'" *New York Times*, October 2, 2017.

31. Matthew L. Wald, "Bush Plan Would End a Monopoly for Amtrak," *New York Times*, June 20, 2002.

32. "Amtrak Reform Council," *Federal Register*, https://www.federalregister.gov/agencies/amtrak-reform-council.

33. "Final Restructuring Plan," Amtrak Reform Council, February 8, 2002, https://govinfo.library.unt.edu/arc/finalreport.html.

34. "Final Restructuring Plan," 49.

35. Matthew L. Wald, "Amtrak Breakup Advances," *New York Times*, October 13, 2005.

36. *Amtrak*, US Senate Committee on Commerce, Science, and Transportation, April 29, 2003, https://www.commerce.senate.gov/2003/4/amtrak.

37. "2004 Republican Party Platform: A Safer World and a More Hopeful America," August 30, 2004, American Presidency Project, University of California, Santa Barbara, https://www.presidency.ucsb.edu/documents/2004-republican-party-platform.

38. "Federal Grants to Amtrak," US Department of Transportation, Federal Railroad Administration, https://railroads.dot.gov/grants-loans/directed-grant-programs/federal-grants-amtrak; "The Budget for Fiscal Year 2006, Historical Tables," table 1.1, https://www.govinfo.gov/content/pkg/BUDGET-2006-TAB/pdf/BUDGET-2006-TAB-3-1.pdf.

39. Matthew L. Wald, "Budget Gives Amtrak Carrots, but Wields Sticks as Well," *New York Times*, November 26, 2005.

40. "Letters for Tuesday, November 13, 2007," *Missoulian*.

41. "Funeral Service for Senator Claiborne Pell," C-Span, January 5, 2009, https://www.c-span.org/video/?283114-1/funeral-service-senator-claiborne-pell.

42. Wayne Miller, *An Uncommon Man: The Life and Times of Senator Claiborne Pell* (Hanover, NH: University Press of New England, 2011), 291–92.

43. Claiborne Pell, *Megalopolis Unbound: The Supercity and the Transportation of Tomorrow* (New York: Praeger, 1966), 9.

44. "Thousands of Passenger Trips," Amtrak, available at Internet Archive, https://web.archive.org/web/20160305084743/http://nec.amtrak.com/sites/default/files/Amtrak_05_Infographics_4_0.png; "Amtrak Route Ridership FY19 vs. FY 18," Amtrak, http://media.amtrak.com/wp-content/uploads/2019/11/FY19-Year-End-Ridership.pdf.

45. Ron Nixon, "Frustrations of Air Travel Push Passengers to Amtrak," *New York Times*, August 15, 2012.

46. Newt Gingrich, Vince Haley, and Rick Tyler, *Real Change: The Fight for America's Future* (Washington, DC: Regnery, 2009), 211.

47. "Why Liberals Love Trains," *Newsweek*, February 27, 2011, https://www.newsweek.com/will-why-liberals-love-trains-68597.

48. "Welcome Aboard!," Amtrak, December 19, 1996, available at Internet Archive, https://web.archive.org/web/19961219142940/http://www.amtrak.com/.

49. Yongsung Lee, Bumsoo Lee, and Md Tanvir Hossain Shubho, "Urban Revival by Millennials? Intraurban Net Migration Patterns of Young Adults, 1980–2010," *Journal of Regional Science* 59, no. 3 (June 2019); "Fewer Young, but More Elderly, Have Driver's License," University of Michigan press release, December 1, 2011, https://news.umich.edu /fewer-young-but-more-elderly-have-drivers-license/.

50. Timothy Aeppel, "Amtrak: White House Wants to Privatize, Congress Subsidize," *Christian Science Monitor*, February 18, 1987.

51. Katharina Grosse, "*psycholustro*: How Can a Train Ride Become a Voyage of Imagi-nation?," Mural Arts Philadelphia, https://www.muralarts.org/artworks/psychylustro/.

52. Sarah Kendzior, "The Peril of Hipster Economics: When Urban Decay Becomes a Set Piece to be Remodeled or Romanticised," *Al Jazeera*, May 28, 2014, https://www .aljazeera.com/opinions/2014/5/28/the-peril-of-hipster-economics.

53. Dushko Petrovich, "Questions of Practice: Approaching *psycholustro*," Pew Center for Arts and Heritage, January 12, 2015, https://www.pewcenterarts.org/post/approaching -psychylustro.

54. Nell McShane Wulfhart, "Bright Passages along the Northeast Corridor," *New York Times*, July 24, 2014.

55. Karl Vick and Don Phillips, "Amtrak Train Derails in New Jersey, Injuring 34," *Washington Post*, November 24, 1996.

56. "A Delayed Transportation Infrastructure Project Moves Forward in the North-east Corridor," PBS NewsHour, October 16, 2021, available at https://www.youtube.com /watch?v=91fqF6XqPgI.

57. Mike Frassinelli, "NJ Transit Boss Defends Decision to Leave Trains in Area Hit Hard by Sandy Flooding," *Star-Ledger*, November 21, 2012.

58. Christopher Flavelle and Jeremy C. F. Lin, "Rising Waters Are Drowning Amtrak's Northeast Corridor," *Bloomberg News*, December 20, 2018.

59. Adrianne Jeffries, "The Amazing Chinatown Bus Network," Motherboard, Novem-ber 27, 2014, https://www.vice.com/en/article/qkve8m/down-to-chinatown; Nicholas J. Klein and Andrew Zitcer, "Everything but the Chickens: Cultural Authenticity Onboard the Chinatown Bus," *Urban Geography* 33, no. 1 (2012): 46–63, available at https://eportfolios .macaulay.cuny.edu/elisha2013/files/2013/01/Everything-But-the-Chickens.pdf.

60. Joseph Schweiterman, "Here Comes the Bus: America's Fastest Growing Form of Intercity Travel," *New Geography*, April 21, 2011, https://www.newgeography.com /content/002195-here%E2%80%99s-comes-bus-america%E2%80%99s-fastest-growing -form-intercity-travel. Amtrak launched a Mandarin version of its website in 2014, https:// zh.amtrak.com/home.

61. Eric Pfanner, "Japan Pitches Its High-Speed Train with an Offer to Finance," *New York Times*, November 18, 2013, https://www.nytimes.com/2013/11/19/business /international/japan-pitches-americans-on-its-maglev-train.html.

62. George Pataki, Ed Rendell, and Christine Todd Whitman, "It's Time for the North-east Corridor to Lead the 'Second Great Railroad Revolution,'" *Philadelphia Inquirer*, August 26, 2021.

63. Matthew Shaer, "The Wreck of Amtrak 188: What Caused the Worst American Rail Disaster in Decades?," *New York Times* January 26, 2016.

64. "Sen. Carper Statement on Amtrak Train Derailment in Northeast Philadelphia," press release, May 12, 2015, https://www.carper.senate.gov/newsroom/press-releases /sen-carper-statement-on-amtrak-train-derailment-in-northeast-philadelphia/.

65. *Amtrak System Timetable: Spring-Fall 2015*, 33, http://www.timetables.org/newpdf /NatT01_20150406_2015_Spring_Fall.pdf.

66. *Accident Report: Derailment of Amtrak Passenger Train 188. Philadelphia, Pennsylvania May 12, 2015* (Washington: National Transportation Safety Board, 2016), 58.

67. *Accident Report*, 7.

68. "All 8 Fatal Victims in Amtrak Crash Identified," Associated Press, May 14, 2015; Jana Kasperkevic and Joanna Walters, "Amtrak Philadelphia Train Crash: Mayor Describes 'Disastrous Mess," *Guardian*, May 13, 2015; Kenneth Hilario, "Chef Eli Kulp Remains Hospitalized," *Philadelphia Business Journal*, May 19, 2015; US Census Bureau, 2015 American Community Survey, Earnings. Census Tract 151.02, Philadelphia County, Pennsylvania. https://data.census.gov/table?t=Earnings+(Individuals)&g=1400000US42101015102 &tid=ACSST5Y2015.S2001.

69. "Statement on the Crash of Amtrak Train 188 in Philadelphia, Pennsylvania," May 13, 2015, American Presidency Project, University of California, Santa Barbara, https://www .presidency.ucsb.edu/documents/statement-the-crash-amtrak-train-188-philadelphia -pennsylvania.

70. Richard Saunders, *Main Lines: Rebirth of the North American Railroads, 1970–2002* (Dekalb: Northern Illinois University Press, 2003), 7.

71. Alan Oser, "About Real Estate," *New York Times*, December 10, 1975; Howard Blum, "Trump: The Development of a Manhattan Developer," *New York Times*, August 26, 1980.

72. Michael Kruse, "The Lost City of Trump," *Politico*, July/August 2018, https://www .politico.com/magazine/story/2018/06/29/trump-robert-moses-new-york-television -city-urban-development-1980s-218836/.

73. David Shepardson, "Trump Unveils Infrastructure Plan, Uphill Battle Awaits in Congress," Reuters, February 12, 2018.

74. Russel Berman, "Donald Trump's Big-Spending Infrastructure Dream," *Atlantic*, August 9, 2016, https://www.theatlantic.com/politics/archive/2016/08/donald-trumps -big-spending-infrastructure-dream/494993/.

75. Marilyn Bender, "The Empire and Ego of Donald Trump," *New York Times*, August 7, 1983.

76. "Joe Biden Takes Amtrak Home," CNN, available at https://www.youtube.com /watch?v=JHwXjmYK1TU.

CODA

1. Walter Benjamin, *The Arcades Project*, trans. Howard Eiland and Kevin McLaughlin (Cambridge, MA: Harvard University Press, 1999), 602.

2. *The Erie Route: A Guide of the New York, Lake Erie & Western Railway* (New York: Taintor Brothers, Merrill, 1882), 43.

3. Dan Herbeck and Michael Beebe, "Town Comes Up Big with a Rail-Car Giant," *Buffalo News* (December 8, 2002).

4. Rachele Huennekens, "CA: Coalition Calls on Amtrak and CA High Speed Rail Authority to Maximize U.S. Job Creation in $3 Billion Bullet Train Manufacturing Contract," *Mass Transit*, May 16, 2014.

5. Bob Johnston, "New Acela Rising: Alstom and Amtrak Give TRAINS First Look at Acela 21, Set to Debut in 2021," *Trains Magazine*, September 2019.

6. Johnston.

7. "Stocks Plunge, with Dow in Bear Market," *New York Times*, March 11, 2020.

8. Amtrak, *Amtrak Five-Year Service Line Plans: Fiscal Years 2020–2025*, 20, https://www .amtrak.com/content/dam/projects/dotcom/english/public/documents/corporate /businessplanning/Amtrak-Service-Line-Plans-FY21-25.pdf.

9. Dan Berry, "No Scrum for Seats. No Quiet-Car Brawls. Is this Really my Commute? The Pandemic has Made New Jersey Transit Unrecognizable," *New York Times Magazine*, May 10, 2021.

10. "How We Call Races," Associated Press, https://www.ap.org/about/our-role-in -elections/how-we-call-races.

11. The White House, "Remarks by President Biden Marking Amtrak's 50th Anniversary," April 30, 2021, https://www.whitehouse.gov/briefing-room/speeches -remarks/2021/04/30/remarks-by-president-biden-at-an-event-marking-amtraks-50th -anniversary/.

12. The White House, "Remarks by President Biden."

13. The White House, "Fact Sheet: The American Jobs Plan," March 31, 2021, https:// www.whitehouse.gov/briefing-room/statements-releases/2021/03/31/fact-sheet-the -american-jobs-plan/.

14. Northeast Corridor Commission, *Connect 2035: A 15-Year Service Development Plan and Infrastructure Planning Process for the Northeast Corridor*, July 2021, 39.

15. *A Rail Investment Plan for the Northeast Corridor: Our Future on Track: Highlights of the Tier 1 Draft Environmental Impact Statement* (Washington, DC: Federal Railroad Administration, 2015), 7.

16. US Department of Transportation, Federal Railroad Administration, *Record of Decision: NEC Future: A Rail Investment Plan for the Northeast Corridor, Washington, D.C., to Boston, Massachusetts, July 2017. Appendix A. Attachment 1—Summary of Elected Official, Agency, and Railroad Operator Feedback*, https://www.fra.dot.gov/necfuture/pdfs/rod /appendix_a1.pdf.

17. Francis X. Clines, "Rediscovering Hell's Kitchen," *New York Times*, November 3, 1985.

18. *The Negro Family: The Case for National Action* (Washington, DC: United States Department of Labor, 1965), 29.

19. Lynn Rosellini, "Capital Station Is Troubled and Empty," *New York Times*, March 1, 1981.

20. Ryan Healy, "The Strange History of NYC's Mighty Hell Gate Bridge," *Gothamist*, February 22, 2016, https://gothamist.com/news/the-strange-history-of-nycs-mighty -hell-gate.

21. "Pennsylvania Station Post Office Opposed," *New York Times*, March 9, 1906.

22. *Planning a Public Future for Sunnyside Yard: Executive Summary* (New York: New York Economic Development Corporation, 2020), 7.

23. "Burnham Place at Union Station," https://burnhamplace.com/.

24. "Burnham Place at Union Station."

25. Aaron Gordon, "Between Gods and Rats, the Moynihan Train Hall Is a Temple to Modern Mediocrity," *Vice Magazine*, January 4, 2021.

26. "Moynihan Train Hall. It's Stunning. And, a First Step," *New York Times*, January 11, 2021.

INDEX

Page numbers in italics refer to figures.

Bonaparte, Joseph, 43–44, 48
Bonaparte, Napoleon, 43
Booth, Edwin, 105
Booth, John Wilkes, 11, 105
Booz Allen Hamilton, 212
Bortz, John, 197
Bostian, Brandon, 213–14
Boston, Massachusetts: electrification
    project in, 200; redevelopment of,
    147; South Station, 71, 79, 147, 163,
    200; transportation in, 40–41
Boston & Albany Railroad, 65
Boston & Maine Railroad, 186
Boston & Providence Railroad (B&P),
    39–43, 56, 65, 66, 124
Boston Redevelopment Authority, 147
Boston Red Sox, 147
Boston Rustlers, 68
Boston Terminal Corporation, 147
Boyd, Allen, 167
braceros, 128
Bradley, Bill, 122
Brandeis, Louis, 69, 124
Bridgeport, Connecticut, 63–65, 71. See
    also East Bridgeport, Connecticut
Bright Victory (film), 115
Bristol Turnpike, 49
Britain, steam engines and railways in,
    35, 40, 56. See also War of 1812
Broad Street Station (Philadelphia),
    71–72, 72, 79, 123, 142–43
Broadway Limited (film), 115
Brower, Henry, 134–36
Brown, Charles Brockden, 27
Brown, George, 57
Brown, Henry, 55
Brown, John, 53–55
Brown, Mary Ann Day, 54
Buckingham, James Silk, 54–55
Buckley, F. H., 4
Budd Company, 165
bullet trains. See high-speed rail travel
Bunker Hill Monument, 35
Burlington Northern Railroad, 178
Burnham, Daniel, 84–85, 196–97
Burnham Place (Washington, DC), 224
Burns, Alexander, 207

Burns, Conrad, 208
Burr, Aaron, 29
Burr, Theodore, 29, 35
Bush, George H. W., 12, 198, 199
Bush, George W., 207–8, 221

Calhoun, John C., 31
Camden & Amboy Railroad (C&A),
    44–51, 53, 58–59, 70, 122
Camp David Peace Accords, 182
Camp Kilmer (New Jersey), 127
canals, 32–35
C&A Railroad. See Camden & Amboy
    Railroad (C&A)
Canton Viaduct, 39–40, 42, 43
Capitol Bus Terminal, 110
Carnegie Institute for Technology, 113
Caro, Robert, 157
Carol, David, 199
Carper, Tom, 213–14
Carroll, Charles, 37–38
Carter, Jimmy, 12, 198
Cassatt, Alexander, 73–74, 79, 85–86,
    88, 92–93, 109
Cassatt, Mary, 73, 86
Castro, Fidel, 144, 145
catenary, 2, 8–9, 104–8, 132, 161, 174,
    183, 193, 198, 205, 212, 214, 222;
    abandonment of, 184; arches in form
    of, 105; geometry of, 104–5; labor
    required for, 111–12; material of, 164;
    problems with, 106–7, 142, 165, 199,
    203; PRR project, 9, 111, 112, 123;
    PWA loans for, 9; structural support
    for, 105, 108, 111, 112, 140, 154, 200
Centennial Exposition (Philadelphia,
    1876), 71–72
Central of New Jersey Railroad, 186
Charles II (king of England), 22–23,
    29, 99
Cheeney, Harriet, 32
Chicago, Illinois, 84
Chinatown Bus, 213
Christie, Chris, 210
Chrysler, 125
Churella, Albert, 58; The Pennsylvania
    Railroad, 70